THE CONSTITUTION AS
POLITICAL STRUCTURE

The Constitution as Political Structure

MARTIN H. REDISH

New York   Oxford
OXFORD UNIVERSITY PRESS
1995

Oxford University Press

Oxford   New York
Athens   Auckland   Bangkok   Bombay
Calcutta   Cape Town   Dar es Salaam   Delhi
Florence   Hong Kong   Istanbul   Karachi
Kuala Lumpur   Madras   Madrid   Melbourne
Mexico City   Nairobi   Paris   Singapore
Taipei   Tokyo   Toronto

and associated companies in
Berlin   Ibadan

Copyright © 1995 by Oxford University Press, Inc.

Published by Oxford University Press, Inc.
198 Madison Avenue, New York, New York 10016-4314

Oxford is a registered trademark of Oxford University Press

Library of Congress Cataloging-in-Publication Data
Redish, Martin H.
The constitution as political structure / Martin H. Redish.
p.   cm.
Includes index.
ISBN 0-19-507060-7
1. Federal government—United States.   2. United States—
Constitutional law.   3. United States—Politics and government.
I. Title.
KF4600.R43   1994
342.73'02—dc20   93-42364
[347.3022]

2 4 6 8 9 7 5 3

Printed in the United States of America
on acid-free paper

Once again, for Caren

PREFACE

This book both synthesizes and expands my work on the constitutional implications of political structure which began in the mid-1980s. It was at that
point that I began to realize the vital symbiotic relationship that exists between matters of political structure and issues of individual liberty and judicial review. The book is designed to provide a thorough exploration of the
intersection of these three fundamental elements of American political and
constitutional theory. In essence, the book stands as a response to those
scholars and jurists who have suggested that judicial enforcement of the
Constitution's provisions concerning governmental structure should be
either reduced or abandoned. It argues that an attempt to draw a dichotomy,
for purposes of judicial review, between issues of liberty and governmental
organization dangerously undermines the complex intersecting network of
protections the Constitution gave us against the onset of tyranny. It further
contends that in any event it is improper, from the perspective of American
political theory, for the judicial branch effectively to repeal constitutional
provisions that its members find to be inadvisable or unwise. This is not a
task for which our judiciary was designed.

The book includes substantially revised and reorganized versions of several previously published articles, a number of which were coauthored with
former students. These individuals deserve substantial credit for their significant contributions to the individual articles that bear their names. In particular, the book has drawn heavily on the following articles:

"Supreme Court Review of State Court 'Federal' Decisions: A Study in
Interactive Federalism," by Martin H. Redish, 19 *Georgia Law Review* 861
(1985); "Constitutional Federalism and Judicial Review: The Role of Textual
Analysis," by Martin H. Redish and Karen L. Drizin (now Karen Levine), 62
N.Y.U. Law Review 1 (1987); "The Dormant Commerce Clause and the
Constitutional Balance of Federalism," by Martin H. Redish and Shane
Nugent, 1987 *Duke Law Journal* 569; and "'If Angels Were to Govern': The
Need for Pragmatic Formalism in Separation of Powers Theory," by Martin
H. Redish and Elizabeth J. Cisar, 41 *Duke Law Journal* 449 (1991). Chapter
5, however, is completely new, and, as already noted, the other chapters

represent revised and reorganized versions of the aforementioned articles. More importantly, the book attempts to provide a theoretical framework and overview at which the individual articles could at most hint.

As usual, the book would not have been possible without the assistance of numerous individuals. Initially, special thanks go to Karen Levine, Shane Nugent, and Elizabeth Cisar, who coauthored the previously published articles. I would also like to thank my colleagues, Gary Lawson and Steve Calabresi, as well as Professor Kathleen Patchell of Northern Illinois Law School, who reviewed portions of the manuscript and spent many hours giving me the benefit of their insights. My secretary, Patricia Franklin, once again made the whole enterprise possible with her now expected (but nevertheless most impressive) proficiency in typing the manuscript. Valuable research assistance was provided by Joseph Miller of the class of 1994 and Christopher Moore of the class of 1995 at Northwestern Law School.

Finally, my wife, Caren, and my daughters, Jessica and Elisa, always remain foremost in my thoughts.

Chicago, Illinois   M. H. R.
November 1993

CONTENTS

THE CONSTITUTION AS
POLITICAL STRUCTURE

1

Introduction: Political Structure, Democratic Theory, and Constitutional Text

The False Dichotomy Between Rights and Structure in Constitutional Theory

It has become fashionable in certain academic circles to urge a dramatically reduced role for the courts in enforcement of the Constitution's structural provisions.[1] In the area of constitutional federalism, the Supreme Court has—with limited aberration[2]—largely followed this scholarly lead, for the most part dropping out of the business of reviewing allegedly unconstitutional federal encroachments on state power.[3] In the separation-of-powers area, however, the modern Court has evinced something of a split personality, seemingly wavering from resort to judicial enforcement with a formalistic vengeance[4] to use of a so-called functional approach that appears to be designed to do little more than rationalize incursions by one branch of the federal government into the domain of another.[5] The Court has gone from one extreme to the other, with the assertion of what are at best tenuous distinctions.[6]

Those constitutional theorists who have urged this stance of judicial indifference toward issues of constitutional structure have chosen instead to focus their attention on issues surrounding the scope of individual rights.[7] The irony in all this is that the body of the Constitution—the document to which the Framers devoted so much time and energy at the Convention in Philadelphia[8]—contained precious few direct references to the protection of individual rights.[9] Rather, the document was primarily devoted to the implementation of an intricate and innovative political theory—a constitutionally limited, federally structured, representative democracy.[10] Although one

3

may, of course, debate the scope or meaning of particular constitutional provisions, it would be difficult to deny that in establishing their complex structure, the Framers were virtually obsessed with a fear—bordering on what some might uncharitably describe as paranoia—of the concentration of political power. Almost every aspect of their ingenious political structure was in some way related to their implicit assumption that, simply put, "power corrupts." Thus, much as a modern urban resident bolts his door shut with several different locks (so that if one fails, another may keep out the dangers of urban life) so, too, did the Framers choose to rely on a number of different structural devices to check what they assumed to be the natural and inherent tendency of government to proceed toward tyranny.

In structuring their unique governmental form, the Framers sought to avoid undue concentrations of power by resort to institutional devices designed to foster three political values: checking, diversification, and accountability. By simultaneously dividing power among the three branches and institutionalizing methods that allow each branch to check the others, the Constitution reduces the likelihood that one faction or interest group that has managed to obtain control of one branch will be able to implement its political agenda in contravention of the wishes of the people. By dividing power on a vertical as well as lateral plane (that is, between the state and federal governments), they sought to assure that not all policy decisions would be made at one political level. And by implementing a diluted form of popular sovereignty, they assured that those in power would be generally responsive to those they represent while they simultaneously reduced the danger that tyrannical majorities would evolve.

That the political structure adopted in the Constitution was designed simultaneously to preserve individual liberty and to avoid tyranny should come as no surprise to anyone reasonably well schooled in the theory of American government. But that fact makes all the more puzzling the modern tendency of both Court and commentators to treat these structural provisions with not-so-benign neglect. Even a casual review of the essence of American constitutional theory reveals that any purported dichotomy between constitutional structure and constitutional rights is a dangerous and false one. When political structure and constitutional rights are viewed as necessary but insufficient parts of a symbiotic, organic whole, one can easily see that in certain ways, the structural provisions are designed to reduce the possibility that individual liberties will, at some future point, be directly assaulted by government. In this manner, it was hoped, direct confrontation between government and liberty could be avoided.[11] In this sense, the Constitution's political structure can be viewed as a means of protecting the rights of the individual against tyrannical majorities. It would be incorrect, however, to view the structural portions of the Constitution solely as a prophylactic protection for minority rights. They may also be seen as prophylactic assurance of the rights of the majority—in other words, as protection against usurpation of sovereign power by those in authority from those whom they represent. One of the primary elements of my thesis is that because the political structure envisioned in the Constitution is so central to the values that inhere in the concept of limited government (namely, the avoidance of tyranny and the preservation of individual liberty), the provisions that dictate that structure need to be enforced by the Supreme Court with considerably more consistency and enthusiasm than they generally have been to date.

Before critiquing the doctrines and theories surrounding the structural portions of the Constitution, it is first necessary to explain the normative theoretical framework against which the examination is undertaken. Initially, I take as a theoretical given the values of both societal self-rule and constitutionalism. I therefore make no effort here to defend what I perceive to be the fundamental political norms historically embodied in American constitutional and democratic theory: (1) that policy choices not preempted by the Constitution are, to the extent possible, to be made by those representative of and accountable to the populace, and (2) that directives contained in the countermajoritarian Constitution preempt simple majoritarian choices.

That a belief in the fundamental notion of some level of popular sovereignty was embedded in our nation's political theory from its beginning can hardly be doubted, as the writings of both modern historians[12] and contemporaneous commentators[13] make clear. If any doubt existed, the establishment of two electorally accountable policy-making branches in the Constitution[14] should have removed it. On the other hand, it is equally clear that majoritarianism was intended to be constrained in our system by countermajoritarian limits established in a Constitution that is in written form, phrased in mandatory terms, and explicitly provides a supermajoritarian method of amendment.[15]

Clearly, the political theory embodied in American constitutional democracy is by no means the only governing structure that a society could adopt. The range of conceivable choices, from ideologically based totalitarianism to monarchy to pure democracy to anarchy, is wide indeed. A great deal of both scholarly thought and writing has, of course, been devoted to the question of political theory's first principle. But at some point, it is necessary to move on, for there are other important and interesting questions to be considered. "Second-level" theoretical analysis—exploration of the governing forms created to implement a society's fundamental governing value choices—is itself worthy of examination. Indeed, undertaking such an examination is the task that legal scholars would seem to be most qualified to perform. Thus, while the value of limited democratic rule can be both articulated and defended,[16] that issue will not be explored in any detail in these pages. Rather, I begin by taking our form of constitutional democracy as a given and proceed to examine the extent to which the Constitution's structural assurances of federalism and separation of powers are necessary to fulfill the underlying goals of our chosen governmental form.

In part, this examination considers what the Framers were attempting to accomplish by insertion of the Constitution's structural provisions. But the fact that the Framers may have intended certain constitutional results is not, standing alone, necessarily a sufficient basis for today adopting a particular constitutional interpretation. Of course, if one adopts an originalist perspective on constitutional analysis,[17] ascertainment of Framers' intent is simultaneously both necessary and sufficient. The point of my analysis, however, is that a reinvigoration of the Constitution's structural provisions is called for, not simply because the Framers intended that these provisions play an important role, but because their vigorous enforcement today remains essential to the attainment of the goals of our political system.

Textualism, Formalism, and Constitutional Structure

At a certain level of analysis, the justification for judicial enforcement of the Constitution's structural provisions moves from the political-normative to the positivistic-textual. For at some point, particular judicial interpretations of constitutional provisions cannot be rationalized by even an arguable construction of constitutional text, and in ignoring unambiguous textual directives the judiciary is ignoring its proper role within our constitutional system. It is at this point that the second element of my thesis becomes relevant: the Supreme Court must intensify its enforcement of the constitutional provisions dealing with political structure, for the simple reason that the Constitution's text unambiguously dictates the existence of a specific governmental form.

Thus, my analysis critiques the modern constitutional doctrines of federalism and separation of powers from two distinct perspectives. Initially, from the perspective of American political theory, it measures the Supreme Court's interpretations of the structural provisions against the political functions that those provisions are capable of performing in furthering the triumvirate of instrumental values they were designed to foster: accountability, diversification, and checking.[18] Secondly, my analysis measures the Court's decisions interpreting the Constitution's structural provisions from the perspective of textual analysis, because I believe that in our form of constitutional democracy the Court's role requires that its constitutional pronouncements not contravene the unambiguous directives contained in the text of the document that the Court interprets and enforces, regardless of the Court's assessment of the political or social merits of those directives.

This two-pronged analytical approach could conceivably be criticized for mixing two very different perspectives. Some might contend that the textual and theoretical critiques of Supreme Court doctrine are mutually exclusive, because issues of textual analysis have no conceptual relevance to an examination of issues of political theory. The focus of this book, however, is not purely on issues of *political* theory, but rather on the implications of American *constitutional* theory as well. As such, it considers all of the elements that enter into that concept. These include analysis of text and textual structure, as well as the normative precepts of political theory that underlie that structure. In construing and enforcing the Constitution, the Court necessarily considers a number of factors. Constitutional text is one of them.[19] Where—

as is likely true in the large majority of cases—text provides only incomplete answers, other considerations must also be taken into account, including issues of normative political theory. But in exploring the importance of governmental structure within our constitutional system, it is both appropriate and advisable to include within one's analysis an examination of the scope of the Constitution's textual directives concerning those issues, for there exist a number of situations—often including constitutional dictates concerning political structure—in which textual analysis will, in fact, be dispositive.[20]

Not everyone has agreed, however, that textual interpretation should serve an important function in judicial enforcement of the Constitution. Indeed, respected scholars have cast doubt on either the feasibility or advisability of textual interpretation in constitutional analysis. Before proceeding to an examination of the constitutional text's specific implications for issues of governmental structure, then, it is necessary to consider the scholarly arguments that have been raised against granting textualism a significant role in constitutional interpretation.

Adherence to Constitutional Text and the Justification for Judicial Review

Prior to the modern generation of constitutional scholars, there probably would have been little need to defend the role of textualism in constitutional analysis. Though the Supreme Court's adherence to constitutional text has traditionally been less than stellar, it is likely that most commentators would have agreed that at least at some outer boundary, text imposes limits on judicial constitutional analysis. Today, however, in order validly to critique the judiciary's constitutional decisions from the perspective of textualism, one must first respond to the wave of modern scholarly attacks on the legitimacy of textualism in constitutional analysis.[21] Any response to the theoretical attacks on textualism, however, should be preceded by an explanation of the arguments in support of judicial adherence to constitutional text. While much of this theoretical defense turns on widely known principles of constitutional and democratic theory, all too often these principles have been ignored by modern constitutional theorists. It is therefore advisable at this point to reexamine them.

The central feature of a democracy is, as a definitional matter, some form of majority rule.[22] While the Framers believed in democratic principles, however, they feared any unchecked power—even power lodged in the majority. Consequently, in order to limit the majority's power, the Framers established a *constitutional* form of democracy. Through a written constitution, subject to stringent amendment procedures, they limited certain governmental action, thereby protecting important values, principles, and rights from control by a simple majority.[23]

The Framers correctly recognized that because of its formal insulation from majoritarian political pressures, the judiciary was the best suited of the three branches to interpret the countermajoritarian Constitution and to protect its principles.[24] The judiciary could best fulfill its function of interpreting the Constitution by remaining free from majoritarian pressure; the Framers therefore attempted to insulate the judiciary from the whims of the majority. The Court became a countermajoritarian body: the only branch of government that is both appointed (rather than elected) and granted the security of salary and tenure protections. The judiciary assumed that along with the power to interpret the Constitution came the power to strike down unconstitutional governmental action. Judicial review, therefore, was recognized as an essential part of the Court's function shortly after the document's ratification.[25]

However, to insure that this countermajoritarian judicial body does not subvert democratic principles, the judiciary must ground invalidation of majoritarian action in the Constitution; it may not replace the will of the politically accountable branches with its own. As Hamilton observed, "The courts must declare the sense of the law; and if they should be disposed to exercise *Will* instead of *Judgment,* the consequence would equally be the substitution of their pleasure to that of the legislative body."[26] Article III's extension of the Court's jurisdiction to cases "arising under this Constitution"[27] manifests the assumption that the Court would be bound by the Constitution's terms.

Unless the unaccountable judiciary is constrained by the outer boundaries of constitutional text in invalidating majoritarian action, it is effectively transformed into a philosopher king, sitting in judgment on the wisdom and morality of all of society's social policy choices. Such a form of government has lost the essential characteristics of a democratic system.

In sum, in a society committed to the value of popular sovereignty, the inertia must lie in favor of the policy choices made by those representative of and accountable to the electorate. It is only when the text of the countermajoritarian governing document provides a rule of behavior or structure that is contravened by majoritarian action that the unaccountable judiciary has license to invalidate that action. Hence, in a democracy the only justification for judicial review by a nonrepresentative governmental organ is the desire to insure that the majoritarian branches adhere to the countermajoritarian limitations imposed by the Constitution. Judicial invalidation of the exercise of majoritarian will on any other grounds would erode the basic democratic principle that nonconstitutional value and policy choices are to be made by those responsive to public will.

On the other hand, while the exercise of judicial review power is justified solely by the Court's role in interpreting the countermajoritarian provisions of the Constitution, the existence of that review power is also logically *dictated* by the concept of a constitutional democracy. If the majoritarian branches could sit in final judgment on the constitutionality of their own actions, there would, as a practical matter, be little point in having imposed formalized countermajoritarian constitutional limitations in the first place.[28] Thus, American political theory simultaneously places significant limitations and obligations on the nonrepresentative federal judiciary. On the one hand, the judiciary derives no logical or moral authority to invalidate the actions of the majoritarian branches on grounds other than inconsistency with constitutional dictates. On the other hand, because of the very nature of a constitutional democracy, the judiciary is, as a matter of American political theory, obligated to invalidate actions of the majoritarian branches that exceed constitutional limits.[29]

The Parameters of Constitutional Textualism

It should be emphasized that a commitment to adherence to text in constitutional interpretation does not necessarily imply acceptance of a kind of static originalism. One can reasonably believe that the outer limits of constitutional text constrain judicial interpretation, yet find that within those limits the interpreter has freedom to adapt and apply concepts to changing conditions. As one scholar has argued,

> [The] leap from the authoritativeness of the constitutional language to that of the intentions or values of those who promulgated the language is an essential ingredient of the originalist dogma, but its justification is not at all clear. Much use of language is characterized by vagueness, ambiguity or both; and knowing the intention with which language was used can often be useful in clarifying vagueness or resolving ambiguity. Words themselves, however, do bring a degree of "objective" meaning with them—a meaning independent of the intentions of any author employing them.[30]

Professor Frederick Schauer has correctly analogized textual interpretation to "a frame without a picture, or better yet a blank canvas. We know when we have gone off the edge of the canvas even though the canvas itself gives us no guidance as to what to put on it."[31] Moreover, the facts both of generally broadly phrased constitutional text and of corroborating historical evidence demonstrates that the Framers actually intended that future generations would provide evolving content to most constitutional provisions[32]—a practice that received expression early in the nation's history in a well-known opinion of Chief Justice John Marshall.[33] It surely does not follow, however, that the words of the constitutional text provide absolutely no interpretive constraints.

Nor does adherence to text necessarily bind one to a concept of rigid "formalism"—that is, a commitment to rigid, noncontextual and abstract legal formulas—in constitutional interpretation. The mode of interpretation I employ throughout my analysis of the Constitution's structural provisions is a type of "pragmatic formalism"—one that rejects the constraints that flow from an all-or-nothing approach to constitutional interpretation. By this I mean that one need not—and should not—be forced to make a choice between rigid, abstract formalism on the one hand and totally unguided and unlimited judicial pragmatism on the other. One may legitimately accept that the nature of a constitutional system imposes on the judiciary an obligation to engage in principled, consistent analysis and to make decisions that are capable of rational reconciliation with governing textual directives, yet simultaneously recognize that within those confines there exists room for the judiciary to take at least some account of pragmatic concerns. The concept of "pragmatic formalism" will be explained in greater detail in the subsequent discussions of the concept's practical operation.[34] Suffice it to note at this point that both textualism and principled analysis leave room—at least to a limited extent—to take into account issues of modern practicality.

Adherence to Text and Linguistic Theory

That outer textual limits should confine the judiciary's constitutional pronouncements is by no means a universally held view. Constitutional theorists have on occasion suggested that judicial adherence to constitutional text is either unnecessary as a matter of political theory[35] or impossible as a matter of linguistic theory.[36] If one adheres to the tenets of linguistic deconstructionism, one of course cannot accept the principle that textual boundaries constrain the judiciary's role, because under this theory words are assumed to be capable of infinite, equally plausible, subjectively derived meanings.[37]

This is not the place to rehearse all of the competing arguments for and against textual deconstructionism in the legal context.[38] Suffice it to say that our legal system has never proceeded on an acceptance of the tenets of deconstructionism,[39] and the facts that the Constitution both appears in written form and provides for a difficult amendment process demonstrate that our nation's constitutional structure eschews deconstructionism. For if it were generally assumed that words in a text are capable of an infinite number of equally plausible meanings, there would have been no point in embodying the Constitution in written form in the first place. Moreover, even if a society were to decide to adopt a written constitution, acceptance of deconstructionism would render a complex amendment process both superfluous and nonsensical: why bother to require amendment, if the words contained in the text can simply be given a completely different—yet nevertheless legitimate—meaning by an authoritative interpreting body?

If one believes that words on a page are capable of an infinite set of equally plausible meanings one will obviously not find persuasive an argument grounded in an appeal to text. Hence, the textual arguments contained in the pages that follow are intended to appeal only to those who believe that the choice of words is capable of setting at least some outer linguistic boundaries on conceivable interpretation.[40]

Textualism and American Political Theory

More puzzling than the deconstructionist attack on the need for judicial adherence to textual outer boundaries in constitutional analysis is the argument that, purely as a matter of political theory, text should not confine the Court's constitutional pronouncements. On occasion, respected scholars have argued that, even assuming that the words of the text are capable of some degree of widely shared definition, the Court is not always morally or politically bound to adhere to these textual contours in exercising its power of judicial review. Among the leading critics of textualism in constitutional analysis is Paul Brest. His attack on textualism turns primarily on considerations of political and moral theory and tradition, rather than on linguistic analysis.[41] Dean Brest's thesis focuses on the distinction between what he calls originalism and nonoriginalist adjudication. The "strict" originalist "purports to construe words and phrases very narrowly and precisely," he contends, while the "moderate" originalist treats the text and original understanding of the Constitution as conclusive "when they speak clearly." For the nonoriginalist, text and evidence of original intent are "important but not determinative . . . in the light of changing public values."[42]

Brest initially attempts to raise doubts about the degree of adherence our written Constitution should properly command. The reason there exists some doubt in Dean Brest's mind concerning the authoritativeness of the Constitution is that "[e]ven if the adopters freely consented to the Constitution . . . this is not an adequate basis for continuing fidelity to the founding document, for their consent cannot bind succeeding generations. We did not adopt the Constitution, and those who did are dead and gone."[43] He concludes that "[g]iven the questionable authority of the American Constitution [at its revolutionary inception] it is only through a history of continuing assent or acquiescence that the document could become law."[44] Brest goes on to argue that the original text of the Constitution has been modified by the "decisions and practices of courts and other institutions," thus undermining the "exclusivity of the written document."[45] Based on this argument, Brest sees no reason to adhere to the original text, even when it speaks clearly, if public values have changed.

On a purely descriptive level, Brest's analysis may be accurate. The Constitution is not self-executing; human action is necessary to implement its dictates, and if an organ of government disregards those dictates and is not stopped by either of the other branches or by the people from doing so, then it is a fact that the Constitution is not being enforced. But the entire point of *written* laws is that they set limits or impose obligations that can be changed only through repeal or subsequent legislative (that is, written) modification. Presumably, for this reason, our nation chose to have a written constitution with an elaborate amendment process, rather than the constantly evolving unwritten constitution of the British model.[46] If one accepts the values of predictability and stability that inhere in the moral dictate of the rule of law, it is by no means clear that incremental and furtive alteration or abandonment of a society's governing document—which has established the organization and structure of government and which itself provides for direct change only through resort to a difficult, formalized process—should be morally or politically acceptable. Otherwise, we would effectively be condoning any governmental usurpation of authority that did not somehow break through the inertia of public passivity. A morally preferable solution would be to accept the force of the governing document, unless it is altered by means of the process ordained in the document itself, or by means of a true revolution, which openly and clearly rejects the document in favor of a new political compact and governing structure.

Once Brest assumes—incorrectly, I believe—that the written Constitution has modern force only if we continually consent to it, he must then prove an additional element. To demonstrate that the Constitution has no force, he must logically establish that, by current practice and tradition, we do not in fact consent to the text of the Constitution, or at least to certain portions of it. This, Brest asserts, is clearly the case:

> Our constitutional tradition . . . has not focused on the document alone, but on the decisions and practices of courts and other institutions. And this tradition has included major elements of nonoriginalism. . . . [Numerous Supreme Court doctrines of constitutional law that depart from originalism] are as well-settled parts of the constitutional landscape as most originalist-based doctrines. They are among the principal subjects that occupy professionals who "do" constitutional law—lawyers, judges, law professors and law students—and are considered part of constitutional law by the media and by the lay public. . . . To make the point affirmatively, the practice of supplementing and derogating from the text and original understanding is itself part of our constitutional tradition.[47]

Several fallacies plague Brest's analysis. First, if—as I suggest—Brest is incorrect in his initial assumption that the authoritativeness of the written Constitution is necessarily tied to the document's continued contemporary acceptance, the fact that accepted Supreme Court practice has departed from that text cannot establish—at least as a normative matter—that the document is no longer binding. Second, Brest fails to account satisfactorily for the fact that the Supreme Court, even in its most sweeping and far-reaching pronouncements—with the possible exception of the constitutional protection of federalism[48]—invariably attempts to clothe its decisions in constitutional text. If modern tradition had clearly rejected the binding nature of the written text, why would the Supreme Court have needed a concept so oxymoronic as "substantive due process"? Why not simply acknowledge that the Court's decisions are not, in reality, "interpreting" the Due Process Clause but simply reflecting the Court's assessment of morality?[49] The Court consistently dons a textual fig leaf, even for its most extreme decisions, quite probably because our society has *not* accepted the principle that the Court or other governmental institutions can simply ignore constitutional text.

Finally, Brest gives insufficient weight to the fact that many elements of society, from private citizens to members of Congress, deny the legitimacy of some of the Supreme Court's decisions, at least in part for the very reason that those decisions have dramatically departed from textual limitations.[50] To date, there has been no formalized public revolt against the Court. But short of overt extralegal action, there is relatively little the public can do once the Supreme Court has spoken. Though the amendment process is extremely difficult, after a number of the Court's most controversial decisions substantial nationwide efforts were made to that end, demonstrating at least a certain degree of public rejection. Congress does possess arguable authority to curb the Court's appellate jurisdiction,[51] but the most Congress can do is curb the Court's jurisdiction, not overrule its prior decisions.[52] Numerous efforts have been made in Congress in recent years to exercise this power and curb the Court's jurisdiction because of dissatisfaction with Supreme Court interpretation of the Constitution.[53] These proposals may have failed less because of agreement that the Court's decisions were legitimate exercises of judicial power than because of fear of eroding the Court's independence in our system of separation of powers.[54]

As a practical matter, there appear to be only two courses of action open to a public dissatisfied with Supreme Court decisions, and substantial segments of the population have taken each. First, at least in certain situations, people can engage in a covert form of civil disobedience—in other words, simply not obey the decisions. Most studies of public compliance with controversial Supreme Court decisions confirm the existence of widespread public rejection.[55] Second, the public can elect a president who promises to appoint justices who will change the controversial decisions, and there can be little doubt that that is exactly what took place, in most of the presidential elections between 1968 and 1988.[56]

Thus, the second element of Brest's argument against the modern authoritativeness of the written Constitution, much like his first, fails. He is incorrect when he asserts that "[t]he fact of this tradition [of nonacceptance of the constitutional text] undermines the exclusivity of the written document."[57] For by ignoring expressions of discontent short of amendment or revolution, he has defined the measuring stick for determining the existence of the "tradition" of rejection far too narrowly.

If one begins with the not-very-startling proposition that society accepts the moral force of the Constitution's text, as I have suggested, and one agrees with the assertion that absence of continuing affirmative consent is not a proper standard by which to judge the legitimacy of a political institution,[58] it seems reasonable to find that no basis exists on which to reject the text's moral force. Since the *only* basis upon which Brest premises his rejection of the force of the text is the absence of continuing consent, a standard that he himself ultimately finds to be an inadequate measure,[59] the text's moral force would appear to remain intact.

Dean Brest is not alone in his belief that accepted public practice may have the legal effect of altering constitutional text. Bruce Ackerman has argued that public acceptance of the New Deal, despite—indeed because of—that program's inconsistency with existing constitutional text, effected a legally binding amendment to the Constitution.[60] While Ackerman of course fully acknowledges that such a process of constitutional alteration is inconsistent with the formal dictates of the amendment process set out in Article V,[61] he contends that similar departures from existing legal standards for alteration occurred when the post–Civil War amendments were adopted and, indeed, at the time of the ratification of the Constitution itself.[62]

Professor Ackerman's logic, one could reasonably suppose, would legitimize, through a process similar to the concept of "adverse possession," governmental conduct that is inconsistent with the dictates of the Constitution's
text when widespread public acceptance of that conduct has been established. Under Ackerman's analysis, then, if the Supreme Court, for whatever
reason, were to refuse to invalidate unambiguous governmental invasions of
the right of free speech[63] and the public as a result fails to vote out of office
those who enacted such invasions, then the First Amendment's protection of
free speech has thereby been "amended."

Such a view of constitutional government effectively abandons the concept of a binding, written Constitution that those who framed and ratified the
document consciously chose over the alternative of the consensus-based,
evolutionary, "unwritten constitution" of England. To be sure, as drafted our
Constitution purposely left substantial room for the processes of legal evolution to work.[64] But the concept of a written and mandatory constitution by its
very nature imposes outer limits on that evolutionary process—limits which
can be altered only by compliance with the complex and difficult process of
amendment set out in the document itself.

The differences in the governmental systems envisioned by the American
and English models are significant. The English model places enormous faith
in both government officials and popular majorities. A society whose governing values are determined by an unwritten process of evolution and consensus building is always subject to the dangers of shifting public attitudes
and is therefore subject to the risks of uncertainty and tyranny. The fact that
the English system has not degenerated in this manner may have more to do
with its largely homogeneous population and long and venerable historical
tradition than anything else—factors wholly inapplicable to our society.

This strong normative basis for preferring a binding, written constitutional structure for our society constitutes at least a partial response to Ackerman's implicit argument from legal positivism, which attempts to deflect an
argument premised on the inconsistency of the New Deal's process of constitutional alteration with the amendment process of Article V: Because we
have chosen to abandon Article V as governing law, the legal positivism
theory goes, any such criticism is meaningless. The most persuasive counter-
argument, then, is that even if one were to accept Ackerman's assertion that
the positive legal framework for altering the document has been changed,
such a change represents a dangerously unwise invitation to governmental
instability and, ultimately, to tyranny.

In any event, it is by no means clear that, purely as a positivistic matter,
public acceptance of the New Deal should be construed as an alteration of
either our constitutional system or the process for amending that system. To
the contrary, to the extent the New Deal is actually assumed to conflict with
preexisting constitutional text,[65] it is the former that is lawless. It is true, of
course, that on a purely positivistic level society may choose to alter its
existing governing form. It is for this reason that our Constitution possessed
political legitimacy at the time of its ratification, despite the inconsistency of

its method of adoption with the alteration procedure established in the Articles of Confederation. The Constitution openly and avowedly superseded the preexisting governing form. Hence, questions about the Constitution's failure to comply with the procedures set out in the Articles of Confederation are rendered legally meaningless. The same cannot be said, however, of the New Deal. Neither President Roosevelt, members of Congress who voted in favor of the New Deal, nor the Supreme Court Justices who ultimately condoned it openly acknowledged either that the program unambiguously departed from the dictates of constitutional text or that the Constitution's procedure for amendment set out in Article V had somehow been legally superseded. To the contrary, the fact that the nation has unhesitatingly continued to adhere to the processes of amendment described in Article V demonstrates that no such change in governing form has taken place.[66]

Thus, while purely as a positivistic matter a society's decision to adopt a wholly new governing form may render meaningless issues about lack of compliance with preexisting ruling processes, there exists absolutely no basis on which to conclude that adoption of the New Deal was either intended by those who adopted it or perceived by those governed by it as anything approaching an open alteration in existing governing form. Surely, if societies may abandon their existing governmental system in favor of a different one, such abandonment should be open and express, rather than furtive and deceptive. No social compact may properly be enforced when the members of society have effectively been tricked into accepting its terms under the guise of supposed consistency with the preexisting form. To condone such an Orwellian process of governmental alteration, as Professor Ackerman apparently does, raises principles of governmental lawlessness and cynicism to new heights.

Professor Ackerman's analogy to the supposedly questionable validity of the post–Civil War amendments is arguably distinguishable from the issue of the validity of the Constitution itself, because the processes by which those amendments were adopted did not in any way purport to abandon the structure imposed by Article V. If, as has been suggested,[67] improper congressional coercion of the Southern state governments in the ratification process renders those amendments inconsistent with the dictates of Article V, then our continued acceptance of those amendments as governing law may be thought to represent tacit alteration of our constitutional amendment process. For several reasons, however, this example fails to support an analogy to the supposedly tacit constitutional alteration claimed by Ackerman to have resulted from public acceptance of the New Deal. First, it is by no means clear that adoption of the post–Civil War amendments should be deemed inconsistent with the dictates of Article V. If one assumes that the governments of the Confederate states were properly viewed as "lawless," it is at least arguable that those governments lacked legitimacy in any event. Second, at the very least one can safely assert that the post–Civil War amendments openly and avowedly altered preexisting constitutional text. Hence the public was aware of the change in governing constitutional textual structure. The same could not be said of the New Deal. Professor Ackerman's analysis, then, fails to justify, on either normative grounds of political theory or positivistic grounds of legal theory, the conclusion that something short of compliance with the amendment process should be deemed to alter unambiguous directives contained in the constitutional text.

It should be noted, however, that as a theoretical matter one could conceivably accept a commitment to textualism in the enforcement of the Constitution's structural provisions without necessarily precluding judicial recognition or enforcement of unenumerated individual rights. This is because one could fashion a reasonable argument that recognition of unenumerated rights is textually authorized by both the Ninth Amendment[68] and the Privileges or Immunities Clause of the Fourteenth Amendment.[69] In any event, such rights are at most *extra*textual, meaning that while the Constitution's text fails to authorize them, it does not expressly prohibit their recognition. In the context of the structural provisions, on the other hand, adherence to textual commands would prevent judicial constitutional pronouncements that are actually *counter*textual—that is, that directly contradict textual directives. Such countertextual decisions arguably threaten the constitutional system more severely than pronouncements that are merely extratextual.[70]

As the analysis in subsequent chapters will demonstrate, rejection of a judicial ability to engage in countertextual constitutional decision making would dramatically affect both existing judicial doctrine and scholarly analysis concerning the structural provisions of the Constitution. This is because large portions of both cannot rationally be reconciled with the unambiguous dictates of constitutional text.

Constitutional Structure, Individual Rights, and the Need to Preserve Institutional Capital

Because, as subsequent analysis will demonstrate, the Constitution's text unambiguously dictates both federalism[71] and separation of powers,[72] rejection of textualism is theoretically essential for abandonment of judicial enforcement of the Constitution's structural directives. It is only if one rejects the need to adhere to the limits of text in constitutional decisionmaking that one may choose to ignore the political structure dictated in the constitutional text. However, while rejection of adherence to text constitutes a necessary condition for abandonment of the structural directives, it is by no means a sufficient one. One must also provide a coherent normative theoretical basis for reaching such a conclusion. For if text is abandoned as a guide to judicial decisionmaking, one must fill the vacuum by providing some alternative normative basis for making constitutional decisions.

The most detailed scholarly attempt to provide a normative basis for judicial nonenforcement of the Constitution's structural provisions has come from Jesse Choper. Professor Choper's theory focuses upon the impact of

Supreme Court structural decisions on the Court's ability to protect individual rights. His concern is that by deciding structural cases, the Court expends its precious limited institutional capital (i.e., good will with the populace) for which there is a more pressing need—to support its individual rights decisions.[73]

Choper applies his theory to judicial enforcement of both the separation-of-powers and federalism provisions. In the context of separation of powers, Choper has developed what he refers to as the "Separation Principle," which proceeds on two key assumptions: (1) that the political branches will effectively police separation-of-powers violations,[74] and (2) that judicial resolution of separation of powers disputes will drain the judiciary's preciously limited institutional capital, needed for the protection of individual rights, where those affected are likely to be unable to protect themselves.[75] Choper's theory has been the subject of substantial scholarly commentary, some of it critical,[76] and with good reason. Neither of Choper's fundamental assumptions comports with either political or constitutional reality.

The Theoretical Legitimacy of Judicial Abstention on Issues of Political Structure

One may initially question whether the Court possesses the moral, political, or legal authority to pick and choose the provisions of the Constitution that it will enforce. Nothing in the constitutional plan in any way contemplated the limitation of judicial review to issues of individual liberty. The primary textual authority for judicial review is the provision of Article III, Section 2, that extends federal judicial power to all cases "arising under this Constitution."[77] Surely nothing in that provision authorizes the Court to decide that certain constitutional provisions are in need of judicial interpretation and enforcement while others are not. Indeed, when the Framers simultaneously protected judicial independence[78] and extended power over cases arising under the Constitution, the Constitution included precious few protections of individual liberty.[79] Most of these protections were subsequently added in the Bill of Rights, which amended the original text. Thus, to the extent the constitutional structure contemplated judicial review, that power was apparently directed primarily at the very types of constitutional issues Professor Choper wishes to exclude from the Court's province.[80]

Moreover, Choper's basic practical assumptions are flawed. Choper believes that through formal and informal checks and influences, the interdependent political branches will be forced toward an equilibrium that reflects the preferences of the majority of citizens. The main actors (the president and Congress) each have sufficient motivation and resources to pursue their constitutional interests. Unless one of these actors violates an individual's rights, Choper believes, the courts should declare these controversies nonjusticiable.[81] Yet, as one commentator has stated: "[I]t is by no means clear that the legislative and executive branches tend toward an equilibrium in which neither branch has a systemic structural advantage over the other."[82] At different times significant imbalances in their relative power may exist.[83] If no tendency toward equilibrium can be established, Choper's faith that separation of powers is self-enforcing seems highly questionable. One of the assumptions underlying Choper's model is that congressional silence signals Congress's approval of executive action. "Because Congress has the power to limit the President's conduct, it is assumed that its failure to do so represents implicit consent to the executive's actions."[84] But this assumption is unwarranted, because institutional barriers may prevent Congress from acting, despite its disapproval of the president's action.[85] Further, the president's veto power limits Congress's ability to control the president's conduct. To restrain an independent-minded executive, two-thirds of the Congress must agree. Moreover, Choper's approach is unable to detect whether or not separation of powers has been maintained, because it makes no attempt to define or examine the concept. He solves the problem of interbranch disputes by simply assuming they do not require judicial resolution.[86] In any event, one may reasonably question whether the assent of one political branch necessarily purifies a usurpation of power by the other political branch, because the concept of branch waiver misses the point of separation-of-powers protections in the first place.[87]

Many of the same problems plague the application of Choper's theory to issues of constitutional federalism. For example, just as troubling as his assumption about the ability of the branches of the federal government to protect their own constitutional interests is his assumption that no serious negative consequences would flow from a total judicial abdication in the area of constitutional federalism.[88] Although Choper has done an admirable job of anticipating and responding to potential criticisms of what he calls his "Federalism Proposal,"[89] he has seriously underestimated the harms that would flow from adoption of his theory.

Choper defends his proposal primarily by arguing that the states need no countermajoritarian constitutional protection because their interests are already adequately represented in the political process, a view previously advocated by Herbert Wechsler.[90] However, whether this argument is empirically correct now, or will continue to be so in the future, is all but impossible to determine, especially by a body as limited in its fact-finding resources as the Supreme Court. Surely it is possible to conceive of a situation in which state interests, at least as the states themselves define them, would be ignored by Congress. The legislative program of the post–Civil War radical Republican Congress is arguably an example.[91] Indeed, some state leaders view the extension to state governments of federal legislation regulating employers as a demonstration that Congress is insufficiently sensitive to their interests.[92] At the very least, it is quite conceivable that a *majority* of states may favor a policy that negatively affects the remaining states. This majority could control the decisions of Congress, leaving the minority unprotected.

More important, even if it is true that in most cases state interests will be adequately represented in Congress, that fact is beside the point as a matter of constitutional theory. All it implies is that relatively few serious constitutional challenges will be made on federalism grounds. As Choper himself notes, the Constitution's Framers were well aware that the political process would protect state interests[93] and, indeed, apparently viewed those political protections as *one* method of assuring the maintenance of an effective system of federalism.[94] That, however, is exactly the point: fully aware that the political process provided the states with some level of protection, the Framers nevertheless provided *additional* protection in the form of a constitutional structure providing for a federal government of enumerated—*and limited*—powers. Had the Framers been confident that the political process, standing alone, would provide sufficient protection to state interests, presumably they would have expressly vested in the federal government carte blanche authority to do what it deemed advisable. They clearly did not do so, and the states themselves, unwilling to rely solely on the enumeration structure of Article I, insisted on insertion of the even more explicit Tenth Amendment as a condition for ratification.[95] Rather than supporting Choper's position, then, evidence of the Framers' understanding of ways in which the political process protects federalism actually undermines his conclusion.

Choper further argues, however, that judicial abdication in federalism disputes need not imply that the federalism provisions of the Constitution are being neither construed nor enforced. Those tasks, he points out, may be performed by the political branches themselves.[96] Such an argument cannot succeed, however, because it proves too much. As a broad theoretical matter exactly the same could be said about *any* constitutional provision, including those protecting individual rights. If the political branches may sit as final arbiters of their own power vis-à-vis the states, the only conceivable barrier to having these branches decide whether they have invaded constitutionally protected enclaves of individual liberty is the assertion that the latter provisions are somehow more valuable. Were the Supreme Court to reject that conclusion, the Constitution would be vulnerable to final interpretation by the very branches intended to be regulated.[97]

Choper contends, however, that vesting final review power in the political branches is appropriate in the federalism area but inappropriate in cases involving individual liberties, because in the latter area (though not the former) we cannot be assured that minority interests will have an effective voice in the political process.[98] But the plan of the Constitution draws absolutely no such distinction. Most provisions of the Constitution, including the federalism provisions, are countermajoritarian in nature, in that they remove from majoritarian discretion certain matters of governmental structure.

In effect, Choper's proposal that state-federal tensions be resolved politically, without judicial intervention, treats the Constitution's enumeration of federal powers as merely advisory. But if this is accurate, it is difficult to understand why the Constitution provides such an elaborate and difficult scheme for amendment, for the structural provisions as well as those protecting individual liberty.[99] If the structural provisions of the Constitution were merely advisory, there would be no need for *any* amendment procedure, since by definition "advice" can be disregarded.

Choper's assumption that the judiciary's institutional capital is transferable from structural cases to individual rights cases is no more credible. Common sense should tell us that the public's reaction to controversial individual rights cases—for example, cases concerning abortion,[100] school prayer,[101] busing,[102] or criminal defendants' rights[103]—will be based largely, if not exclusively, on its feelings concerning those particular issues. There exist no grounds to believe that the public's acceptance or rejection of these individual rights rulings would somehow be affected by anything the Court says about wholly unrelated structural issues.

Perhaps the most fundamental difficulty with Choper's approach is his assumption that the paramount purpose of the judiciary is to protect individual rights. This represents a highly anachronistic view of the intended judicial role, since the Bill of Rights did not exist as part of the Constitution when Article III first vested in the judiciary the power to adjudicate cases arising under the Constitution. Moreover, Choper's theory ignores the fact that the entire Constitution was created to avoid tyranny and protect liberty.[104] To separate out the individual rights provisions for special judicial protection undermines the document's careful intertwining of "back-up" systems. His theory thus reflects acceptance of a false dichotomy between the role of the individual rights and structural provisions of the Constitution.

Finally, Choper's judicial abdication model improperly implies that the Court is free to pick and choose the constitutional provisions it is willing to enforce. Nothing in the proper nature of the judiciary's role authorizes it effectively to repeal provisions of the Constitution. Because of its uniquely insulated position,[105] the judiciary is especially suited to enforce the provisions of a countermajoritarian Constitution.[106] And since all constitutional provisions, not merely those protecting individual liberty, are subject to Article V's supermajoritarian amendment process, there is no basis in either constitutional text or theory to justify selective judicial abdication.

Conclusion

A synthesis of the textual and political analyses advocated in these pages establishes the need for vigorous judicial enforcement of the Constitution's directives concerning political structure. As the following chapters will demonstrate, acceptance of this thesis would dictate substantial alteration in the Supreme Court's current interpretation and enforcement of the Constitution's structural provisions. Generally, this change should come in the form of an increase in judicial enforcement of these provisions, in order to help assure that our system fulfills and maintains its democratic promise.[107] On occasion, however, the Court's intervention into the relations between federal and state governments should be restrained, so that the federal system may function in its proper and intended manner.[108]

Those who framed the Constitution wisely recognized the fragile and vulnerable nature of the form of limited, federalistic democracy they were creating. The safety nets that they inserted into our system, however, are themselves vulnerable, and once they are dissipated, the system itself becomes exposed and threatened by erosion. Despite assertions to the contrary by respected scholars, absent judicial protection and enforcement the viability of these structural provisions cannot be assured. It is therefore time for the Supreme Court to assume an active role in assuring governmental adherence to the structural protections of democratic government embodied in the Constitution.

The next two chapters focus on the "vertical" aspect of American political structure, concerning the relationship between the two levels of sovereign political authority in our system, the state and federal governments. These chapters explore how the Constitution deals with the contradictions inherent in a system in which one governmental level is simultaneously sovereign yet subordinate. Chapters 4 and 5 concern the "lateral" form of government interaction, concerning the delicately structured system of separation of powers, by which the Framers sought to reduce the dangers of tyranny through careful allocation of political and legal authority among the three branches of the federal government.

2

Federalism, the Constitution, and American Political Theory

To say that the Supreme Court's efforts to develop a principled, coherent approach to its role as the constitutional arbiter of interfederal disputes have been less than successful is surely a significant understatement. During the early and middle decades of this century, the Court moved from one extreme—substantial judicial intervention to protect state interests against federal encroachment[1]—to the other—judicial reluctance to scrutinize federal accretion of powers that had for many years been deemed exclusive to the states.[2]

The inconsistency in the Court's approach to issues of constitutional federalism intensified when, in the relatively brief span of nine years, the court flip-flopped from a dramatic reassertion of a strong constitutional enclave protecting states' rights in the controversial 1976 decision in *National League of Cities v. Usery*[3] to what probably amounted to an almost total judicial abdication of any role in enforcing constitutional protections of federalism in *Garcia v. San Antonio Metropolitan Transit Authority*[4] in 1985. In reaching its conclusion, the *Garcia* Court made reference to Professor Choper's view that judicial protection of federalism is largely unnecessary because the states can protect their interests through the constitutionally mandated political process.[5] Recently, the Court in *New York v. United States*[6] invalidated portions of a federal law effectively forcing state legislatures to adopt specific legislation on the grounds that it violated the Tenth Amendment. This decision appears to signal the Court's re-entry into the area of constitutional federalism, at least to a certain extent.

National League of Cities may be criticized on grounds of both social policy and political theory.[7] In particular, it could be argued that the decision created cryptic and unworkable standards for shielding state interests that might threaten the ability of the federal government to achieve its national

23

goals.[8] On the other hand, similar problems also plague the opposite view, that the judiciary should abstain on issues of constitutional federalism.[9] Yet there exists an even more dispositive reason to reject both the extreme interventionist model of *National League of Cities* and the abdication model advocated by Choper: neither represents a rational or legitimate construction of the constitutional text.

Textual analysis reveals that the Constitution protects state power against federal encroachment solely by prohibiting the federal government from usurping state authority beyond the limits implicit in the "checklist" of enumerated powers.[10] Striking down the extension of federal wage and hours regulations to the states as employers in *National League of Cities* violated this textual construction, because once the Court concedes that the federal government was delegated the power to regulate hours and wages under the Commerce Clause, then Congress's exercise of that power is textually incapable of undermining state sovereignty in an unconstitutional manner. Likewise, the Court's abdication of review of federalism issues unjustifiably ignores textual language—in this case, by turning it into a guide for Congress's "conscience" rather than construing it as an enforceable, countermajoritarian constraint on federal power.

There are, of course, arguments that may be raised to undermine these textual critiques. First, if one denies either the viability or necessity of the Court's adherence to text, then these criticisms are naturally rendered irrelevant. For reasons already discussed,[11] however, such a complete rejection of textualism in constitutional interpretation is both politically and linguistically improper. Yet it might be further argued that the criticism of the abdication model on textual grounds amounts to what is largely an academic enterprise, because much the same "policy" results could be achieved by a legitimate alternative construction of constitutional text. Indeed, it can be argued that prior to both *National League of Cities* and *Garcia,* the Supreme Court had effectively employed the judicial abdication model in Commerce Clause cases through the use of such a textual analysis.[12] However, while the text admittedly does not prevent the Court's engaging in substantial deference to congressional extensions of federal authority, any construction of the commerce power logically dictated by the text would differ, both qualitatively and quantitatively, from a total abdication of judicial authority.[13]

Before one explores in detail the implications of textual analysis for the scope of constitutional federalism, it is advisable to understand the nature and value of the American federal system, purely as a matter of American political theory. For it is through a synthesis of both textual and policy analyses that constitutional interpretation is properly conducted, so in light of the textual ambiguities that invariably arise in constitutional interpretation one's perspective on the political values of federalism may at some point properly influence judicial construction of the Constitution. Hence the first section of this chapter examines the broad theoretical scope, nature, and value of American federalism. The following section focuses on the implications of the Constitution for the structure of American federalism. It explains why both the enclave and abdication models represent illegitimate constructions of constitutional text. The final section examines how the constitutional text should be interpreted in order to fulfill the valuable goals of federalism while simultaneously adhering to the Constitution's textual dictates.

Federalism as Political Theory: The Nature and Value of American Federalism

The theoretical and pragmatic functions designed to be served by a federal system are not difficult to discern. The decentralization of political power makes perfect sense in a system premised on the fear of, and the desire to avoid, tyranny. Placing all sovereign authority in one governmental unit is an invitation to dictatorial rule. Federalism tends to avoid tyranny in two ways. First, by dividing sovereign power between two levels of government, a federal system reduces the likelihood that the superior governmental level will be able to control all aspects of its citizens' lives. Second, if the inferior governmental level attempts to impose tyrannical rule, its citizens have available the safety valve of interstate mobility.

To the extent that federalism is seen as a means to assure individual liberty, it could be argued that the concept should not be relied upon as a basis for resisting attempts by the superior governmental level to protect its citizens' liberty from encroachment by state government. To a large extent, of course, it is this logic that prompted adoption of the Fourteenth and Fifteenth Amendments, severely restricting state governmental power to infringe upon individual liberty. However, federalism may be thought to serve values wholly apart from the deterrence of tyranny and the protection of liberty, and in any event many of the federal attempts to encroach on state power have nothing to do with the protection of individual liberty.

The political diversity inherent in a federal system potentially fosters all of the social and economic benefits that may flow from the use of different governmental units to address social problems. Because of its unique qualities, each system brings different perspectives to such concerns. As a result of its size, resources, and national perspective, the federal government is able to deal with certain problems that extend across the borders of the individual states. Yet because state governments can focus on the unique impact that a problem may have in a particular geographical or economic area, are closer to popular will, and can engage in social experimentation without the costs and risks incurred by conducting untested social programs at the national level, they provide a perspective that the federal government is unable to maintain. That, basically, is the crux of American federalism.

The Relationship Between State and Federal Governments: Choosing Between the "Dual" and "Cooperative" Models of Federalism

Recognition of the social values that federalism can provide may imply a great deal about the desired nature of the relationship between the two levels of sovereignty. Scholars have long debated this issue. On the one hand, certain commentators have argued that ours is fundamentally a system premised on a concept of "dual federalism." This term has been described as a concept of "two separate federal and state streams flowing in distinct but closely parallel channels."[14] Under this approach to the theory of federalism, "each of the two sovereignties has its own exclusive area of authority and jurisdiction, with few powers held concurrently."[15]

According to Professor Edward Corwin's seminal article, the theory of "dual federalism" represents the synthesis of four axioms:

> 1. The national government is one of enumerated powers only; 2. Also the purposes which it may constitutionally promote are few; 3. Within their respective spheres the two centers of government are "sovereign" and hence "equal"; 4. The relation of the two centers with each other is one of tension rather than collaboration.[16]

Note that in Professor Corwin's analysis, relations between the two sovereigns are always viewed as being in a state of competitive tension. Any overlap of functions is therefore quite naturally viewed as a threat of possible usurpation of one sovereign's authority by the other. This view is confirmed by another commentator's suggestion that "dual federalism" envisions "two mutually exclusive, reciprocally limiting fields of power—that of the national government and of the States. The two authorities confront each other as equals across a precise constitutional line, defining their respective jurisdictions."[17]

On the other hand, the competing concept of "cooperative" federalism, according to Professor Corwin, posits that "the National government and the States are mutually complementary parts of a single governmental mechanism all of whose powers are intended to realize the current purposes of government according to their applicability to the problem in hand."[18] This system envisions "a sort of informal give and take"[19] between state and federal governments addressing the many problems common to both governmental systems. This theory views American government not as a "layer cake," but, in the words of Professor Morton Grodzins, as a "marble cake": societal problems generally do not affect only one governmental system, and therefore the appropriate response to these problems cannot be so neatly divided between the two systems.[20] Professor Richard Leach has noted this fact: "Shared functions, without regard to neat allocations of responsibility, is . . . the core of American governmental operation and of the theory of federalism as well. Intergovernmental levels is the working principle of the federal system."[21]

The Impact of the Choice of Federalism Theory on the
State-Federal Relationship: Making the Case for
Interactive Federalism

The preceding discussion has described, in basic form, the essential elements of the two primary competing theories of American federalism. Before one can decide which—if either[22]—represents the historically or normatively valid characterization, however, one must understand the implications of each theory for the nature of the state-federal relationship. The issue is especially important because it appears that many political theorists have mischaracterized the impact of one or the other theory on the relative strengths of the state and federal governments. An examination of the true impact of the choice of either the dual or the cooperative federalism model demonstrates that the suggested dangers of cooperative federalism have been substantially overstated by the model's critics. Some form of the concept of cooperative federalism is the only realistic model to govern most areas of modern state-federal relations, and, if properly applied, can do much to maximize the social welfare of both state and federal systems.

As Professor Corwin's description of the concept indicates,[23] dual federalism is generally assumed to imply an inherent equality between the two distinct sovereigns in the federal system. Thus, any rejection of dual federalism in favor of some form of cooperative federalism is thought to permit a reduction in state power relative to that of the federal government.[24]

Of course, if one includes as an essential element of the definition of dual federalism the equal stature of the competing sovereigns, then to suggest that the concept inherently requires equality amounts to a tautology. But, if one instead focuses upon the abstract nature of the state-federal relation under the structures of both dual and cooperative federalism, then it is by no means clear that viewing the two sovereigns as distinct and antagonistic entities with discrete jurisdictions necessarily provides greater power to the states than does a system in which the two sovereigns interact in the exercise of their often concurrent jurisdictions. One could just as easily imagine a "dual" system in which the two jurisdictions do not overlap, but the jurisdiction of the federal government is considerably broader than that of the state government. Indeed, given modern developments in transportation and technology, resulting in a substantial increase in the number of problems that require governmental attention crossing state lines, it is highly likely that any current "dual" system, premised on a concept of mutually exclusive state and federal powers, would necessarily result in a significant decrease in state power vis-à-vis the federal government. It is unrealistic to expect interstate problems to be solved without performance of an important role by the federal government. If, under a dual system, recognition of power in one sovereign inherently implies an absence of concurrent power in the other sovereign, then recognition of an expanded federal role in these areas would at the same time necessarily diminish correspondingly the scope of state authority over the same matters. If, on the other hand, a cooperative or "sharing" concept of federalism were recognized, state and federal authorities could each perform an important function in attempting to deal with such problems.[25] Hence, expansion of the scope of potential federal power would not automatically reduce state power.

Further, a concept of federalism in which state and federal governments engage in a give-and-take, both in terms of ideas and resources, does not necessarily undermine the theory of state integrity. Indeed, such a concept would seem to fit well with the model of states as social laboratories—often described as a value of a federal system.[26] Under this view, states may experiment with social policies in ways that would be too risky or expensive for the federal government to attempt initially. Yet the federal government may learn and benefit from such experiments, borrowing the more successful ones for national use. Such borrowing necessarily involves an interfederal sharing of information and techniques, yet simultaneously recognizes the states as valuable integral units within the federal system.[27] In any event, when the interfederal interchange takes the form purely of communication of advice and information from the federal government to the states, there surely can be no claim that the practice somehow threatens state integrity.

Even in the effectuation of existing federal programs, the view of federalism as sharing may underscore the importance of the states as units within the federal system. One illustration is the enforcement of environmental legislation where, according to Professor Richard Stewart, "[t]he inadequacy of federal resources in comparison to the magnitude of environmental problems inevitably results in federal dependence on state and local authorities."[28] Thus, the concept of cooperative federalism does not view governmental power as a limited pie, to be divided between antagonistic state and federal governments. Rather, the assumption is that it is possible for all governments to grow in power simultaneously.[29] This example underscores the basically "symbiotic"[30] nature of the state-federal relationship.

Certain caveats must be noted in this analysis of cooperative federalism, lest the discussion be deemed naive or disingenuous. First, there can be little doubt that the reach of federal power has substantially expanded in the last century, both in legal theory and political fact. New Deal legislation brought the federal government into areas where it had traditionally not ventured, and, as subsequent discussion will demonstrate, corresponding Supreme Court expansions of Congress's commerce power[31] constitutionally justified such legislation, as well as arguably even more expansive modern congressional action.[32] Whether these constructions of the Commerce Clause are legitimate is the subject of subsequent discussion. The point for present purposes is that such an expansive reading of the commerce power is neither inherently commanded by a cooperative theory of federalism nor necessarily precluded by the abstract concept of a "dual" state-federal relationship. The only practical difference between the two theories of federalism in this context is that under a cooperative model expansion of federal power does not automatically imply a reduction of state power. In contrast, a dual model presumably would require such a reduction, because the essence of the dual structure is the mutually exclusive exercise of state and federal power.

A second caveat concerns the arguably euphemistic nature of the "cooperative" label. As the name suggests, scholars who advocate this view of federalism tend to disregard the significant conflicts and tensions that have arisen over the years between state and federal systems. Surely the relations between state and federal governments throughout the nation's history could not be exclusively described with such positive terms as "cooperation" and "sharing." The long and controversial judicial history of hard-fought battles over federal preemption in the commerce[33] and intellectual property[34] areas belies any assumption of a continuous, tension-free cooperative relationship between state and federal governments. The same could be said in the area of judicial federalism, where the interrelation of state and federal courts has most assuredly not always been free from conflict.[35]

Yet these facts do not necessarily demonstrate that the dual federalism model more accurately depicts the nature of American federalism. Such a conclusion would suffer from the fallacious assumption that the only conceivable alternative to the totally cooperative model is the dual model. The true alternative to the rigid "parallel function" theory of dual federalism is more appropriately labeled "interactive" federalism—a term more neutral than "cooperative" and one that recognizes the inevitable intertwining of the state and federal systems as they both go about the business of governing.[36] At times, this interaction will be combative in nature, where the governing decisions of one sovereign differ from the other's and threaten the social and economic policies sought to be advanced by the other's decisions. Yet, at other times the actions of the respective sovereigns will be supplementary or complementary to each other, combining to meet the same problem in different but not conflicting ways. At still other times the problems facing government will call for some form of cooperative action—either through direct joint action, or more indirectly, through the exchange of information, ideas, and experiences.[37] There is no reason to believe that combative and cooperative federalism are mutually exclusive; both are manifestations of the dynamic interaction of the state and federal systems.[38]

A final caveat concerns the avoidance of absolutes in the federalism debate. Whether one believes, as a normative matter, that the dual or interactive models should be deemed the appropriate theory, there can be little doubt that neither is—or ever was—the exclusive form of American federalism. Just as it is inconceivable that all matters falling within the federal government's commerce power are automatically and totally excluded from the state province[39] (rendering an absolute dualism highly dubious), so, too, is it difficult to imagine the states exercising no powers free from federal control.[40] One need only examine the pervasive statutory structure and common law of any state today to realize that, as a practical matter if not a constitutional one,[41] state government remains a viable independent policymaking force in the modern federal system. Thus, any discussion of what I have called "interactive" federalism must implicitly recognize the continued relevance of at least some practical level of dualism.

Historical Evidence and the Federalism Debate

In a certain sense, examination of the historical data in the debate between the "dualists" and the "cooperativists" is fundamentally an academic exercise. Even those scholars who firmly believe in the historical dominance of dual federalism, like Professors Corwin and Scheiber, acknowledge that the modern concept of American federalism has departed dramatically from the system's historical origins as they view them.[42] If one accepts Professor Friedrich's description of federalism as a dynamic, rather than static process,[43] then the mere fact that the current structure departs from its historical origins does not necessarily imply—at least as a matter of political theory[44]—that the current system is invalid.

Of course, one might reject the modern federalism structure as a normative matter, but historical assumptions would seem to be at best only marginally relevant to normative issues. An examination of the historical data is nevertheless helpful, if only to provide a context in which to understand the development of the current model. Therefore, the analysis now turns to such an historical examination.

The Framing of the Constitution

Though several scholars find in the Convention debates and the Federalist Papers strong support for one or the other view of federalism, ultimately the evidence appears either cloudy or contradictory. Although Professor Friedrich suggests that "[i]t is no exaggeration to say that federalism was the most central issue of the constitutional convention at Philadelphia,"[45] other scholars contend that the Framers gave precious little attention to the theoretical nature of the state-federal relationship.[46] As K. C. Wheare pointed out, "[It] is interesting to note that the words 'federal' or 'federation' occur nowhere in the American Constitution."[47]

Whatever assumptions were made by the Framers about federalism, it does not appear that the Constitution on its face dictates the dual federalism model. It is true that one reasonably can construe the Constitution to preserve certain governmental power for exclusive state authority, whether one reaches this conclusion through a reading of the Tenth Amendment or simply by finding outer limits in the enumerated federal powers.[48] But this fact, even if accepted, does not tell us anything about the nature of possible state-federal interaction on matters deemed to be within federal power, nor does it tell us exactly how broad federal power is or how narrow the state enclaves actually are. Thus, even if one were to concede that the Framers had no firm concept of cooperative or interactive federalism, it would not necessarily follow that such a theory was unconstitutional, but merely that it was not constitutionally compelled.[49] What this analysis does tell us about the scope of constitutional federalism, however, is that, to the extent constitutional limits on federal power to preempt state authority are discerned,[50] such recognition does not necessarily dictate adoption of a rigid dual federalist model.

Indeed, a strong argument can be fashioned to support the view that on the contrary, the constitutional text is actually inconsistent with the dual federalism model. In Article I, Section 8, the Constitution enumerates most of Congress's powers. Yet Article I, Section 10[51] explicitly prohibits to the states specified powers granted to Congress under Section 8. If the Framers had assumed the existence of dual federalism, there arguably would have been no reason to include Section 10, because it would have been universally understood that the express grant of a particular power to the federal government would have automatically deprived the states of that power. Even if one assumes that Section 10 was inserted solely for purposes of emphasis (in much the same manner as the Tenth Amendment is designed to emphasize the limited nature of federal power),[52] the inclusion within that express prohibition of state power of only a few of the powers enumerated in Section 8[53] logically belies an intent to expressly codify dual federalism. If the Framers had intended to reach that result, presumably they would simply have stated that the grant of a power to the federal government automatically excludes a similar state power. In contrast, the fact that Section 10 expressly excludes only selected federal powers would seem to imply that to the contrary, the exercise of state authority in the areas of federal power *not* expressly prohibited was to be permitted (subject, of course, to the possibility of federal legislative preemption).[54]

Advocates of dual federalism have ignored this powerful textual argument, however, instead seeking historical support in extratextual sources. Professor Scheiber, for example, claims that strong historical support for a dual federalism model can be found in the Federalist Papers. He points to *The Federalist* No. 46, where Madison noted that the states were to be "'constituent and essential parts' of the new federal system, whereas the central government was 'no wise essential to the operation or organization' of the states."[55] It is not clear, however, how this statement is thought to endorse a dual system in anything more than its most minimal sense. Madison's statement might be relevant in an argument over whether the federal government has authority effectively to destroy the states, but it says little about the nature of future state-federal interaction.

Madison also stated in *The Federalist* No. 46 that "the State governments could have little to apprehend, because it is only within a certain sphere that the federal power can, in the nature of things, be advantageously administered."[56] This statement, however, establishes only that the federal government was intended to be one of limited powers. It says nothing about the possibly mutually exclusive nature of state and federal power; nor does it really say anything about the actual extent of those "limited" federal powers. It also says nothing about the possibly antagonistic relationship between state and federal governments. Indeed, much of *The Federalist* No. 46 appears to constitute an attempt to calm the fears of those who believed the federal government might undermine the states.[57]

Professor Scheiber may find stronger support for his assertion in Madison's statement that "[t]he Federal and State governments are . . . constituted with different powers and designed for different purposes."[58] But to focus exclusively upon these words is to take them out of context. An examination of the surrounding language demonstrates that Madison was thinking little about the issue of dual federalism.[59] Rather, he was attempting to defuse the issue of potential antagonism between state and federal governments, emphasizing that:

> [T]he ultimate authority, wherever the derivative may be found, resides in the people alone, and that it will not depend merely on the comparative ambition or address of the different governments whether either, or which of them, will be able to enlarge its sphere or jurisdiction at the expense of the other.[60]

It is true that, on occasion, supporters of the Constitution attempted to respond to the fears of anti-Federalists by arguing that "[t]he two governments act in different manners, and for different purposes," that is, "the general government in great national concerns, in which we are interested in common with other members of the Union; the state legislature in our mere local concerns. . . . They can no more clash than two parallel lines can meet."[61] But, at least in the absence of some firm basis in constitutional text, random statements by individual Framers cannot be taken to prove the case for dual federalism. In any event, this view, like Madison's, does not appear to represent a coherent political theory as much as an attempt "to explain the new system and to make sense of the 'concurrent jurisdiction' of two legislatures over the same people."[62] Ultimately, the Federalists resolved their theoretical ambiguity by focusing upon the people, rather than the states, as the source of political sovereignty.[63] Such a theory does not compel acceptance of the dual model. Rather, by emphasizing a single source of all state and federal authority, this position suggests a recognition of the overlapping powers of the two levels of government.[64]

From the Framing of the Constitution to the Reconstruction Era

The historical debate over the theory of federalism reaches its zenith in a discussion of the post-Constitution to Reconstruction periods. Although Professor Scheiber summarily dismisses any view of the period's history as one of cooperative federalism,[65] other respected scholars contend that while the accepted myth of the period was one of dual federalism, the reality involved the evolution of the modern concept of cooperative federalism.[66] The Supreme Court, too, has more recently recognized the long history of state-federal cooperation.[67]

Determining the winner in this debate requires a great deal more expertise in American history than I possess, and a detailed historical analysis is not really called for in any event, in light of both the clear implication of constitutional text[68] and the overriding importance of the normative aspect of the issue and the general acknowledgement that something akin to the cooperative federalism model currently dominates. One possible explanation for the historical difference of opinion, however, is that the early evidence of cooperative federalism is slim, not because that model had been rejected in favor of a dual structure, but simply because the scope of the federal government's power was thought at the time to be so limited, or at least was not widely exercised.[69] Once Congress's power was expanded in the twentieth century, primarily through an expanded judicial construction of the Commerce Clause,[70] the evidence of state-federal interaction, not surprisingly, increased significantly.[71]

The Theory of American Federalism in the Judicial Context

Though certain commentators now challenge the point,[72] there can be no serious doubt that the interactive model has dominated judicial federalism since the nation's beginnings. Indeed, the ultimate irony of the position taken by supporters of dual federalism in the judicial context is demonstrated by Professor Scheiber's reliance upon language in the Supreme Court's decision in *Younger v. Harris*[73] to support the separation of state and federal judicial power,[74] in total disregard of the fact that the decision's essence concerned the fungibility of state and federal courts as enforcers of federal law.[75] It is difficult to understand, then, how Professor Scheiber can point to *Younger* to support the proposition that "our jurists are no more ready than our historians or legal scholars to . . . accept blandly that 'sharing' was the norm in historic federal-state relations in the United States."[76] Though *Younger* recognized a need for state discretion to attain legislative goals free from undue federal constitutional limitation,[77] such a view in no way constitutes a rejection of federalistic "sharing." The Court's conclusion that equity would not act because of the availability of an adequate defense at law in the state criminal prosecution[78] necessarily assumes both the ability and obligation of the state court system to provide a *federal* constitutional remedy in the same manner that a federal court would. The tradition of state-federal cross-pollination and interchange in the judicial context is a long and venerable one, both in the sense that state courts have been called upon to adjudicate federal law and that federal courts have regularly adjudicated issues of state law.

Federal Law in the State Courts

As I and others have detailed,[79] from the time of the Constitution's framing the assumption has been that state courts constitute a legitimate judicial forum for the adjudication and enforcement of federal law. It was apparently for this reason that the Framers compromised by refusing to require the creation of lower federal courts in Article III of the Constitution.[80] The Constitution's Supremacy Clause[81] demonstrates the Framers' assumption that state courts could—and indeed must—adjudicate issues of federal law, an obligation and authority that was confirmed by the Supreme Court early in the nation's history.[82] As Professor Henry Hart stated: "In the scheme of the Constitution, [state courts] are the primary guarantors of constitutional rights, and in many cases they may be the ultimate ones."[83]

The constitutional authority of the state courts to adjudicate issues of federal law formed the basis for the Supreme Court's decision in *Claflin v. Houseman*.[84] This case established that in the face of congressional silence a presumption of concurrent state and federal court jurisdiction would exist to enforce federal causes of action,[85] a presumption that the modern-day Supreme Court has reaffirmed.[86] In cases such as *Testa v. Katt*[87] the Supreme Court has recognized a corresponding state court *duty* to adjudicate federal claims, except in the rare case when a "valid excuse" for failing to do so is provided.[88]

This historical description of state and federal judicial "sharing" of the power to adjudicate and enforce federal law is so well established that normally I would have thought it unnecessary to include even this relatively brief discussion of the point. However, the assumption that state courts are constitutionally empowered to exercise federal judicial power has been challenged by one commentator,[89] and in large part for that reason he rejected the holding in *Michigan v. Long*[90] that an ambiguous state decision will be presumed to rest on federal, rather than state, constitutional grounds.[91] Robert Welsh explains his rejection of the traditional view of the role of state courts in the federal system in the following manner. First, he relies on his interpretation of the data surrounding the framing of the Constitution.[92] Second, he relies on the theoretical analysis contained in several Civil War–period Supreme Court decisions.[93] Finally, he focuses upon what he considers the linguistic nuances of the phrase, "federal judicial power."[94]

In rejecting the traditional historical analysis, Welsh argues that "[t]he historical record, skimpy and contradictory as it sometimes is, offers scant support for such a broad interpretation of state court authority under the federal Constitution."[95] Curiously, however, he appears to accept the history of the Madisonian Compromise, in which the Framers agreed to allow Congress to decide whether or not to create lower federal courts, much as the history has been described by others.[96] Yet if he accepts that the Framers assumed that Congress need not create lower federal courts, how could he possibly question the additional assumption made by the Framers that state courts could interpret and enforce federal law, in the event Congress chose not to create lower federal courts in the first place? Who, other than the state courts, could the Framers possibly have assumed would provide the initial forum for adjudication of federal claims in such an event?

Welsh's analysis disregards the post-Convention congressional history, in which Congress chose to vest the overwhelming portion of the power to adjudicate federal claims in the state courts, rather than in the recently created lower federal courts.[97] It was not until 1875, almost ninety years later, that Congress enacted the first long-lasting general federal question jurisdiction statute for the lower federal courts.[98] It is beyond understanding how, in light of this undisputed history of state court enforcement of federal law, anyone can seriously question the constitutional authority of the state judiciaries to adjudicate federal rights and claims.[99] Why else does the Constitution contain a supremacy clause?

Welsh fails to respond directly to these contentions, but may have done so by implication. Though he unconvincingly suggests that "much of the evidence suggests that article III was written to *preclude* reliance on state courts altogether,"[100] his fallback position is that "even assuming that the Constitution allowed a limited role for state courts, [the mere fact that] Congress could permit state courts to hear federal claims [does] not suggest that the Constitution or Congress could empower tribunals to exercise 'the Judicial power of the United States.'"[101] Under Welsh's interpretation of Article III, "because state courts were constitutionally ineligible to serve as lower federal courts, Congress could either create independent federal tribunals or leave federal enforcement to the state judicial process. Congress did not have the option . . . to vest 'the Judicial power of the United States' in state courts."[102]

Welsh thus appears to concede, at least as a fall-back stance, that state courts actually can adjudicate federal law and enforce federal claims (a wise concession, since they have done so from 1789 to the present day). He seems to believe, however, that in doing so the state courts—unlike the federal courts—are not exercising the federal "judicial power." One may reasonably inquire whether he intends to suggest that when a *federal* court adjudicates a claim under the Federal Employers' Liability Act or one of the federal civil rights acts, it is exercising the federal "judicial power," yet when a *state* court does so it is not exercising that same power.[103] If so, his argument amounts to little more than an empty, irrelevant formalism: in both cases, the courts perform the exact same functions, exercise the identical authority, and operate under the exact same obligations. Thus, the use of the label, "judicial power," would seem to have absolutely no relevance to the realities of the situation.

Welsh's reliance on the analysis of Chief Justice Taney in *Ableman v. Booth*,[104] at least as a prima facie matter, appears to provide stronger support for his position. The same could be said for the post–Civil War decision in *Tarble's Case*,[105] which relied heavily on *Ableman* in holding that a state court lacked authority to issue writs of habeas corpus to federal military officers. In *Ableman*, the Supreme Court held that state courts lacked authority to issue a writ of habeas corpus to require federal authorities to produce a prisoner held in federal custody. In so holding, Taney's opinion provided an articulation of the dual federalism model in the judicial context:

There can be no such thing as judicial authority, unless it is conferred by a Government or sovereignty; and if the judges and courts of Wisconsin possess the jurisdiction they claim, they must derive it either from the United States or the State. It certainly has not been conferred on them by the United States; and it is equally clear it was not in the power of the State to confer it, even if it had attempted to do so; for no State can authorize one of its judges or courts to exercise judicial power, by *habeas corpus* or otherwise, within the jurisdiction of another and independent Government. [106]

Welsh fails to acknowledge, however, that the *Ableman-Tarble* dual sovereignty analysis has been heavily criticized by respected commentators, for the very reason that it departs so strikingly from traditional assumptions about the role of state courts as enforcers of federal rights. [107] In his important historical study, Judge Gibbons noted:

Until *Abelman* [sic] *v. Booth,* the assumption always had been that state courts had unlimited jurisdiction within their respective territories, subject only to the congressional power to provide for federal exclusivity, pretrial removal, or appellate review. Thus the Court's holding that state courts lacked authority to consider the legality of confinement under federal process was a remarkable instance of judicial creativity. [108]

Hence, *Ableman* and *Tarble* may be viewed simply as judicial overreactions to the preconflict tensions and aftermath of the Civil War, rather than as representatives of established American federalism theory. Ironically, the two decisions underscore the point, made earlier, [109] that use of a dual federalism model may be employed just as easily as a means of *increasing* federal power at the expense of state institutions as the other way around. In historical context, however, they do not establish the judicial duality that Welsh asserts.

I should emphasize that while I consider *Ableman* and *Tarble* to represent poorly reasoned aberrations from long-established tradition, I have always accepted their ultimate conclusions. I reach this result by rejecting their dubious dual federalism analysis in favor of an inference, in the face of congressional silence, of an implied congressional decision to render exclusively federal the judicial power directly to control the conduct of federal officers. [110] In fact, much of my writing has argued against modern acceptance of the principles of state-federal court fungibility. [111] But this view in no way undermines recognition of either the historical or modern shared role of state and federal courts as enforcers and interpreters of federal law.

There is, I submit, no inconsistency in these two positions. One can readily accept both *Tarble* and *Testa v. Katt,* [112] even though under the former state courts are denied power to enforce federal law, while under the latter they are compelled to do so. This seeming inconsistency is reconciled by recognizing the existence of both the combative and cooperative elements of interactive federalism in the judicial context: [113] in certain situations, the interaction of state court with federal law will undermine an overriding federal legislative scheme,[114] while in others cooperative interaction will be required to facilitate attainment of federal policies.

It should also be emphasized that to suggest that state courts may contribute to the development of federal law does not necessarily imply that they be viewed as the equal of the federal courts in performance of this task, any more than the federal courts' contributions to the development of state law in the exercise of their diversity jurisdiction[115] imply equality with the state courts as the shapers of state law. The Supreme Court's fashioning of jurisdictional doctrine[116] on the unsupported assumption that state and federal courts are fungible as protectors of federal rights is plainly inaccurate today,[117] just as it was in 1871, when the major statutory protection of civil rights against incursion by state officers was enacted.[118] More importantly, judge-made doctrines premised on this assumption of fungibility undermine the congressional determination to afford an individual the option of choosing between state and federal courts for the enforcement of his federal rights.[119] But the fact that state courts are both theoretically and practically unequal to the federal courts as enforcers of federal rights does not alter the long history of state court involvement in the interpretation and enforcement of federal law, which continues to this day. Nor does it suggest that state courts would in all cases be unable to make contributions to the development of federal law when given the opportunity.

Finally, it should be noted that rejection of Welsh's rigid dichotomy between state and federal judicial authority does not lead—as Welsh believes—"to the federalization of state courts."[120] Whatever role the state courts ultimately play as enforcers of federal law, their primary responsibility will always be the development and interpretation of state law. Nor is there any reason to believe that recognition of the shared federal power of state and federal courts necessarily precludes state court discretion to rely on state, rather than federal constitutional protections, as long as they do not undermine federal law. The fluid and dynamic nature of interactive federalism prevents use of such rigid categorization.

State Law in the Federal Courts

Equally beyond dispute is the important role the federal courts have played in the adjudication and development of state law. Pursuant to their diversity jurisdiction,[121] the federal courts have long contributed to state law construction.[122] In fact, one of the arguments currently relied upon by respected advocates of the continued maintenance of diversity jurisdiction is the important contribution made by the federal courts to the growth and improvement of state law.[123] This growth is accomplished through a type of interfederal judicial dialogue, conducted through the decisional process that is typical of the tradition of interactive federalism.[124] Moreover, in addition to the diversity jurisdiction, federal courts contribute to the development of state substantive law in the exercise of their supplemental jurisdiction, which authorizes them to adjudicate issues of state law that arise out of the same set of factual circumstances as a federal case already before them.[125]

Finally, note should be taken of the manner in which both state and federal judicial systems have borrowed from each other in the development of judicial procedures.[126] Thus, the role of state courts as interpreters of federal law is to a large extent mirrored in the federal judicial exposition of state law.

Federalism as Constitutional Theory: Textual Analysis, the Commerce Clause, and the Theory of Enumerated Powers

The preceding discussion is devoted to the nature of interaction between the two levels of sovereignty in the American federal system. Although to a certain extent that analysis implicates issues of constitutional text and structure, its focus is primarily on the normative political theory that underlies American federalism. The values sought to be attained by that political theory might be seriously threatened, however, if the constitutional protections of federalism were ignored, thereby enabling the federal government effectively to consume the states by completely preempting their policymaking authority. At the same time, the carefully structured constitutional balance of federalism could be upset if the judiciary were to impose constitutional limitations on federal power that could not be grounded in the Constitution's text. Moreover, for reasons explored in chapter 1,[127] Supreme Court constitutional interpretations that fail to comport with legitimate constructions of constitutional text undermine the judiciary's proper role in American political theory. Hence the analysis now moves from the predominantly normative-political level of inquiry to an examination of the Constitution's implications in its exploration of American federalism.

On a constitutional level, while state and federal power have clashed on numerous fronts, the primary battle between state and federal governments has come in the construction of Congress's enumerated power to regulate interstate commerce.[128] It is generally through the exercise of this power, combined with its auxiliary authority under the Necessary-and-Proper Clause,[129] that Congress today seeks to regulate countless aspects of the commercial and personal lives of the citizenry. An understanding of the proper scope of federal authority under the Commerce Clause begins with an analysis of the constitutional text.

The Enclave and Abdication Models: A Textual Critique

The Doctrinal Background

In *National League of Cities v. Usery*,[130] the Court considered the constitutionality of the 1974 amendments[131] to the federal Fair Labor Standards Act,[132] which extended minimum wage and maximum hour legislation to state and local government employees. The Court began its analysis by explicitly recognizing Congress's power under the Commerce Clause to regulate minimum wage and maximum hour standards for private employees. In recognizing Congress's power in this area, the Court cited a long line of decisions establishing this precedent and, in addition, noted that the plaintiffs challenging the constitutionality of the 1974 amendment did not question Congress's ability to regulate the wages and hours of private employees.[133] Nevertheless, Justice Rehnquist, writing for the majority, reasoned that "there are attributes of sovereignty attaching to every state government which may not be impaired by Congress, not because Congress may lack an affirmative grant of legislative authority to reach the matter, but because the Constitution prohibits it from exercising the authority in that manner."[134] He concluded that

> [o]ne undoubted attribute of state sovereignty is the States' power to determine the wages which shall be paid to those whom they employ in order to carry out their governmental functions, what hours those persons will work, and what compensation will be provided where these employees may be called upon to work overtime.[135]

The majority held that "insofar as the challenged amendments operate to directly displace the States' freedom to structure integral operations in areas of traditional governmental functions," they violate the constitutionally based protection of state sovereignty. The Court explicitly confined its decision to cases arising under the Commerce Clause and did not consider whether the result would be different if Congress were to affect state sovereignty by exercising authority granted under other sections of the Constitution, such as the Spending Clause.[136] Justice Blackmun concluded in a brief concurrence that the Court had adopted a balancing approach. Under such an approach, he reasoned, the Court would not "outlaw federal power in areas such as environmental protection, where the federal interest is demonstrably greater and where state facility compliance with imposed federal standards would be essential."[137]

In *Garcia v. San Antonio Metropolitan Transit Authority*,[138] nine years later, the Court overturned *National League of Cities* in upholding the extension of minimum wage and maximum hour legislation to metropolitan mass transit employees. Justice Blackmun, writing for the majority, concluded that *National League of Cities* had not only failed to develop an adequate standard for defining the scope of traditional governmental functions but had also reached inconsistent results in attempting to apply that standard.[139] He concluded that "the attempt to draw the boundaries of state regulatory immunity in terms of 'traditional governmental functions' is not only unworkable but is also inconsistent with established principles of federalism."[140] According to Justice Blackmun, the Framers chose to rely on a federal system in which special restraints on federal power over the states "inhered principally in the workings of the National Government itself, rather than in discrete limitations on the objects of federal authority."[141]

Hence, state sovereign interests "are more properly protected by procedural safeguards inherent in the structure of the federal system than by judicially created limitations on federal power."[142] As a result, "[a]ny substantive restraint on the exercise of Commerce Clause powers must find its justification in the procedural nature of this basic limitation."[143] In sum, the Court in *Garcia* concluded that except under the rare circumstance of a failure in the political process,[144] the Court should refrain from interfering with congressional legislation on the grounds that it exceeds Commerce Clause limitations.

A certain degree of ambiguity exists in the Court's opinion in *Garcia* as to exactly how the ability of the states to protect themselves in the political process affects the Court's interpretation of the Commerce Clause. For example, the Court cited the structure of the national government itself as "the principal means chosen by the Framers to ensure the role of the States in the federal system," apart from "the limitation on federal authority inherent in the delegated nature of Congress's Article I powers."[145] The opinion thus seemed to acknowledge the existence of limitations on the federal government deriving from the concept of limited powers, and appears to refer to the structural ability of the states to protect themselves merely as an *additional* form of protection. Later in the opinion, however, the Court might be thought to imply that any limitations on Congress's power it finds in the Commerce Clause have nothing to do with interpretation of the terms "commerce" or "among the several States":

> [W]e are convinced that the fundamental limitation that the constitutional scheme imposes on the Commerce Clause to protect the "States as States" is one of process rather than one of result. Any substantive restraint on the exercise of Commerce Clause powers must find its justification in the procedural nature of this basic limitation, and it must be tailored to compensate for possible failings in the national political process rather than to dictate a "sacred province of state autonomy."[146]

It is true that in the first sentence quoted above, the Court refers to the protections of the "States as States." This language suggests that the Court's "political process" analysis of the commerce power was intended to be limited to situations in which Congress attempts to employ that power to regulate state governments directly—the specific issue involved in *National League of Cities*. The second quoted sentence, however, expressly refers to "[a]*ny* substantive restraint of the exercise of Commerce Clause powers" (emphasis added), apparently extending its reach to *all* exercises of the commerce power. Moreover, at another point in the opinion, the Court stated that "the principal and basic limit on the federal commerce power is that inherent in all congressional action—the built-in restraints that our system provides through state participation in federal governmental action."[147] Nothing in this sentence confines the Court's "political process" analysis to direct regulations of state governments. Rather, it appears to apply to *any* congressional exercise of the commerce power. Moreover, Professor Choper, who was cited by the Court, had relied upon the "political process" analysis in support of a total judicial abdication of the review function in Commerce Clause cases, regardless of whether the federal regulation is of state governments or private authority.[148] Thus, it may be that the *Garcia* Court's hypothetical treatment of the Commerce Clause's reach to private activity was as brief and conclusory as it was[149] precisely because of its belief in the "political process" rationale. The fact remains, however, that the Court's primary, if not exclusive, focus in *Garcia* was on the special sovereignty protection against *direct* federal regulation recognized in *National League of Cities*, rather than on the more traditional situation of federal reliance on the commerce power to regulate private activity. Subsequent decisions seem to make clear that the Court sees *Garcia* solely as a case that rejected the concept of a special state enclave against direct federal regulation.[150]

More recently, the Court has demonstrated its willingness to intervene, at least under limited circumstances, to protect the states from what it deems unconstitutional federal coercion. But the Court appeared to limit its intervention to a narrow class of cases, in which the federal government effectively commandeers the state's legislative process. In *New York v. United States*,[151] the Court held unconstitutional the so-called "take title" provision of the Low-Level Radioactive Waste Policy Amendments Act of 1985[152] on the grounds that it violated the Tenth Amendment. The provision specified that a state or regional compact of states that failed to provide for the disposal of all internally generated radioactive waste by a particular date must, upon the request of the waste's generator or owner, take title and possession of the waste and become liable for all damages suffered by the generator or owner as a result of the state's failure promptly to take possession.[153] In invalidating this provision, the Court, in an opinion by Justice O'Connor, reasoned that "Congress may not simply 'commandee[r] the legislative processes of the States by directly compelling them to enact and enforce a federal regulatory program.'"[154] The Court found no inconsistency between its holdings in *New York* and *Garcia*, because *Garcia* "concerned the authority of Congress to subject state governments to generally applicable laws."[155] Therefore *New York*, wrote Justice O'Connor, "presents no occasion to apply or revisit" the holding of either *Garcia* or any similar decision, because "this is not a case in which Congress has subjected a State to the same legislation applicable to private parties."[156]

In dissent, Justice White found this suggested distinction unpersuasive, asserting that the Court "builds its rule around an insupportable and illogical distinction in the types of alleged incursions on state sovereignty. . . ."[157] He correctly noted that "[t]he Court's distinction between a federal statute's regulation of States and private parties for general purposes, as opposed to a regulation solely on the activities of States, is unsupported by our recent Tenth Amendment cases."[158] More importantly, he correctly noted that "the

Court makes no effort to explain why this purported distinction should affect the analysis of Congress' power under general principles of federalism and the Tenth Amendment. The distinction, facilely thrown out, is not based on any defensible theory."[159] In attacking the Court's distinction, Justice White persuasively argued that "[t]he alleged diminution in state authority is not any less because the federal mandate restricts the activities of private parties."[160]

Whether or not the *New York* Court's asserted distinction of *Garcia* is deemed persuasive, it appears likely that on a purely doctrinal level its underlying logic will leave the *Garcia* holding largely intact. In effect, the Court's invalidation of the "take title" provision in *New York* will mean only that Congress may not directly coerce a state government into legislating.[161] When the federal government simply imposes the same regulatory burdens on the state governments that it has imposed on private parties, or when the federal government has merely preempted state authority to regulate private conduct, it is likely that the deference accorded the federal government in *Garcia* will remain intact. To be sure, the Court's decision in *New York* does undermine the coherence of the logic of judicial abstention that appeared to underly *Garcia* by recognizing at least a limited area appropriate for judicial intervention. Nevertheless, as a practical matter it is likely that for the most part, the Court will continue to abstain from controversies implicating issues of constitutional federalism.

It is true, of course, that the Court in *Garcia* implied that it will intervene if there is a breakdown in the processes by which the legislation was adopted. But at no point does the Court indicate exactly what processes must be followed in order to insure that the states are adequately represented in the decisionmaking process. It is therefore doubtful that the Court's standard, to the extent that it was designed to represent anything other than total abandonment of the enclave of state protection, would be workable.

While the Court appears to have abandoned the special insulation of state governments from federal regulation it had recognized in *National League of Cities*, it has never formally adopted Professor Choper's abdication model for cases involving exercises of the commerce power to regulate private activity. One may reasonably question, however, whether as a practical matter the Court has not reached a result in Commerce Clause cases that is tantamount to judicial abdication. The Court has not invalidated a congressional regulation of private commerce since the 1930s,[162] and while this fact alone may be dispositive of nothing, the Court's doctrinal analysis in upholding these laws could easily be extrapolated to amount to an all-but-total judicial deference to congressional decisionmaking. Such a doctrinal approach, however, cannot be reconciled with the Constitution's text, when read as a whole. The same can be said of the construction of constitutional protection of states by the Court in *National League of Cities*. This can be demonstrated by contrasting both of these doctrinal models with the language and structure of the relevant provisions of the Constitution.

National League of Cities, *the Tenth Amendment,*
and Constitutional Text

In *National League of Cities*,[163] Justice Rehnquist acknowledged for the majority that, when applied to the private sector, federal wage and hours laws constitute legitimate exercises of the federal commerce power.[164] Thus, in barring the application of such laws to state governments, Justice Rehnquist clearly did not rely on a construction of the Commerce Clause, because that clause provides no distinction in its scope based on whether the subject of regulation is private or state operated.[165] Rather, he based his decision on what he saw as the constitutional structure of federalism embodied in the Tenth Amendment. That amendment provides that "[t]he powers not delegated to the United States by the Constitution, nor prohibited by it to the States, are reserved to the States respectively, or to the people."[166]

For many years the Court construed the Tenth Amendment to perform a function similar to that performed by other provisions in the first ten amendments: to provide an "enclave" against what would otherwise be an authorized exercise of governmental power.[167] For example, if Congress were to enact a law providing that no newspaper traveling in interstate commerce could criticize the president of the United States, it is likely (at least under current standards of interpretation) that such an act would be found to be authorized by the Constitution's grant of authority to Congress to regulate interstate commerce.[168] The law, in other words, falls within the "checklist"[169] of enumerated congressional powers. But while falling within the constitutional checklist is a *necessary* condition for an enactment's constitutional validity, it is not a *sufficient* one. For the Constitution also contains various additional limitations on governmental authority—"enclaves" of activity insulated from governmental control. In the case of the hypothetical congressional enactment, then, the fact that the statute was found to be authorized by Article I would answer only part of the constitutional inquiry; the First Amendment's free press protection[170] would undoubtedly invalidate the law, despite its prima facie authorization by the Commerce Clause.

Similarly, early judicial pronouncements treated the Tenth Amendment as "a second line of constitutional defense against federal overreaching, a sort of enclave of 'local affairs' committed exclusively to state regulation and therefore, whatever the checklist might imply, beyond the reach of the central government."[171] During the New Deal period, however, the Court rejected this construction of the Tenth Amendment and instead recognized it for what, as a linguistic matter, it appears to be: a truism.[172] In other words, all the amendment provides is that the states retain powers not given to the federal government. The only means of determining whether a particular power is reserved to the states, then, is by first deciding whether the power has been granted to the federal government in its checklist of powers. If a particular power has been given to the federal government, in Article I or elsewhere in the Constitution, that power is tautologically not reserved to the states by the Tenth Amendment.

By conceding in *National League of Cities* that Congress's regulation of wages and hours was in fact authorized by the Commerce Clause,[173] Justice Rehnquist effectively conceded the Tenth Amendment argument. Because the power in question was admittedly *granted* to the federal government, it could not be simultaneously *retained* by the states. Justice Rehnquist made no meaningful attempt to respond to this dispositive textual argument. He relied instead on the Court's statement about the Tenth Amendment one year earlier in *Fry v. United States:*[174]

> While the Tenth Amendment has been characterized as a "truism," stating merely that "all is retained which has not been surrendered," . . . it is not without significance. The Amendment expressly declares the constitutional policy that Congress may not exercise power in a fashion that impairs the States' integrity or their ability to function effectively in a federal system.[175]

But this ultimately amounts to an obfuscation of the textual argument, rather than a response to it. The amendment "expressly declares" absolutely nothing about Congress's power to impair the states' integrity, except to reaffirm that the federal government is one of limited powers. Unless Congress's exercise of a constitutionally delegated power violates a limitation imposed by another constitutional provision, its action cannot be unconstitutional. Since the Tenth Amendment imposes no additional limitations, the exercise of one of Congress's enumerated powers cannot unconstitutionally undermine state integrity.[176]

One may legitimately ask, of course, why the Tenth Amendment was ratified in the first place if it only stated a truism that presumably would have been understood in any case. The answer is quite probably that the amendment represented what amounted to an exclamation point to the concept of limited federal powers embodied in the original text of the Constitution. The amendment served to allay the fears of state representatives, who wished to leave no doubt that the federal government was one of limited powers.[177] While in a technical sense the amendment adds nothing that we probably could not have derived from the text itself, then, in a more practical, political sense it accomplished a great deal at the time of its adoption.[178]

Although the amendment served an important political purpose, its text provides absolutely no basis for the creation of a distinct enclave of state power that inhibits the exercise of a grant of power to the federal government. Thus, Justice Rehnquist, a jurist traditionally associated with a view of the judiciary's role as extremely limited in a democratic society,[179] invalidated the actions of the majoritarian branches of government without any supporting basis in the Constitution's text.

The Supreme Court's recent limited reassertion of a Tenth Amendment enclave for state power in *New York v. United States*[180] is no more acceptable as a matter of textual construction. There, in invalidating the "take title" provision of the Low-Level Radioactive Waste Policy Amendments Act of 1985,[181] Justice O'Connor did nothing more than conclusorily assert that Congress may not "commandeer" the state legislatures by requiring them to enact legislation.[182] There can be little doubt that in so holding, she was assuming the existence of some sort of enclave of state sovereign power in the Tenth Amendment, above and beyond the limits inherent in the concept of enumerated powers[183]—an enclave that cannot be discerned from the provision's text.

Perhaps an argument could be fashioned that Justice O'Connor's reasoning was simply that Congress's enumerated powers should not be construed to extend to requiring enactment of state legislation. If so, the decision in *New York* could be rationalized as simply a construction of the enumerated powers of Article I, Section 8, rather than as an assertion of an enclave of state authority, immune from federal incursion. But such a suggestion would amount to little more than a play or words. The Court's analysis in *New York* does not inquire whether Congress's legislation is actually designed to affect or regulate interstate commerce, but rather poses the same inquiry posed by the "enclave" concept of the Tenth Amendment: whether state governments are improperly burdened by federal legislation that requires them to legislate to some preordained end.

In her opinion, Justice O'Connor attempted to blur the enumerated power-enclave choice, by suggesting that the supposed dichotomy was a false one. "[I]t makes no difference," she asserted, "whether one views the question at issue in this case as one of ascertaining the limits of the power delegated to the Federal Government under the affirmative provisions of the Constitution or one of discerning the core of sovereignty retained by the States under the Tenth Amendment. Either way, we must determine whether any of the three challenged provisions . . . oversteps the boundary between federal and state authority."[184] She argued that "the two inquiries are mirror images of each other," because "if a power is an attribute of state sovereignty reserved by the Tenth Amendment, it is necessarily a power the Constitution has not conferred on Congress."[185]

Her assertion that the Tenth Amendment and enumerated powers analyses are mirror images of each other is accurate, however, only if one views the Tenth Amendment as nothing more than a reassertion of the concept of limited powers, as the post–New Deal Commerce Clause cases held.[186] But if this had been Justice O'Connor's view, she would have inquired solely whether the means chosen by Congress furthered its constitutionally dictated goal of regulating interstate commerce. Instead, she inquired solely whether Congress's chosen means of enforcing its commerce power improperly burdened the states.[187] This inquiry is derived from an enclave analysis, not from an examination of the scope of Congress's enumerated powers. Such an enclave analysis, however, cannot be squared with the explicit text of the Tenth Amendment, which by its terms unambiguously establishes that its limitation on federal power is coterminous with the limitations inherent in the concept of enumerated powers.

Justice O'Connor justified her conclusion that the federal government could not require state legislation in part on her finding that the Framers consciously chose not to authorize such a practice. At least to a certain extent, however, she appears to have turned history on its head. The history to which she points concerns primarily the Framers' decision to depart from prior practice under the Articles of Confederation, which required Congress to act through state legislatures.[188] There is, of course, all the difference in the world between *requiring* Congress to act only through state legislatures on the one hand and *permitting* Congress to do so.

Though it has recently been argued that Justice O'Connor's understanding of Framers' intent is largely accurate,[189] even if true this fact is largely beside the point. Unless the Framers actually embodied their goal in constitutional text, that goal has no constitutional status, because it has not been subjected to the ratification process; only the text has received such treatment. At most,[190] then, original intent can play a role in *interpreting ambiguous constitutional text*. In the case of congressional power to require state legislation, however, even if Justice O'Connor's conclusion as to the Framers' intent were correct, no provision of constitutional text can even arguably be thought to embody the Framers' goal. If the Framers had in fact decided that Congress could not require state legislation, one would think that they would have included an explicit prohibition on such a power in the text. At the very least, they could reasonably have been expected to insert some special protection of state sovereignty, framed in general terms. With the possible exception of the Guarantee Clause, which at most applies only in truly extreme circumstances, they did neither. Indeed, when, in the Tenth Amendment, the Constitution's drafters finally did make some reference to protection of the states, it was only to reaffirm the concept of enumerated powers. Thus, the history to which Justice O'Connor points—even if it were not as questionable as it is—cannot support a finding of a prohibition on federal power to require state legislation.

Justice O'Connor expressly declined to ground her protection of state power in the Guarantee Clause, which provides that "[t]he United States shall guarantee to every State in this Union a Republican Form of Government. . . ."[191] While the conclusion may not be textually inevitable, the provision could reasonably be construed to prohibit the federal government from forcing a state legislature to adopt legislation which it might not have chosen to adopt of its own free will. Under these circumstances, one could argue that the electorates of the individual states had been deprived of the representation and accountability that inhere in the concept of republican government. And since the Guarantee Clause requires that the federal government "guarantee to the states a republican form of government," a fortiori the provision prohibits the federal government from itself *destroying* republican government in the states. But it is highly doubtful that a proper analysis of the Guarantee Clause would lead to invalidation of the take title provision.[192] One might argue that by requiring a state legislature to enact legislation that it would not otherwise enact, Congress is subverting the representative and accountability processes that are central to the concept of republican government. But when one recalls that Congress unquestionably has constitutional power to preempt *all* state regulation (or nonregulation) of nuclear waste, regardless of the contrary will of particular state legislatures, the "nonrepublican" aspect of the "take title" provision appears less damning. Ultimately, the primary regulatory policy choice is made by Congress and the President, both representative and accountable bodies. In the tradition of "interactive" federalism, state legislatures are "conscripted" to enact implementing legislation, and to the extent they have freedom to shape the method of achieving that federal policy choice to the specific needs of their states they, too, are acting in a representative and accountable manner. In any event, Justice O'Connor chose not to rely on the Guarantee Clause because the issue had been rendered moot by her construction of the Tenth Amendment.[193] It is clear, however, that as a textual matter the Guarantee Clause is at least arguably capable of a construction consistent with Justice O'Connor's view. The Tenth Amendment, upon which Justice O'Connor chose to rely, is not.

It should be emphasized, however, that at most the Guarantee Clause could justify invalidation of the relatively unique form of regulation involved in *New York* and not serve as a textual substitute for the Tenth Amendment in support of the enclave recognized in *National League of Cities*. In *New York* the Court found that the federal statute effectively forced the state legislature to enact a statute. As noted, such a result could be thought to violate the Guarantee Clause, because the legislators are required—perhaps against their will—to fashion substantive legislation, and thus cannot be held accountable for that legislative policy choice by those whom they represent—the fundamental premise of republican government. However, to invalidate on Guarantee Clause grounds any congressional legislation imposing direct regulatory limits that the states may not contravene would be to allow the Guarantee Clause to swallow the Supremacy Clause. Congress, in the valid exercise of its powers, may impose limits that the states may not contravene. Arguably, however, Congress could be thought to violate the Guarantee Clause when it indirectly coerces the state legislature into enactment of particular substantive legislation.

Under an enumerated powers analysis, to decide whether Congress's requirement that states take title to waste for which they had not made disposal provisions is unconstitutional, one would have to determine whether imposition of such a requirement falls within one or more of Congress's enumerated powers in Article I, read in combination with the Necessary-and-Proper Clause.[194] No doubt, Congress could reasonably conclude that radioactive waste presents a problem of national proportions, thereby triggering the congressional power to regulate interstate commerce. The difficult question under this "enumerated powers" analysis, however, is whether Congress must choose between preempting state regulatory power through the enactment of controlling substantive federal legislation on the one hand or leaving the problem to regulation by the individual states on the other—the likelihood of which, of course, varies from state to state. One might argue that the Constitution should be construed to impose this either-or choice on the federal government. Yet it is surely conceivable that Congress might conclude that while the problem is one that must be dealt with, individualized state treatment is likely to prove the most efficient and effective method of regulation. As long as it is agreed that the Necessary-and-Proper Clause should be given something more than a narrow and grudging interpretation, it would seem that Congress should not be forced into the position of choosing between a possibly inefficient nationwide regulatory scheme and the risk that, if left to their own devices, individual states would choose to leave the problem unaddressed. Viewed in this manner, the congressional action invalidated in *New York* could be deemed simply an example of the "interactive" federalism that has existed throughout the nation's history.

The Abdication Model and Constitutional Text

While Justice Rehnquist's adoption of the "enclave" model of federalism in *National League of Cities* improperly construed the text of the Tenth Amendment to provide states with an additional level of constitutional protection of their sovereignty, the conclusion that protection of federalism should be relegated exclusively to the Darwinism of the political process does not logically follow. Once again, analysis of the textual structure demonstrates that the Constitution contemplates a different course.

The Constitution's drafters had three options open to them in addressing the issue of state protection against federal incursion. First, they could have simply ignored the problem. The federal government could have been vested with general open-ended powers that it could exercise as it deemed necessary. Second, as previously discussed, they could have chosen to protect the states by creating an "enclave." Whatever powers they ultimately chose to vest in the federal government, they could have prohibited that government from invading certain specified state prerogatives. Finally, they could have chosen to protect the states merely by limiting the scope of the federal government's powers. While the states would receive no special, direct constitutional protection, they would be protected indirectly, because the federal government would be prohibited from usurping state authority beyond the limits implicit in its checklist of enumerated powers. An examination of the text demonstrates that the drafters in fact chose this final option.

Two constitutional provisions are central to an examination of the Constitution's allocation of power between state and federal governments: Article I, Section 8 (which delegates power to Congress), and the Tenth Amendment. Any legitimate interpretation of the constitutional protection of federalism, therefore, must not only be compatible with the language of each provision but must also explain how these provisions interact to form a cohesive and consistent formulation of the division of power; that is, the interpretation must be justified by the "textual structure."

Article I, Section 8 contains eighteen clauses, each bestowing a discrete power on the national government.[195] Article I, Section 8's language forms a checklist that invests Congress with specific powers rather than a more general, open-ended authority, along the lines of "The United States may enact any law it deems necessary and proper."[196] This checklist structure necessarily implies a limitation on congressional authority. Had the document not presumed that the powers of the federal government be limited, enumerating specific powers would have been a pointless exercise. As Chief Justice Marshall correctly noted in *Gibbons v. Ogden,* "[E]numeration presupposes something not enumerated. . . ."[197] Thus, examination of the four corners of the document reveals a textual structure that rejects the concept of unlimited federal power.

One could conceivably argue that the enumeration was intended to be merely suggestive, rather than exhaustive, but there is no basis in the text of Article I to support such a contention. Moreover, it is at this point the Tenth Amendment plays what was probably its intended role. That provision explicitly precludes such a construction of Article I, which would have been highly dubious even without that amendment. The amendment's text underscores the fact that what has not been delegated—that is, what is not on the congressional checklist—is left to the states. Under the structure imposed by the text, any analysis of whether the national government has unconstitutionally encroached upon state authority must focus solely on the nature of the national activity. If the activity falls within the scope of a checklisted power, it is legitimate. An activity outside the checklist is beyond the national government's authority.

The abdication model of constitutional federalism is, then, inconsistent with the clear directives of the text. Had those who drafted and ratified the Constitution believed that the states could adequately protect themselves in the political arena, they would have chosen the option of ignoring the issue of federalism completely and vesting Congress with unlimited legislative authority. The text is clear that this was not the chosen course, and thus inescapably reflects the belief that the states require at least a certain degree of countermajoritarian constitutional protection, above and beyond what they could achieve for themselves through the political process.

The Alleged Futility of Judicial Review: Construing the Scope of the Commerce Power

Perhaps the most persuasive response to the textual attack on judicial abdication in issues of constitutional federalism is that requiring judicial review in such cases amounts to a victory of form over substance.[198] After all, the Court has, in the name of construction of the Commerce and Necessary-and-Proper Clauses, given Congress tremendous latitude. It is certainly true that the Court's modern construction of the Commerce Clause has, as a practical matter, often led to the same results that would be achieved by express judicial adoption of the abstention model.[199] However, to the extent that a combined construction of the Commerce and Necessary-and-Proper Clauses produces results equivalent to the abdication model, they represent improper interpretations of both the textual structure of Article I, in which

Congress's powers are enumerated, and the Tenth Amendment. Moreover, even where the substantive outcomes would prove identical, the very availability and process of judicial review would probably have beneficial effects on federal legislative and administrative activity.

The Commerce Clause gives Congress power "to regulate commerce with foreign Nations, and among the several States, and with the Indian Tribes." To meet the requirements of legitimate textual interpretation, the clause must be properly limited by its language. At a minimum, in order to be an appropriate subject for regulation, the regulated activity must be rationally definable as "commerce," and that commerce must in some sense either cross state lines or at least have a non-negligible impact upon commerce that does so. Although it would be both unrealistic and unwise to attempt to develop rigid, abstract definitions of the terms "commerce" and "among the several States," it is not difficult to provide some "common-sense" content to these constitutional terms, based on the outer reaches of our society's shared linguistic conventions. The term "commerce" connotes some connection to the manufacture or sale of goods or to the provision of services for pay. The phrase, "among the several States" must be construed to require some meaningful impact across state lines—from one state to another.

The potential textual open-endedness derives not so much from the Commerce Clause itself, however, but rather from that clause read in conjunction with the Necessary-and-Proper Clause, which authorizes Congress to "make all laws which shall be necessary and proper for carrying into execution the foregoing powers . . . ."[200] In employing this power, Congress may regulate subjects that are themselves not interstate commerce, as long as their regulation will affect interstate commerce, thereby implicating the commerce power. If Congress is permitted unlimited discretion to determine the impact of its regulations on interstate commerce, there is effectively nothing left of either the enumerated powers concept or the Tenth Amendment, which reflects and affirms that concept. The unambiguous message derived from a synthesis of these textual provisions is that the federal government is designed to be one of limited powers. Although the outer reaches of those limits may conceivably expand, a conclusion that one of the enumerated powers effectively vests authority to attain any and all legislative ends surely violates the explicit command of the textual structure. For if that were not the case, neither the specific enumeration of congressional powers in Article I nor the express reservation of all "remaining" power to the states in the Tenth Amendment would have any meaning.

To be sure, since Chief Justice Marshall's opinion in *McCulloch v. Maryland*,[201] the Necessary-and-Proper Clause has received an extremely broad construction. "[W]e think," Marshall wrote, "the sound construction of the constitution must allow to the national legislature that discretion, with respect to the means by which the powers it confers are to be carried into execution, which will enable that body to perform the high duties assigned to it, in the manner most beneficial to the people."[202] He then stated what has become the foundation for a broad construction of the clause:

> Let the end be legitimate, let it be within the scope of the constitution, and all means which are appropriate which are plainly adapted to that end, which are not prohibited, but consistent with the letter and spirit of the constitution, are constitutional.[203]

The fact remains, however, that a reading of the Necessary-and-Proper Clause which effectively transforms Congress's limited enumerated powers into a blanket authorization of unlimited federal legislation cannot withstand textual analysis.

In light of its traditionally broad interpretation, the terms of the Necessary-and-Proper Clause are at least potentially subject to broad construction. However, when one places them in the context of the constitutional structure revealed from a holistic examination of the text, it becomes clear that an unlimited construction is impermissible; there must be *some* conceivable federal legislation that would fall outside the clause's terms, lest federal power become unlimited, in contravention of the limits inherent in the concept of enumerated powers provided for in both Article I, Section 8, and the Tenth Amendment. Thus, the Court must draw *some* stopping point, derived from the meaning of the governing language. For example, if Congress were to enact the proposed domestic violence legislation rendering family violence a federal crime, and were to purport to ground the act in its commerce power, the Court should hold the legislation unconstitutional. Any connection between the act and commerce of any kind, much less interstate commerce, is simply too remote. If such a law were upheld, it would be difficult to imagine *any* federal legislation that would fall outside the scope of the commerce power. And it is this inquiry that the Court must make when asked to review the constitutionality of statutes grounded in the commerce power that affect interstate commerce in at most speculative or remote ways. Before upholding such laws, the Court must be able to contemplate conceivable statutes that would exceed constitutional limits. While this mode of analysis is admittedly both awkward and difficult, there would seem to exist no viable alternative to a Court that simultaneously wishes to extend Congress's power yet adhere to the limits of the Constitution.

The Court did not have occasion to examine the scope of the commerce power, except in so-called dormant Commerce Clause settings,[204] until the turn of the century, when the Interstate Commerce Act[205] and the Sherman Act[206] were enacted. The Court's early approach to the Commerce Clause was quite narrow.[207] To a certain extent, it was based on an "enclave" conception—an approach, as already shown, that exceeds textual limits[208]— and on distinctions between "direct" and "indirect" effects on interstate commerce. Direct effects on commerce, such as price fixing in livestock markets, could be prohibited under the Sherman Act, but indirect effects, such as manufacturing an object for commerce, were beyond the scope of the clause.[209] Although the direct-indirect distinction did not violate any explicit textual directive, it reflected an unnecessarily narrow conception of the clause.

In the early part of the century the Court also relied on a "dual federalism" interpretation of the Commerce Clause: if the activity that the federal government sought to regulate was one traditionally regulated by the states, it could not simultaneously fall within the scope of federal power.[210] As already demonstrated, however, the "dual federalism" model is consistent neither with the textual structure of the Constitution nor the history of American political theory. Nor can it be justified by the text of the Tenth Amendment, which directs that the scope of power reserved to the states is determined by first examining the scope of federal power, rather than the reverse, which would be dictated by a "dual federalism" model.

In the early 1940s the Court reevaluated the scope of the commerce power. It held in *Wickard v. Filburn*[211] that acts which, taken in isolation, did not affect interstate commerce could be regulated if their aggregate economic effect was nationally significant. This principle became known as the "cumulative effects doctrine." Under this approach, an activity did not have to cross interstate lines to be subject to regulation. It was enough that the "cumulative effect" of such activities affected the national economy.[212]

In *United States v. Darby*,[213] the other major decision expanding the commerce power, the Court concluded that the power enabled Congress to legislate for the general welfare, untied to specific commercial objectives:

> Congress, following its own conception of public policy concerning the restrictions which may appropriately be imposed on interstate commerce, is free to exclude from [such] commerce articles whose use in the States for which they are destined it may conceive to be injurious to the public health, morals, or welfare, even though the State has not sought to regulate their use.[214]

It is important to note that neither *Wickard* nor this aspect of *Darby* necessarily constitutes a clear departure from explicit textual limitations. As for *Darby*, nothing in the text unambiguously establishes that the congressional purpose in regulating interstate commerce must focus upon purely commercial or economic interests. Once the textual requirements that what is regulated be "commerce" and that the commerce be "among the several States" are satisfied, the text is silent on the issue of limitations on Congress's purpose in establishing such a regulation. When one views the issue from political or social perspectives, modern economic and technological developments make reasonable the conclusion that Congress must be given expanded leeway to deal with problems that previously were not thought to be matters of federal concern. As long as the expansive interpretations fit within the textual perameters of both the Commerce Clause and the enumerated powers concept, they are not inconsistent with the basic tenets of constitutional federalism.

Wickard may seem to represent a more substantial stretching of the text, but it, too, can withstand textual analysis. Although the commerce regulated in that case concededly did not flow interstate, the contention was that, cumulatively, this type of commerce did affect interstate commerce. Pursuant to the Necessary-and-Proper Clause of Article I,[215] Congress may do more than merely exercise its specifically enumerated powers; it may also do anything that is "necessary and proper" to the effective exercise of those powers. Though that phrase is rationally susceptible to interpretations of varying breadth,[216] as both a normative and textual matter it is not unreasonable to construe it to allow Congress to regulate commerce that is purely intrastate, in order to avoid or attain a potential effect on commerce that is, in fact, interstate. Indeed, if Congress were denied this power, it might well be deprived of its ability to regulate matters of significant national concern, merely because when viewed in an individualized manner the subjects of regulation do not implicate interstate commerce.

Two aspects of the Court's modern Commerce Clause jurisprudence, however, potentially give rise to difficulties because both could conceivably lead to a construction of federal power that has an unlimited reach. One of these potential problem areas involves determination of whether federal regulation of something other than interstate commerce actually will affect commerce that crosses state lines. This problem arises in assessing the constitutionality of statutes both facially and as applied in particular cases. The Court has applied a "rational basis" test to determine whether federal legislation enacted pursuant to the commerce power ultimately affects interstate commerce:

> The Court must defer to a congressional finding that a regulated activity affects interstate commerce, if there is any rational basis for such a finding. . . . This established, the only remaining question for judicial inquiry is whether "the means chosen by [Congress] must be reasonably adapted to the end permitted by the Constitution."... The judicial task is at an end once the Court determines that Congress acted rationally in adopting a particular regulatory scheme.[217]

One may ask why the Court has chosen such a deferential course in reviewing congressional judgments that interstate commerce will ultimately be affected by particular federal legislation. There is little reason to believe that Congress possesses some special expertise on this matter that the Supreme Court lacks, or that Congress has available to it certain information to which the Court is denied access. Indeed, in a number of cases in which individual liberty was threatened, the Court disregarded another branch's judgment that regulation was necessary, despite its clear institutional deficiencies in reviewing matters within legislative or executive expertise.[218] In those individual liberty cases in which the Court *has* deferred to the superior expertise of one of the other branches, the pragmatic justification for deference was considerably clearer than in the case of commerce regulation.[219] The likeliest reason for the great deference given Congress in the commerce area is that a majority of the Court had concluded that federalism guarantees are simply

not as important to the maintenance of the values underlying our governmental system as are constitutional provisions protecting individual liberty.[220] As noted previously, however,[221] the dichotomy between constitutional guarantees of individual liberty on the one hand and of political
structure on the other dangerously ignores the important role that our political structure plays in insuring those protections of liberty. Thus, while use of
a rational basis test, at least in the abstract, is not inconsistent with the
implications of a purely textual analysis of the Commerce Clause, it appears
inadvisable as a matter of federalism theory.

One might respond to the validity of a rational basis test on the grounds
that Congress needs substantial discretion in order to deal with rapidly
changing socioeconomic conditions. Even if such an argument were accepted, however, the question remains as to how as a practical matter the
Court should apply its rational basis test. If the test is invoked simply as a
euphemism for effective abdication, the approach would as a practical matter
differ little from the more candid abdication advocated by Professor
Choper.[222] But to the extent that the use of the rational basis test in Commerce Clause cases actually did amount to judicial abstention, it would represent a violation of the textual directive derived from the concept of enumerated powers. If Congress is given unreviewable discretion to assume that
any activity has an effect on interstate commerce, then Congress's enumerated and limited powers are effectively transformed into a grant of unlimited
federal legislative power. Disregarding textual limitations on federal power,
this approach would thus be subject to the same theoretical criticisms previously leveled at the judicial abdication model.[223]

While a rational basis test could be, and on occasion has been, used
merely to disguise abstention, it is important to recognize that this need not
be the case. An examination of the use of a rational basis test in other areas of
constitutional analysis is instructive. The Court's use of a rationality test to
disguise abstention is illustrated by *Korematsu v. United States*,[224] where the
Court accepted, with effectively no review, the military's factual assertion
that military necessity justified the internment of Japanese Americans in
California at the outbreak of World War II.[225] The Court did not, as dissenting Justice Jackson urged,[226] formally refuse to rule on the validity of the
government's action. Rather, it *purported* to decide the necessity issue on its
merits, but did so by doing little more than repeating the government's
conclusory assertions.[227] Had the Court employed a *meaningful* rational
basis standard, it would have made at least some independent, objective
examination of the factual basis used by the government in making its finding
of necessity.[228] To be sure, the decision to invoke a rational basis test, rather
than a more searching form of scrutiny, can allow the reviewing court to
resolve all close questions, both factual and predictive, in favor of the government. But a test that asks the government to do no more than assert as a
conclusion the finding required to render its action constitutional amounts to
no judicial review at all.

Although the Court's invocation of the rational basis test in equal protection analysis traditionally amounted to a euphemism for abstention,[229] in several recent decisions the Court actually invoked minimum rationality review to invalidate state regulation on equal protection grounds.[230] In so doing, the Court demonstrated how, by engaging in limited but meaningful review, it may provide the majoritarian branches wide latitude to act without eviscerating a constitutional provision designed to limit those branches.[231]

Use of a *meaningful* rational basis test is, as a matter of constitutional theory, more important for federalism than for equal protection issues. Even if the Court were effectively to abstain from *certain* equal protection cases, the provision would not be rendered devoid of all meaning as a result, because of its continued application to cases involving suspect classifications and "fundamental rights."[232] If the Court abstains in the federalism area, however, those provisions are effectively rendered meaningless as limitations on congressional authority, which was their clearly intended purpose.

It is arguable that one of the Court's pre-*Garcia* efforts in the area of Commerce Clause review manifests just such a form of meaningful rational basis review. In *Hodel v. Virginia Surface Mining & Reclamation Association*,[233] the Court upheld the Surface Mining Control and Reclamation Act of 1977[234] against a Commerce Clause challenge. The act, designed to "establish a nationwide program to protect society and the environment from the adverse effects of surface coal mining operations,"[235] created

> a two-stage program for the regulation of surface coal mining: an initial, or interim regulatory phase, and a subsequent, permanent phase. The interim program mandates immediate promulgation and federal enforcement of some of the Act's environmental protection performance standards, complemented by continuing state regulation. Under the permanent phase, a regulatory program is to be adopted for each State, mandating compliance with the full panoply of federal performance standards, with enforcement responsibility lying with either the State or Federal Government.[236]

The plaintiffs in *Hodel* challenged the act partially on the grounds that it exceeded Congress's power under the Commerce Clause. In considering this challenge, the Court stated clearly its limited standard of review: "[W]hen Congress has determined that an activity affects interstate commerce, the courts need inquire only whether the finding is rational."[237] The Court concluded that "the District Court properly deferred to Congress' express findings, set out in the Act itself, about the effects of surface coal mining on interstate commerce."[238] Such language may seem to imply that rationality review is being used as a mere euphemism for abstention, since the Court appears to accept the congressional findings without probing them even slightly. The Court repeated the explicit congressional finding that

> many surface mining operations result in disturbances of surface areas "that burden and adversely affect commerce and the public welfare by destroying or diminishing the utility of land for commercial, industrial, residential, recreational, agricultural, and forestry purposes, by causing erosion and landslides, by contributing to floods, by polluting the water, by destroying

fish and wildlife habitats, by impairing natural beauty, by damaging the property of citizens, by creating hazards dangerous to life and property by degrading the quality of life in local communities, and by counteracting governmental programs and efforts to conserve soil, water, and other natural resources."[239]

Had the Court ended its inquiry simply by citing Congress's detailed but clearly conclusory findings, its rationality review would have been disconcertingly similar to the *Korematsu* approach.[240] But the Court did not end its inquiry at that point. It added that "[t]he legislative record provides ample support for these statutory findings."[241] The Court noted that the act "became law only after six years of the most thorough legislative consideration."[242] The opinion then referred to congressional committees' "detailed findings"[243] about the effect of surface mining on the nation's economy, and to specific congressional documentation of "the adverse effects of surface coal mining on interstate commerce."[244]

Whether the deference inherent in the use of a rational basis standard of review is appropriate in constitutional federalism cases is debatable. But once that standard is accepted, the Court in *Hodel* appears to have done an adequate job of reconciling use of such a test with its role as independent arbiter of constitutional limitations on the majoritarian branches of government. It is, of course, conceivable that the congressional findings were factually inaccurate, and if so it might be difficult for the Court to discover the inaccuracy. But it is not unreasonable for the Court to impose on those parties challenging the constitutionality of the legislation the burden of establishing that inaccuracy.[245]

There can be little doubt that, under a rationality standard of review, challenged federal legislation will be upheld in the overwhelming majority of cases. This is as it should be, because it would be most distressing to discover that our national legislature consistently acts in an irrational manner. It is also probably true (though likely not provable) that the states gain a certain degree of protection against federal overreaching through the workings of the political process. But it does not follow that *every* constitutional challenge will be rejected, at least under a meaningful rationality standard. More important, even if all, or virtually all, constitutional challenges are rejected on the merits, the very expectation of review encourages Congress to engage in the kind of searching inquiry it apparently undertook prior to passing the Surface Mining Act. Such an inquiry serves to ensure that Congress stays within the limitations on its power established by the Constitution in the name of federalism.

The second aspect of the Court's modern Commerce Clause jurisprudence that could easily lead to an unlimited reach of federal power can be described as the "class of activities" doctrine, articulated in *Darby*. There the Court construed certain provisions of the Fair Labor Standards Act of 1938[246] to apply to "an employer engaged . . . in the manufacture and shipment of goods in filling orders of extrastate customers, [who] manufactures his product with the intent or expectation that according to the normal course of his business all or some part of it will be selected for shipment to those customers,"[247] even if ultimately the product was shipped only interstate. "Congress was not unaware," said the Court,

> that most manufacturing businesses shipping their product in interstate commerce make it in their shops without reference to its ultimate destination and then after manufacture select some of it for shipment interstate and some intrastate according to the daily demands of their business, and that it would be practically impossible, without disrupting manufacturing businesses, to restrict the prohibited kind of production to the particular pieces of lumber, cloth, furniture or the like which later move in interstate rather than intrastate Commerce.[248]

In so holding, the Court relied on the decision in the so-called *Shreveport Case*[249] for the proposition that Congress may regulate "intrastate transactions which are so commingled with or related to interstate commerce that all must be regulated if the interstate commerce is to be effectively controlled."[250]

Such a conclusion appears to represent a reasonable construction of the Necessary-and-Proper Clause, as applied to Congress's commerce power. When it is impractical for Congress to separate those members of the regulated class who are in interstate commerce from those who are not, Congress's power to regulate interstate commerce could not be effectively exercised unless Congress is allowed also to regulate those members of the class who do not affect interstate commerce.

It should not follow, however, that Congress may rely on this logic when the two elements of the class are not so intermingled as to render regulation of only the interstate element impractical. The danger in the use of the "class of activities" doctrine, then, is that Congress will rely on it to regulate all elements of a subject class, including those that are not in interstate commerce, even when the drawing of a regulatory distinction would not be truly impractical.

A possible example of such unacceptable bootstrapping is *Perez v. United States*.[251] There the defendant had been convicted of "loan sharking" activities in violation of the Consumer Credit Protection Act.[252] The defendant argued that Congress could not reach his activities under the Commerce Clause, because all of his activities had been conducted intrastate. The Court, relying heavily on *Darby*, upheld the conviction because the defendant "is clearly *a member of the class* which engages in 'extortionate credit transactions' as defined by Congress. . . ."[253] It concluded that "[w]hen the *class of activities* is regulated and that *class* is within the reach of federal power, the courts have no power 'to excise, as trivial, individual instances of the class.'"[254] The question, however, is why does the Court not have the *obligation* to "excise" such activities, unless Congress can establish that separation would be impractical? After all, unless the members of the class are thus intermingled, the entire rationale for congressional regulation of the members not themselves in interstate commerce disappears.

While finding "impracticality" may present some doctrinal problems, a relatively simple method of determining impracticality would be to inquire first whether federal enforcement of Congress's regulation required an individualized adjudicatory process, and second whether *all* of the subject's regulated activities were intrastate. Where Congress either has chosen or is constitutionally required to provide such an individualized process, as in the case of criminal prosecutions such as *Perez,* and defendants can establish that their own activities were *entirely* intrastate (rather than intermingled with interstate activities), it surely is not impracticable to separate the members of the class who can be constitutionally regulated from those who cannot. While making such a defense available to a subject of regulation will no doubt increase the federal regulatory burden somewhat, it will do so only minimally, especially if the burden of proof is placed on the subjects of regulation to establish that their activities were entirely intrastate. Thought it would of course be more *convenient,* for purposes of federal regulation, to allow wholesale grouping of similar activities, whether or not they all constitute interstate commerce, such convenience would be gained at the price of the concept of limited federal power. The standard for application of the "class of activities" doctrine should be as restrictive as in its first articulation in the *Shreveport Case:* it is only where "the interstate and intrastate transactions . . . are so related that the government of one involves the control of the other,"[255] that the doctrine may be invoked. As Justice Stewart, dissenting in *Perez,* persuasively argued:

> [U]nder the statute before us a man can be convicted without any proof of
> interstate movement, of the use of the facilities of interstate commerce, or of
> facts showing that his conduct affected interstate commerce. I think the
> Framers of the Constitution never intended that the National Government
> might define as a crime and prosecute such wholly local activity through the
> enactment of federal criminal laws.[256]

It is true that the Court in *Perez* also found that "[e]xtortionate credit transactions, though purely intrastate, may in the judgment of Congress affect interstate commerce," because Congress had found that loan sharking was 'the second largest source of revenue for organized crime . . . and is one way by which the underworld obtains control of legitimate businesses."[257] But it is in such situations that the Court must ask itself whether its logic proves too much—in other words, whether such reasoning would authorize the federalization of *all* activity.[258] If so, then the Court's reasoning would effectively allow Congress's commerce power, read in conjunction with the Necessary-and-Proper Clause, to consume the textually dictated and politically sound principle of limited federal power.[259] As Justice Stewart noted:

> [I]t is not enough to say that loan sharking is a national problem for all crime
> is a national problem. It is not enough to say that some loan sharking has

interstate characteristics, for any crime may have an interstate setting. And the circumstance that loan sharking has an adverse impact on interstate business is not a distinguishing attribute, for interstate business suffers from almost all criminal activity, be it shoplifting or violence in the streets.[260]

Justice Stewart correctly asserted that "[i]n order to sustain this law we would . . . have to be able at the least to say that Congress could rationally have concluded that loan sharking is an activity with interstate attributes that distinguish it in some substantial respect from other local crime."[261]

Federalism, the Court And the Constitution

It might be argued that today the concepts of "interstate" and "intrastate" commerce are meaningless and that, in light of advances in transportation and technology, there is no longer any commerce that can be truly deemed "intrastate." It might further be contended that the political values traditionally thought to be fostered by use of a federal system [262] are no longer valid, if they ever were, or that federalism does not serve those values. But neither of these arguments justifies the abandonment of judicial review in constitutional federalism cases.

Acceptance of the view that today all commerce is interstate effectively rejects the carefully structured constitutional scheme of limited federal power and supplants it with a structure in which the power of the federal government knows no limitations. There is no rational means of construing the textual structure to allow such a result. Such a change would therefore require resort to the formal amendment process, a recourse that would surely face significant political opposition. To avoid construing the Constitution in a manner inconsistent with any rational form of textual construction, the Court today should require that Congress have some real factual basis to support an assertion of impact on interstate commerce. This form of review, although limited, would invalidate legislation enacted on merely conjectural or remote commerce-impact grounds.

As for the argument questioning the continuing political merits of a federal system, one should recall the link between federalism and the values of political diversification, accountability and checking that underly our system.[263] While socioeconomic conditions today are of course substantially different from the time of the Constitution's framing, the values designed to be fostered by that document remain central elements of our political fabric. In any event, such an inquiry is simply not the Court's to make, at least for purposes of deciding whether to enforce specific constitutional provisions. A court that is authorized to reject explicit constitutional mandates concerning federalism because of its opinion regarding the value—or lack thereof—of those protections may just as logically refuse to enforce the First Amendment guarantee of free speech because of its conclusion that protection of free expression causes more harm than it is worth.[264] We might debate the merits of the Court's judgment, but, as a logical matter, if the Court were allowed such discretion in regard to the Constitution's directives concerning federalism, it would be difficult to challenge its ultimate authority to reach a similar conclusion regarding free speech.

The Court's function in our governmental system is to enforce and interpret the Constitution, not to repeal provisions it views as unwise or outmoded. Surely such a result was never intended, as clearly evidenced by the Constitution's written form, its imposition of an extremely arduous amendment process, and its limitations on the subject matter jurisdiction of the federal judiciary. And there can be little doubt that by abdicating its function of reviewing the actions of the majoritarian branches to ensure compliance with constitutional dictates, the Court would effectively repeal the constitutional provision in question; the majoritarian branches would be left free to ignore countermajoritarian constitutional restrictions if they so desired.

Conclusion

The system of federalism established by our constitutional structure contemplates a synergistic and symbiotic interaction of the state and federal governments, so that societal knowledge and welfare can be maximized. Use of a federal system can also have the beneficial result of reducing the dangers of tyranny that inhere in the concentration of political power. While the importance of federalism has understandably decreased as the problems facing the nation have become more complex and national in scope and as technology has effectively made the nation smaller, the values originally designed to be fostered by the choice of a federal system remain significant. Moreover, these values have been constitutionalized in the synthesis of the enumeration of federal power and the Tenth Amendment's reservation of unenumerated power to the states. It is this textual directive which the Supreme Court must enforce, as it must enforce all the Constitution's directives.

Given the generally broad language of the Constitution's text, a reviewing court will inevitably have substantial power to incorporate into the interpretive process many normative judgments concerning social policy and political theory. Such a result is unavoidable, once we recognize both that the provisions of a written constitution must be broadly phrased to allow for unforeseen developments and situations and that the only governmental body truly suited to the exercise of the interpretive power is the largely independent judicial branch. Unless the very existence of a written constitution is to be rendered totally meaningless, however, the language of its provisions must be assumed to retain at least some degree of ascertainable meaning. The textual structure gleaned from a combined reading of Article I, Section 8, and the Tenth Amendment is a classic illustration of this point. As is true of most constitutional concepts, "interstate commerce" is not self-defining and thus leaves a great deal of room for judicial elaboration. But it is clear from a reading of the text that the Tenth Amendment imposes no limitations on congressional power to protect state sovereignty that are not already implicitly protected by the limitations imposed in the "interstate commerce" concept itself. It is also clear from an examination of the textual structure that whatever its outer reaches, the commerce power cannot be unlimited, lest the carefully developed constitutional scheme of protection for federalism through enumeration of limited federal powers be forsaken.

The Court has an important role to play in ensuring congressional adherence to the limits of the Constitution. The concept of a government whose actions are limited by an overriding constitutional structure, so important to the government's continued legitimacy, is severely undermined by the Court's abandonment of this role. In the area of constitutional federalism, the difficult problem facing the Court is to allow the Constitution to grow in recognition of the need for expanded federal power to meet new social needs while simultaneously preserving the values of federalism unambiguously embodied in the Constitution's text. Neither the unduly restrictive "enclave" model adopted in *National League of Cities* nor the judicial abdication model of *Garcia* represent satisfactory solutions of that problem.

3

The Dormant Commerce Clause and the Constitutional Balance of Federalism

As explained in the previous chapter, Congress's power to regulate interstate commerce has grown through judicial interpretation to the point where today it is virtually unlimited in its reach.[1] As is the case with all of Congress's powers enumerated in Article I Section 8, of the Constitution, however, the commerce power need not be exercised by Congress. Thus, despite the power's all-but-total extension, Congress has continued to leave numerous areas free from federal statutory regulation. Even in certain areas in which Congress has invoked its authority, substantial room has been left for state regulation.[2]

In a number of instances, however, even when Congress has failed to invoke its commerce power to preempt state regulation of interstate commerce by means of federal statute, the Supreme Court has struck down state regulation as a direct violation of the Commerce Clause itself.[3] The Court has done so when it finds that such regulation either discriminates against out-of-state interests or unduly burdens the free flow of commerce among the states.[4] The Commerce Clause in its "dormant" state[5] is thought to invalidate such state regulation, though it is accepted that Congress may choose to overrule the judicial invalidation of a particular state regulation by statutorily authorizing it.[6] This, then, briefly describes the concept of the "dormant Commerce Clause."

The literature on the dormant Commerce Clause has been anything but dormant in recent years. Traditionally considered an arcane aspect of American constitutional law that fell far behind individual liberties as a generator of academic or student interest, the dormant Commerce Clause has in recent years been the subject of a resurgence of both scholarly[7] and judicial[8] concern. Leading constitutional scholars have once again recognized that ours is a complex federal system, giving rise to numerous constitutional problems inherent in the division of authority between two levels of political sovereignty.

Much of the recent literature has focused largely on the substantive standards to be employed in deciding whether state regulation is permissible. To that end, these works have attempted primarily to determine both the proper purposes to be served by the clause and the specific content that Supreme Court doctrine should possess, often reaching conflicting conclusions on these issues.[9] Such efforts, however, are reminiscent of an argument over the proper lapel widths to be placed on the emperor's new clothes. With limited exception,[10] the modern literature expends relatively little effort in an attempt to explain either the textual source or legitimacy of the dormant Commerce Clause. However, no such valid constitutional source exists: the simple fact is that there is no dormant Commerce Clause to be found within the text or textual structure of the Constitution. It is true, of course, that on occasion scholars have argued that the Court may "read into" the Constitution broad precepts that lack a specific basis in text—what has been referred to as the "unwritten constitution."[11] Such a position has in fact been specifically urged as a justification for the dormant Commerce Clause.[12] As I have previously argued, however, this is an approach that lacks any basis in constitutional democratic theory.[13] The concept of a federal constitutional democracy vests in an unrepresentative federal judiciary the authority to invalidate majoritarian decisions of state legislative bodies only when such a result is dictated by some provision or combination of provisions of the countermajoritarian Constitution, or when clearly preempted by congressional action.[14] Absent textual foundation, the dormant Commerce Clause cannot stand, regardless of whatever valuable social, economic, or political policies the concept might be thought to foster.

But even if one were to assume that a judicial supplement to the text may, under certain circumstances, be accepted, such a view could not justify recognition of the dormant Commerce Clause. For subsequent analysis will demonstrate that not only is there no textual basis to support recognition of such a concept, but the dormant Commerce Clause actually contradicts, and therefore directly undermines, the Constitution's carefully established textual structure for allocating power between federal and state sovereigns. If this is the case, as I believe it is, then invocation of the dormant Commerce Clause would constitute a considerably greater judicial usurpation of constitutional authority than would a mere judicial supplement to a text otherwise silent on the matter.

That the dormant Commerce Clause conflicts with the balance of federalism established in the Constitution can be proven by gleaning from various provisions a textual infrastructure of federalism.[15] Examination of the Constitution's text reveals that the Framers employed several very different forms of limitation on the exercise of state power. Some provisions directly and absolutely limit the exercise of state authority, effectively precluding congressional authorization of such state behavior.[16] Others explicitly condition the exercise of state power on an affirmative authorization by Congress,[17] while still others impose no explicit limit on state power, but rather vest in Congress the authority to act, thereby providing Congress the *option* of preempting or precluding objectionable state legislative action in the field.[18] The power to regulate interstate commerce clearly falls within the third category of limitation on state authority. Though the text expressly renders a number of actions beyond state power, the general power to regulate interstate commerce is not among them. The only textual reference to the regulation of interstate commerce, at least in the broad sense,[19] is contained in Article I's affirmative grant of power to Congress.

The differences in the nature of these constitutional limitations on state authority are by no means merely formalistic or technical. Initially, there is an obvious and important difference between constitutional limitations that apply directly and those that may be overcome by congressional action: the former can be removed only by resort to the all-but-impossible amendment process,[20] and are thus insulated from congressional intervention. Hence the first category is qualitatively different from the other two varieties.

The practical differences between the two remaining forms of limitation are also significant, however. It is a practical reality of the legislative process that the enactment of legislation is a long, difficult, and cumbersome task. Thus, where the political inertia is initially to be placed can make an enormous difference in the level of activity allowed the states. State power that requires an affirmative grant of authorization by Congress is much less likely to be allowed than authority that is vested unless and until Congress affirmatively revokes it. Both constitutional language and history make clear that the regulation of commerce was intended to be of the latter variety.[21]

The dormant Commerce Clause reverses the political inertia established by the Constitution in favor of state power to regulate interstate commerce: it is an unrepresentive federal judiciary—the organ of the federal government most insulated from state influence and the organ traditionally feared most by the states[22]—that makes the initial legislative judgment whether the state regulation of interstate commerce is reasonable, forcing the states to attempt to overcome the substantial political inertia of the legislative process in order to regain the power denied them by the federal judiciary. This is clearly not the plan of the Constitution. State power to regulate interstate commerce was designed to be judged solely by the political judgment of Congress, where the states have long been thought to exercise substantial power through resort to the political process.[23]

Of course, it nevertheless might be argued that, as a policy matter, it is unwise to allow the states the benefit of congressional inertia because the states may do much to inhibit the free flow of commerce among the states and thereby undermine the principle of free trade, bring about the "Balkanization" of the nation, or impose burdens on those who have no say in the legislative process.[24] The initial—and most obvious—answer to these contentions is that such considerations are irrelevant in the face of unambiguous constitutional text to the contrary, and, if sufficiently strong, should be applied through the amendment process. Such an appeal to text may be accused of being overly positivistic. Yet if the unambiguous commands of constitutional text can be so easily ignored or modified short of resort to the amendment process, then little of substance is left of our constitutional system, and any other constitutional directive can at a later date be similarly ignored.

Moreover, as a matter of normative political theory, the system of federalism gleaned from the Constitution's text makes substantial economic and political sense as an attempt to attain the goals that we as a nation have established. Allowing the states to further the principle of political and economic diversity produces all of the attendant benefits that derive from both economic experimentation and the ensuing decentralization of power.[25] At the same time, the political branches of the federal government may legislatively curb state authority when the dangers of disuniformity are deemed to be too great. Thus, purely as a matter of policy, it is doubtful that regulation of state power through the dormant Commerce Clause is preferable to the exclusive political check explicitly set out in the Constitution. Judicial invalidation of state regulation solely on the grounds that it interrupts the flow of commerce[26] effectively undermines many of the basic advantages thought to be derived from use of a federal system. This benefit of federalism should be sacrificed only when the negative impact on the nation's economy is so severe that the hurdles of political inertia toward preempting congressional action can be overcome.

If the dormant Commerce Clause were abandoned, the interests of the nation need not suffer. The Privileges-and-Immunities Clause of Article IV[27] provides a firm textual grounding for judicial invalidation of the most egregious form of state regulation, that discriminating against out-of-staters, and Congress remains a viable safety net for nondiscriminatory state legislation whose benefits are outweighed by its negative impact upon the free flow of interstate commerce.

Certain commentators, largely on grounds of political theory, have argued that the dormant Commerce Clause can properly serve only one value, namely, the "democratic process" concern that state legislation might disproportionately affect out-of-staters, who were unrepresented in the legislative process.[28] As so revised, the clause would protect only against state legislation discriminating against out-of-state residents. This has led one of these commentators to suggest that the dormant Commerce Clause, as a separate concept, is no longer necessary, since the Privileges-and-Immunities Clause may be construed to perform the same function.[29] Purely in terms of result, this conclusion is similar to the one reached here. However, despite this coincidental similarity in result, the internal logic of this theoretical critique is fundamentally flawed in several respects, and in any event ultimately fails because of its lack of grounding in constitutional text.[30]

The first section of this chapter examines the growth and development of the dormant Commerce Clause. It traces the origins of the clause, beginning with Chief Justice Marshall's first declarations on its nature. The following section explains why the dormant Commerce Clause finds no basis in constitutional text. In reaching this conclusion, the analysis considers and rejects the conceivable arguments for finding a textual authorization for the dormant Commerce Clause.

The chapter next proceeds to establish the clause's inconsistency with the text's allocation of authority within the nation's structure of federalism. It then critiques and rejects the arguable nontextual justifications for the dormant Commerce Clause. The chapter proceeds to examine the Constitution's textual structure for the federal and state regulation of interstate commerce that would remain after the demise of the dormant Commerce Clause. It examines how the Constitution's textual structure, absent the dormant Commerce Clause, can adequately prohibit state economic legislation that discriminates against out-of-state individuals engaged in commerce or that places undue burdens on interstate commerce. Finally, it discusses and rejects the "democratic process" critique of the dormant Commerce Clause.

The Growth and Development of the Dormant Commerce Clause

The dormant Commerce Clause has been utilized to invalidate a myriad of state regulations affecting interstate commerce. For example, the Court, relying on the clause, has invalidated state licensing requirements,[31] train length restrictions,[32] mudguard requirements,[33] truck length prohibitions,[34] and various produce regulations.[35] In so doing, the Court has enunciated several tests to review state regulations.[36] The content of these tests does not concern us here, since the focus at this point is the constitutional legitimacy of the dormant Commerce Clause, rather than its application. However, it is readily apparent from an examination of the decisions developing the doctrine that the Court has been unable to articulate a justification for the dormant Commerce Clause that finds a basis in the Constitution's text. Instead, the Court has either improperly circumvented or completely ignored constitutional text in its attempts to justify the clause's existence.

In light of this longstanding judicial failure adequately to ground the concept in the constitutional text, one may wonder what basis the Court has asserted in support of the doctrine in its origins. Because the Court has for many years simply assumed the dormant Commerce Clause's constitutional legitimacy, it is not as easy as one might think to discover the original constitutional theory behind the concept's creation. In the search for the origins of the dormant Commerce Clause, the investigation begins with two of the first Commerce Clause cases decided by the Court, then under the guidance of Chief Justice John Marshall.

Chief Justice Marshall and the Dormant Commerce Clause

In *Gibbons v. Ogden*,[37] the New York legislature had granted a monopoly to operate steamships between New Jersey and New York. Gibbons argued that the monopoly was invalid under the Commerce Clause, as well as under federal navigation legislation.[38] The Court dismissed the question whether a state could, in accordance with the Constitution, regulate commerce among the several states.[39] Chief Justice Marshall maintained that the "sole question" before the Court was: "[C]an a State regulate commerce . . . among the States, while Congress is regulating it?"[40] The Court answered this question in the negative, holding that Congress had enacted a consitutionally valid law pursuant to the Commerce Clause, regulating the same subject matter as the New York act, and therefore the federal act controlled under the Supremacy Clause.[41]

Although the Court purported to avoid deciding the question whether the states could constitutionally regulate commerce in the absence of preemptive federal legislation, the Chief Justice's opinion is famous for answering this very question in dicta.[42] Marshall did not establish the dormant Commerce Clause in *Gibbons*, although according to Justice Frankfurter, he could have garnered the votes to do so.[43] Still, the opinion contributed to the concept's development.

Before reaching the Court's actual decision, the Chief Justice flirted with the concept that the Constitution's grant of power to Congress to regulate commerce among the states necessarily precluded the states from exercising a concurrent power over the same object.[44] Marshall appears to have believed the state and federal governments possess very different powers over interstate commerce. In considering the argument that the state and federal governments had concurrent power to regulate interstate commerce, just as the state and federal governments had concurrent power to levy taxes,[45] he raised a possible distinction between the two sovereign powers:

> In imposing taxes for State purposes, they are not doing what Congress is empowered to do. Congress is not empowered to tax for those purposes which are within the exclusive province of the States. When, then, each government exercises the power of taxation, neither is exercising the power of the other. But, when a State proceeds to regulate commerce . . . among the several States, it is exercising the very power that is granted to Congress, and is doing the very thing that Congress is authorized to do.[46]

Marshall found "great force in this argument," and noted that "the Court is not satisfied that it has been refuted."[47] He admitted that the states could enact various laws that "form a portion of that immense mass of legislation, which embraces everything within the territory of a State, not surrendered to the general government . . . ." "Inspection laws, quarantine laws, health laws of every description, as well as laws for regulating the internal commerce of a State, and those which respect turnpikes roads, ferries, &c., are component parts of this mass."[48] He further acknowledged that

> [i]t is obvious, that the government of the Union, in the exercise of its express powers, . . . for example of regulating commerce . . . among the States, may use means that may also be employed by a State, in the

exercise of its acknowledged powers . . . , for example, of regulating commerce within the State."[49]

However, he countered, "All experience shows, that the same measures, or measures scarcely distinguishable from one another, may flow from distinct powers; but it does not prove that the powers themselves are identical."[50]

It is the Chief Justice's opinion in *Willson v. Black-Bird Creek Marsh Co.*[51] that can most directly be relied upon for the proposition that Marshall recognized the negative aspect of the commerce power. It is in this decision that the Chief Justice first used the term "dormant" in connection with the Commerce Clause. Delaware had authorized the building of a dam across a navigable creek.[52] The plaintiffs contended that the authorizing act was in conflict with the federal government's power to regulate interstate commerce.[53] The Court rejected the challenge to the statute and summarily declared:

> We do not think that the act empowering the Black Bird Creek Marsh Company to place a dam across the creek, can, under all the circumstances of the case be considered as repugnant to the [federal] power to regulate commerce in its *dormant* state, or as being in conflict with any law passed on the subject.[54]

However, Marshall provided no guidance as to the nature of the "dormant state" of the Commerce Clause in *Black-Bird Creek*,[55] nor was he able to pass on any other questions regarding the Commerce Clause.[56]

The Growth of the Dormant Commerce Clause

Though in the years after *Gibbons* the Court on occasion expressed reluctance to invoke the dormant Commerce Clause,[57] it was in *Cooley v. Board of Wardens*[58] that the doctrine was firmly established in Supreme Court jurisprudence. *Cooley* at first glance appears an unlikely case from which so enduring a doctrine as the dormant Commerce Clause would emerge. The controversy centered upon a Pennsylvania statute requiring ships to engage a local pilot when entering or departing the port of Philadelphia, or incur a sixty-dollar penalty for failing to do so.[59] Justice Curtis, writing for the majority, rejected three attacks upon the statute[60] and upheld it as a constitutional regulation of commerce.[61] More importantly, the opinion established an enduring standard for the review of state regulations of interstate commerce in the absence of preemptive federal legislation.[62]

Interestingly, the dormant Commerce Clause emerged in *Cooley* from the Court's *rejection* of the argument that the statute was an invalid regulation of interstate commerce on the grounds that Congress had been granted an exclusive power to regulate such commerce under Article I, Section 8, clause 3.[63] Justice Curtis declared that it was well settled that the power to regulate commerce included the power to regulate navigation in the manner in which the Pennsylvania statute regulated pilotage.[64] But he rejected the exclusive view of the Commerce Clause by referring to a federal statute enacted in 1789[65] permitting state regulation of pilotage by then-existing or thereafter-enacted state statutes.[66] He maintained that if the states were stripped of any power to regulate commerce by the Commerce Clause, Congress could not delegate such a power to the states, and that since the 1789 act sanctioned such state statutes, there was "necessarily implie[d] a constitutional power [on the part of the state] to legislate."[67]

Justice Curtis then turned to *The Federalist* No. 32 for the proposition that

> the mere grant of such a power to Congress, did not imply a prohibition on the States to exercise the same power; that it is not the mere existence of such a power, but its exercise of the same power by the Congress, which may be incompatible with the exercise of the same power by the States, and that the States may legislate in the absence of congressional regulations.[68]

He continued that

> when the nature of a power like this is spoken of, when it is said that the nature of the power requires that it should be exercised exclusively by Congress, it must be intended to refer to the subjects of that power, and to say they are of such a nature as to require exclusive legislation by Congress. Now the power to regulate commerce, embraces a vast field, containing not only many, but exceedingly various subjects, quite unalike in their nature; some imperitively demanding a single uniform rule, operating equally on the commerce of the United States in every port; and some, like the subject now in question, as imperitively demanding that diversity, which alone can meet the local necessities of navigation.[69]

From this Curtis deduced that

> [e]ither absolutely to affirm, or to deny that the nature of . . . [the commerce] power requires exclusive legislation by Congress is to lose sight of the nature of the subjects of this power, and to assert concerning all of them, what is really applicable but to a part. Whatever the subjects of this power are in their nature national, or admit only of one uniform system, or plan of regulation, may justly be said to be of such a nature as to require exclusive legislation by Congress.[70]

Thus, Justice Curtis ultimately avoided answering the difficult question whether Congress's power to regulate commerce was exclusive. Instead, he struck what appears to have been a pre-Civil War judicial compromise. Rather than decide that the federal commerce power was exclusive, thereby possibly alienating the more fervent states' rights advocates and further dividing the nation, he adopted a selective approach to federal exclusivity under the Commerce Clause. This approach simultaneously avoided confrontation yet reserved for the Court the ability to invalidate objectionable state legislation under a theory of *partial* exclusivity. Moreover, the case before the Court provided the perfect vehicle for the articulation of the selective doctrine with little contemporary objection, since the Court there found that Congress had permitted the states to regulate the commerce in question.

By focusing on the objects of commerce, rather than the power itself, Curtis was able to avoid interpreting the relevant textual provision of the Constitution, the Commerce Clause. He appealed to reason to state that the commerce power was exclusive only as to those objects of commerce that required, presumably upon a showing of objective proof, exclusive federal legislation.

At the close of his opinion, Curtis reemphasized the Court's adoption of the "selective" approach to questions concerning the regulation of interstate commerce. He rationalized that the Court's opinion was confined to the precise question before it[71] and did not extend "to the question what other subjects, under the commercial power, are within the exclusive control of Congress, or may be regulated by the States in the absence of all congressional legislation . . . ."[72] Thus was born the "*Cooley* Rule of Selective Exclusiveness."[73] Under the *Cooley* Rule, only those state regulations of interstate commerce whose very nature required exclusive federal regulation would be invalid directly under the Commerce Clause.

Conspicuously absent from Justice Curtis's opinion is any cogent examination of the Constitution's text. Yet his theory of "selective exclusiveness"—in addition to amounting to a conceptual oxymoron—is curiously incapable of rationalization with the terms of the Commerce Clause. The clause's language clearly says nothing that *directly* prohibits the exercise of concurrent state power in *any* instance. It is perhaps possible to construe a constitutional *grant* of power to Congress as an automatic, corresponding *prohibition* of the exercise of state power on the same subject (though, for reasons discussed below,[74] such a construction must ultimately be rejected). But it is important to emphasize that that is not the construction adopted by Justice Curtis. Rather, it is only those subjects that, by their "nature," demand exclusive federal control that are constitutionally removed from state regulation. Surely, there is no rational means of construing the broad language of the Commerce Clause to authorize the creation of such a dichotomy in the exercise of state power, premised on some vague judicial perception of the "nature" of the commerce being regulated. Instead of grounding his doctrine in the text, Curtis attempted to circumvent the Constitution's language, because a candid interpretation of the Commerce Clause would have required him to find the commerce power to be either exclusive or concurrent—a choice which he apparently took great pains to avoid.

Nearly twenty-five years later, the Court supplemented the justification fashioned in *Cooley* for the dormant Commerce Clause. In its 1875 decision in *Welton v. Missouri*,[75] the Court invalidated, pursuant to the dormant Commerce Clause, a Missouri statute requiring nonresident "peddlers" to purchase licenses before selling their wares. The Court recognized the *Cooley* doctrine, stating that "it has been held that the States may provide regulations until Congress acts with reference to them; but where the subject to which the power applies is national in its character, or of such a nature as to admit of uniformity of regulation, the power is exclusive of all State authority."[76] Later in the Court's opinion, however, Justice Field declared that "[t]he fact that Congress has not seen fit to prescribe any specific rules to govern inter-State commerce does not affect the question. *Its inaction on the subject . . . is equivalent to a declaration that inter-State commerce shall be free and untrammelled.*"[77]

Thus Justice Field, possibly recognizing the dormant Commerce Clause's tenuous textual basis, attempted to characterize the concept as an inference of congressional intent from Congress's failure to enact its own regulatory legislation. As a matter of statutory construction, this represents a highly dubious approach.[78] Disturbingly, the Court never fully explicated this supplemental justification for the dormant Commerce Clause. Nonetheless, it became a firm part of dormant Commerce Clause jurisprudence.

The modern Court appears untroubled by the lack of any textual justification for the dormant Commerce Clause. In *Southern Pacific Co. v. Arizona*,[79] the Court noted that the states could neither impede the "free flow" of commerce nor regulate elements of interstate commerce requiring national uniformity. The Court refused to choose between its previously articulated justifications for the dormant Commerce Clause, because "[w]hether . . . this long-recognized distribution of power between the national and state governments is predicated upon the implications of the Commerce Clause itself . . . or upon the presumed intention of Congress, where Congress has not spoken . . . the result is the same."[80] Instead, the Court continued to employ the dormant Commerce Clause, regardless of its constitutional justification, by summarily adhering to precedent:

> For a hundred years it has been accepted constitutional doctrine that the Commerce Clause, without the aid of Congressional legislation, thus affords some protection from state legislation inimical to the national commerce, and in such cases, where Congress has not acted, this Court, and not the state legislature, is under the Commerce Clause the final arbiter of the competing demands of state and national interests.[81]

Since *Southern Pacific*, the Court has failed to reconsider the constitutional basis of the dormant Commerce Clause. Rather, in unquestioning reliance on the clause, the Court has continued to invalidate certain state regulations affecting interstate commerce.[82]

The Dormant Commerce Clause and the Constitutional Text

In some respects, there seems to be little remarkable about the *Cooley* doctrine. When Congress expressly determines, as it did in *Cooley*, that the nature of the commerce in quesion does not require exclusive regulation, the states may exercise power over that commerce. Alternatively, when Congress determines, by the enactment of federal legislation, that certain objects of commerce require exclusive federal regulation, the conflicting state regulations are clearly invalid under the Supremacy Clause.[83] It is, however, under a third scenario that the troubling effect of the *Cooley* doctrine is revealed. Under *Cooley*, when Congress has not regulated the objects of commerce in question, *the Court itself* determines whether the nature of the commerce requires exclusive federal regulation. Thus, the Court, in reviewing state legislation, essentially makes what amounts to an intrinsically legislative determination as to whether a particular type of commerce requires exclusive federal regulation.

The analysis that follows will demonstrate that the dormant Commerce Clause lacks a basis in either the Constitution's text or history. In so doing, the analysis will critically examine—and reject—the two conceivable arguments for rationalizing the dormant Commerce Clause with the Constitution's text: (1) that the textual grant of the commerce power to Congress automatically provides an implicit constitutional negation of concurrent state power, and (2) that Congress's failure to regulate a particular aspect of interstate commerce necessarily implies a congressional decision to leave the subject unregulated, thereby rendering any state regulation inherently inconsistent with congressional intent and therefore invalidated by the Supremacy Clause.

The Dormant Commerce Clause and the Text of the Commerce Power

Examination of the text makes clear that the Constitution imposes certain express prohibitions on state action. For example, Article I, Section 10 declares:

> No State shall enter into any treaty, alliance, or confederation; grant letters of marque and reprisal; coin money; emit bills of credit; make anything but gold and silver coin a tender in payment of debts; pass any bill of attainder, ex-post-facto law, or law impairing the obligation of contracts, or grant any title of nobility.
>
> No State shall, without the consent of the Congress, lay any imposts or duties on imports or exports, except what may be absolutely necessary for executing its inspection laws; and the net produce of all duties and imposts, laid by any State on imports or exports, shall be for the use of the treasury of the United States and all such laws shall be subject to the revision and control of the Congress.
>
> No State shall, without the consent of the Congress, lay any duties of tonnage, keep troops, or ships of war, in time of peace, enter into any agreement or compact with another state, or with a foreign power, or engage in war, unless actually invaded, or in such imminent danger as will not admit of delay.[84]

Similarly, the Privileges-and-Immunities Clause of Article IV[85] imposes certain limits on state behavior.[86]

None of these prohibitions, however can be (or has been) relied upon as a basis for recognition of the dormant Commerce Clause.[87] Under *Cooley's* rationale of that clause,[88] the states may not regulate certain objects of commerce when the Court determines that these objects of commerce require exclusive federal regulation.[89] Nothing in the above-cited provisions authorizes such a practice. Moreover, the Court has made clear that Congress may authorize state economic regulations that have been invalidated under the dormant Commerce Clause.[90] Clearly, most of the constitutional prohibitions previously referred to do not provide a textual basis for this element of the doctrine, either. Rather, the Court has maintained that the dormant Commerce Clause derives directly from the Article I, Section 8 grant to Congress of a power to regulate interstate commerce.[91] That provision states: "Congress shall have power . . . [t]o regulate commerce with foreign Nations, and among the several States, and with the Indian tribes."[92] The Commerce Clause is not a self-executing power; rather, it is a power that is given to Congress, to use or not, as it deems necessary. Nowhere does the Constitution or its amendments textually deny the exercise of this same power to the states.[93]

On the basis of the text, then, one of two conclusions may be reached. One possibility is that the very existence of this constitutional grant of power to the federal government necessarily prevents the states from exercising *any* power over interstate commerce. This view amounts to adoption of what is generally referred to as the "dual federalism" model of the constitutional allocation of power between the state and national governments: "[t]wo mutually exclusive, reciprocally limiting fields of power—that of the national government and of the states."[94] Alternatively, the clause may be taken to mean that while the grant of power to Congress *enables* Congress to override state regulations of interstate commerce and, at times, preempt state regulations of commerce under the Supremecy Clause.[95] Absent such affirmative congressional action, the states are free to regulate interstate commerce (subject, of course, to traditional limitations on states' exercise of legislative jurisdiction).[96] This second theory constitutes an application of the "cooperative" model of federalism.[97]

In the "dual federalism" model of American constitutional government, the state and federal governments each exercise their own exclusive area of jurisdiction.[98] As noted in the previous chapter, according to Professor Edward Corwin, the dual federalism model is composed of four principles:

> 1. The national government is one of enumerated powers only; 2. Also the purposes which it may constitutionally promote are few; 3. Within their respective spheres the two centers of government are "sovereign" and hence "equal"; 4. The relation of the two centers with each other is one of tension rather than collaboration.[99]

For present purposes, the important component of the dual federalism model is the assumption that if a power is committed to one sovereign, it cannot be exercised by the other sovereign. Thus, under this model granting a power to the federal government automatically denies that power to the state governments.

Even if one were to accept the dual federalism model as the controlling theory of American federalism,[100] the dormant Commerce Clause still cannot survive, at least in its current doctrinal state. Under this model, the Constitution's textual grant of power to Congress would simultaneously deprive the states of *any* power to regulate interstate commerce—a result substantially different from established dormant Commerce Clause doctrine.[101] Moreover, Congress could not constitutionally authorize the states to enact legislation affecting commerce if the constitutional grant of power to regulate commerce deprived the states of *all* power to enact any legislation affecting interstate commerce, for Congress presumably cannot cure such a lack of constitutional power on the part of the states.

In any event, as previously explained, the dual federalism model of American constitutional government is not the accepted theory of American federalism.[102] Indeed, it is questionable whether it ever represented the controlling model of constitutional government.[103] That the Constitution itself does not contemplate so rigid a division of sovereign power is, ironically, established by the very existence of the direct constitutional prohibitions on state power contained in Article I, Section 10. If the Constitution's drafters had contemplated a dual federalism model, the prohibitions contained in Article I, Section 10, would have been superfluous; the very grant of those powers to Congress in Article I, Section 8, would have automatically precluded the concurrent exercise of state power in any of these areas. It might be responded that the enumeration of powers prohibited to the states in Article I, Section 10, is included solely for purposes of emphasis. But this argument breaks down once it is recalled that the listing of prohibited powers in Article I, Section 10, corresponds only partially to the powers granted to Congress in Article I, Section 8. Moreover, the Commerce Clause is one of those congressional powers in Section 8 that is not explicitly prohibited to the states in Section 10. Thus, the facts that the Framers deemed it necessary to include the express prohibitions of Article I, Section 10, despite the express grant of congressional power in Article I, Section 8, over many of the same subjects, and that in a number of instances (including, in particular, the commerce power) the grant of a power to Congress in Section 8 is not matched by a corresponding prohibition of state power in Section 10 make clear that the Constitution contemplates at least a certain potential overlap of state and federal legislative power.

If one were to reject the dual federalism model and instead adopt the alternative view that the states can exercise a "concurrent power" over commerce, the existence of the constitutional grant of power to Congress to regulate commerce breaks down as textual support for the dormant Commerce Clause. Assuming that the states and the federal government both retain power over interstate commerce, there exists no principled basis for the Court *ever* to invalidate state regulation, at least in the absence of congressional preemption, on the basis of the text of the Commerce Clause.[104]

Though it is impossible to construe the text of the Commerce Clause to justify the dormant Commerce Clause concept, the clause's advocates have found support in various contemporaneous statements of the Framers. Even if such evidence existed, however, one should seriously question the relevance of any Framers' understandings not manifested somewhere in the text. For it was the text, not some unstated understanding, that was ratified into law. Nonetheless, Professor Donald Regan has argued that the Framers did assume the existence of the dormant Commerce Clause. He remarks that "[t]here is much evidence that the main point of [the] grant [of power over interstate commerce] . . . was not to empower Congress, but rather to disable the states from regulating commerce themselves."[105] He further notes that "[t]he framers wanted commerce among the states to be free of state-originated mercantilist impositions. Giving Congress the power to regulate internal commerce was one way of denying the states that power under the view . . . that the granted powers were exclusive."[106] Regan acknowledges that "as Congress' power over interstate commerce is now understood, we cannot treat that power as exclusive. But that does not mean the framers could not have regarded as exclusive the much narrower power they were thinking of."[107]

One might reasonably inquire, however, why, if the Framers intended such a result, did they fail to incorporate this principle into the text? Why, instead of convolutedly phrasing their intended *prohibition* on *state* power in terms of a *grant* of *federal* power, did the Framers not simply include a direct prohibition on the exercise of state power? After all, in both Article I, Section 10, and Article IV, Section 2, the Framers expressly imposed numerous direct prohibitions on state power. Their failure to do the same for the general power to regulate interstate commerce, then, represents strong counterevidence to Professor Regan's assertion concerning their intent.

Professor Regan notes that there is evidence suggesting that Congress was given the commerce authority in order to prevent state economic protectionism. But that is exactly the point—*Congress* was given the power. That Congress was constitutionally vested with the legislative power to disable the states from regulating interstate commerce in no way implies either that *the Constitution itself* automatically denies the states such power or that *the federal judiciary* has such a power. In this context, it is important to note that the historical references generally cited in support of the dormant Commerce Clause speak only of the potential dangers to national unity caused by interstate economic friction. They do not specifically refer to the need for an initial *judicial* power of oversight to prevent this problem in the total absence of congressional action.[108] Thus, since the Framers were clearly aware of the dangers of interstate economic friction, and chose to deal with the problem textually *only* by the vesting of a power in Congress, rather than by imposition of a direct constitutional prohibition (other than the Privileges-and-Immunities Clause) it appears clear that they saw the exercise of congressional authority as the sole means of dealing with the problem, to the extent it fell beyond the reach of the Privileges-and-Immunities Clause.

Even if one were to accept Professor Regan's argument that the Framers intended a mutual exclusivity between state and federal power to regulate commerce, such a theory could not justify the dormant Commerce Clause as it has always existed. This is because as structured the concept does not impose such a mutual exclusivity. Professor Regan responds, however, that the Framers understood that the Constitution vested Congress with an exclusive power to regulate commerce under a much narrower understanding of the term "commerce" than is the case today.[109] Therefore while we can no longer regard the commerce power as exclusive under today's broader understanding, we *can* do so for that which the Framers themselves defined as "commerce." It is certainly true that the modern expansive interpretation of both the terms "commerce" and "among the several States" in the Commerce Clause is considerably broader than those terms were understood in the late eighteenth century, though one might nevertheless argue that the Framers themselves may well have contemplated the possibility of changes in interpretation over time.[110] But as previously argued, the view that the Framers assumed the commerce power to be exclusive is undermined by the explicit prohibitions of Article I, Section 10. In any event, it is difficult to understand why any constitutional consequences should flow from such a distinction. Either we adopt an "originalist" model of constitutional interpretation, in which event all of Congress's exercises of that power beyond the original understanding are invalid, or we do not, in which event all of Congress's exercises of the power are equally valid, and no distinction at all would be drawn on this basis. Professor Regan's suggested distinction, then, represents a wholly unprincipled and narrowly result-oriented mode of constitutional analysis.

Finally, even if one were to accept Professor Regan's argument, it would not justify the dormant Commerce Clause, either in its origins or its modern construction, since the Court has never drawn such an originalist/nonoriginalist distinction in applying the clause. Most importantly, Professor Regan's analysis ignores the fact that, as subsequent discussion will demonstrate,[111] the dormant Commerce Clause actually contradicts and undermines the textual structure of federalism. In terms of the Constitution's plan, there is all the difference in the world between a direct prohibition on state power, on the one hand, and the vesting in Congress of an option to invalidate state action, on the other.

The Dormant Commerce Clause as an Inference of Congressional Intent

Perhaps because of the decision's tenuous logic, the Court subsequently attempted to supplement the *Cooley* justification for the dormant Commerce Clause by maintaining that Congress's failure to regulate a particular type of interstate commerce implicitly manifests Congress's intention that that particular type of commerce remain unregulated. The Court has thereby avoided interpreting the text of the Commerce Clause, because of its assumption that Congress has somehow "acted" pursuant to its commerce power and thus manifested its "intent." State legislation, then, is invalidated pursuant to the Supremacy Clause, rather than pursuant to the commerce power itself; it is a simple matter of federal preemption. Alternatively, one might argue that Congress's failure to overrule the Court's dormant Commerce Clause decisions manifests Congress's intention to condone both the judicial exercise of the power and the propriety of the result. Under either scenario, however, congressional failure to legislate cannot legitimately be transformed into legislation, for both theoretical and practical reasons.

When it invalidates state regulations of commerce under the dormant Commerce Clause by relying on a congressional failure to regulate a particular type of commerce, the Court relies on what can only be the most abstract of legislative intentions. The Court apparently need not point to a specific congressional refusal to regulate the particular type of commerce—a failure to pass a specific piece of legislation.[112] Instead, the Court relies merely on the fact that this type of commerce has not been regulated by Congress. Based on this fact alone, the Court *assumes* that Congress was aware of possible problems arising in this area of commerce, but nevertheless intended that it remain unregulated. No theoretical canon of legislative construction nor any practical reality of the legislative process can justify so sweeping an assumption about congressional intent.

The Court's interpretation of Congress's intention in the matter ignores two plausible explanations for the congressional failure to legislate. Initially, Congress may not be aware that a particular type of commerce is being regulated by the states, much less that uniform national regulation (or the lack thereof) is required. Further, in light of the complete absence of a record or text upon which to derive Congress's intent, it is at least equally probable that Congress intended that the regulation of the particular type of commerce be left to the individual states to regulate as they see fit, rather than that it be left completely unregulated.

Regardless of the Court's interpretation of Congress's intent, it is improper to transform a congressional failure to legislate into the equivalent of legislation.[113] Under the terms of the Constitution, only the "Constitution, and the laws of the United States which shall be made in pursuance thereof . . . shall be the supreme Law of the Land . . . ."[114] Before Congress enacts a law, the proposed legislation must undergo thorough examination, debate and, ultimately, enactment in both Houses of Congress. Congressional failures to legislate are not, by definition, subject to this process.

No more persuasive is the argument that congressional failure to overrule a judicial invalidation of state legislation amounts to congressional acceptance of the Court's action. As I have previously argued, "[r]eliance on a congressional failure to overrule a limiting judge-made doctrine . . . effectively condones through legislative inertia what was initially an improper and unauthorized judicial usurpation of legislative authority."[115] When the Court usurps congressional power in this way, as it does under the dormant Commerce Clause, it attempts to transform this usurpation into the status of constitutionally enacted legislation—absent the constitutional passage of the legislation.[116] As Thomas Merrill has aptly noted:

> The argument based on the possibility of congressional override ignores the institutional reality that, given its crowded agenda, Congress is far more likely not to act than to act with respect to any particular issue presented for its attention. Thus, the theoretical possibility of congressional override cannot disguise the fact that lawmaking by federal courts would in most cases result in the federal courts, rather than Congress, having the last say. In practice therefore, institutionalization of the practice of lawmaking by federal courts would represent a major shift in policymaking power away from Congress toward the federal judiciary—in violation of the constitutional scheme.[117]

Congress simply does not have available to it the time and resources adequately to police the Court's jurisprudence while at the same time consider the vast amount of legislation that is introduced each session.[118]

The Dormant Commerce Clause and the Constitution's Structure of Federalism

The Constitution's Three-Level Structure for Controlling State Power

The Constitution's text establishes an intricate, three-level structure for the allocation of power between the state and federal governments. In one category of situations the states are expressly and absolutely prohibited from enacting certain types of legislation. In the second category, the states must overcome Congress's institutional inertia in order to obtain congressional authorization for the state legislation. In the third category, the states are free to enact legislation, because they do not have to overcome a federal legislative barrier before doing so. Congress, however, has authority to preempt or overrule such state action by legislation enacted pursuant to one of its enumerated powers.

First, the Constitution expressly precludes certain types of state legislation. The states, for example, are prohibited from "coining money; emitting bills of credit; mak[ing] anything but gold or silver coin a tender in the payment of debts; [or] pass[ing] any . . . law impairing the obligation of contracts . . . ."[119] Additionally, a state cannot discriminate against citizens of other states.[120] These provisions place absolute constitutional prohibitions on state power to enact these measures. Consequently, absent constitutional amendment, the states are permanently enjoined from enacting such measures; Congress, by itself, lacks authority to authorize such state action.

Second, the Constitution places several prohibitions on the exercise of state power that are conditional. Article I, Section 10 provides that

> No State shall, without the consent of Congress, lay any imposts or duties on imports or exports, except what may be absolutely necessary for executing its inspection laws; and the net produce of all duties and imposts, laid by any State on imports or exports, shall be for the use of the treasury of the United States and all such laws shall be subject to the revision and control of the Congress.
>
> No State shall, without the consent of Congress, lay any duties of tonnage. . . .[121]

Thus, the states cannot act in these areas absent affirmative authorization by Congress, unless the state enactment falls under one of the enumerated exceptions. In this context, the political inertia falls against the exercise of state power, because of the inherent difficulty in obtaining affirmative congressional action.[122]

Finally, Congress's enumerated powers in Article I, Section 8, when read in conjunction with the terms of the Supremacy Clause,[123] make clear that those powers neither expressly nor conditionally denied to the states may be exercised by them, subject to reversal or preemption by legislation enacted pursuant to one of Congress's enumerated powers. These constitutional provisions, when taken together, make up the Constitution's textual structure for allocating governmental power between the state and federal systems.

The dormant Commerce Clause substantially undermines this constitutional balance of federalism, by imposing a judge-made barrier to state regulations of interstate commerce that can be overcome only by means of affirmative congressional action. There are two basic reasons why the reversal of political inertia brought about by the dormant Commerce Clause so fundamentally conflicts with the workings of this three-level constitutional structure. It is to an examination of these reasons that the analysis now turns.

The Benefit of Political Inertia: Barriers to the Legislative Process

Absent the dormant Commerce Clause, the states would be able to enact economic legislation unless it ran afoul of the Constitution's direct textual prohibitions on state economic legislation or was preempted by act of Congress. Under these circumstances, the Constitution establishes the inertia *in favor* of the exercise of state power, because the states do not need to overcome any federal barrier before they enact their economic legislation; affirmative congressional action (either before or after enactment of the state law) is required to invalidate the legislation. The result in cases in which the Court invokes the dormant Commerce Clause is that the Court has reversed the inertia, turning the constitutional balance of federalism against the states.

Any attempt to obtain a specific piece of legislation from Congress presents a nearly insurmountable task for the state, given the realities of the federal legislative process. During each Congress, thousands of measures are introduced into each house. Of the thousands of measures introduced, only a small percentage are enacted into law.[124] The congressional legislative process is an arduous one that may entail a series of compromises from the time the bill is introduced until it is finally voted upon by the members of each house.[125] Further, the process is lengthy, time-consuming, and replete with opportunities for delaying or killing a bill.[126] The process, however, contains a time constraint. Each bill introduced must be passed by both houses before the expiration of that Congress's two-year term.[127] If the bill is not passed within the two-year period, it automatically dies and must be reintroduced in the following Congress, and the process begins once again.[128]

These difficulties can only be aggravated by the Court's initial determination that the state enactment places an undue burden on commerce, regardless of whether the Court has made the correct decision. As a general matter, "Congress is far more likely not to act than to act with respect to any particular issue presented for its attention."[129] When the Supreme Court has already spoken on the matter, it is even less likely that Congress will take issue with the Court's determination that the invalidated state statute placed an undue burden on interstate commerce.

Thus, the most obvious reason that states would prefer congressional to judicial oversight of their regulation of interstate commerce is the considerably greater likelihood of congressional inaction than of congressional action. While the judiciary cannot itself initiate a review proceeding, once a legal challenge is privately instituted (a very likely event, given that state economic regulations will negatively affect at least some private industry) the courts will be required to rule, one way or the other, on the validity of a state's interstate economic regulation. In contrast, the bureaucracy of Congress will be provoked to action only in those instances in which the harm deriving from the state's regulation is deemed truly substantial.

Comparing Congressional and Judicial Oversight: The States' Perspective

There exist important political reasons why the states would prefer congressional to judicial control of their interstate economic regulations, above and beyond the simple difference in political inertia. Initially, a strong argument could be fashioned that Congress, as an institution, is better equipped to make the type of policy decision that the Court now makes under the dormant Commerce Clause when it determines that an evenhanded[130] economic regulation places an undue burden on commerce. "Congress has the superior institutional capability to gather the relevant economic information, and Congress operates on the political basis most appropriate for resolving normative questions."[131] Several members of the Court have expressed this same thought:

> Unconfined by the "narrow scope of judicial proceedings" Congress alone
> can, in the exercise of its plenary constitutional control over interstate com-
> merce, not only consider whether the [state enactment] is consistent with
> the best interests of our national economy, but can also on the basis of full
> exploration of the many aspects of a complicated problem devise a national
> policy fair alike to the States and our Union.[132]

Congress can marshall its committee and agency resources to collect relevant
information from a much broader spectrum of sources than can the judiciary
before holding hearings and engaging in debate to decide the matter at hand.
While this can be said of any decision of the Court, it is of particular import in
dormant Commerce Clause cases, because the decision made under the
dormant Commerce Clause is essentially a legislative determination.

Even if one were to reject the conclusion that Congress is better
equipped to make the proper determination under the Commerce Clause,
there is still a substantial factor weighing against the Court's use of the
dormant Commerce Clause. The view has been widely held, at the time of
ratification as well as in modern times, that the states have a special ability to
protect their interests through resort to the national political process. The
modern basis for this view was articulated by Professor Herbert Wechsler,
who contended that "the states are the strategic yardsticks for the measurement of interest and opinion, the special centers of political activity, the
separate geographical determinants of national as well as local politics."[133]
The states play a "crucial role" in the selection of the president and the
members of Congress, Wechsler argued, despite the ratification of the Seventeenth Amendment,[134] which requires the popular election of senators.
State electors select the president in the electoral college and senators and
representatives are selected by the populations of the individual states.

Wechsler noted that Congress evinces an inherent tendency to avoid new
intrusions into the affairs of the states. The constitutional distribution of
power between the three branches of the federal government, particularly
the allocation of the lawmaking power to Congress, he reasoned, is an essential means of protecting the states from federal intrusions.[135] Wechsler concluded that "[f]ederal intervention as against the states is thus primarily a
matter for congressional determination as it stands."[136] More recently, as
already explored in chapter 1, Professor Choper has become an effective
advocate of the same position,[137] and the current Supreme Court has itself
relied upon the unique political relationship between the states and Congress in fashioning its doctrines of constitutional federalism.[138]

Nor did recognition of the states' potential influence in Congress go
unnoticed by the Framers. Madison, for example, argued that

> as a security of the rights and powers of the states in their individual capacity
> against an undue preponderance of the powers granted to the Government
> over them in their collective capacity, the Constitution has relied
> on . . . the responsibility of the Senators and Representatives in the Leg-
> islature of the U.S. to the Legislatures and peoples of the states.[139]

Indeed, state influence was thought by some to be so great that the fear was expressed that Congress might at some point actually be "captured" by the states.[140] To be sure, I have already made clear my view that this reasoning provides an inadequate basis to justify judicial abdication in the enforcement of the Constitution's guarantees of federalism.[141] As most, it suggests that relatively few instances of state-federal conflict will arise; it says nothing about how the judiciary should react when such a conflict does arise. But this logic does have substantial relevance for the validity of the dormant Commerce Clause, because it explains why those who drafted the Constitution chose to structure the text to leave Congress as the primary supervisor of state exercise of power that overlaps federal authority.

In striking contrast to the traditionally close political relationship between the states and Congress is the long history of antagonism between the states and the federal judiciary. In fact, it was the lack of restraints on the federal judicial power that gave rise to much of the opposition to the adoption of the Constitution. While the Framers agreed that there should be one supreme judicial tribunal for the United States,[142] the establishment of inferior federal courts met with opposition from both within and without the Convention. For example, the mandatory creation of inferior federal courts was opposed in the Convention because the creation of the lower federal courts "would make an unnecessary encroachment on the jurisdiction of the States . . . ."[143] Lower federal courts were also seen as "creat[ing] jealousies & oppositions in the state tribunals, with the jurisdiction of which they will interfere."[144] James Monroe saw the creation of lower federal courts as "highly improper and altogether unnecessary."[145] Even creation of the Supreme Court was opposed, because it was feared that the Court would "swallow up all the other courts of the judicature"—mainly the state courts—and would deprive the citizens of the states of their civil liberties.[146] The fear was expressed that because of the existence of the federal judiciary the state courts would "soon be annihilated," and that the federal courts would destroy the rights that the states guaranteed to their citizens.[147]

The states' mistrust of the federal judiciary continued well after the Constitution's ratification. In fact, modern commentators[148] have suggested that the sole purpose of the Eleventh Amendment's[149] adoption was the fear that the federal courts would themselves extend their jurisdiction to include states, despite the absence of congressional authorization. Thus, at the time of ratification as well as in modern times, significant differences existed between the states' relationship with Congress and with the federal judiciary.

It should now be clear why the Constitution left to Congress the power to review most efforts by the states to regulate interstate commerce. While the Framers selected what they deemed especially egregious or disruptive state economic practices for express constitutional prohibition,[150] they apparently decided that in the great majority of situations the exercise of state authority should be presumed valid, subject solely to the political check of Congress's preemptive power.[151]

The Constitutional Preference for Congressional Control and the Value of Federalism

One might argue, of course, that it is for the very reason that state regulation of interstate commerce is more likely to stand under exclusive congressional review that judicial oversight is preferable. But when constitutional text is unambiguous, policy issues are beside the point. I have argued that (1) the Constitution's text clearly provides for initial congressional, rather than judicial, review of state regulation of interstate commerce (assuming the regulation violates no other constitutional prohibition),[152] and (2) there are important practical differences between the two forms of review. Once the constitutional preference is clearly ascertained, it is not appropriate—short of resort to the amendment process—for the courts to question constitutional choice.

If one were to debate the issue purely as a matter of federalism policy, however, it is highly doubtful that judicial oversight should be deemed preferable to exclusive congressional review. Initially, as already noted, examination of the relative fact-gathering capabilities of the two institutions demonstrates the probable superiority of the legislative branch. Moreover, the fact that exclusive congressional control, for reasons already discussed, is likely to result in considerably fewer invalidations of state regulation of interstate commerce is wholly consistent with the values sought to be fostered by the choice of a federal system in the first place. Under the dormant Commerce Clause, the Supreme Court invalidates state regulations when they either discriminate against out-of-staters or when they unduly burden interstate commerce, even though in a nondiscriminatory manner. Because discriminatory state regulations may be satisfactorily dealt with through resort to other constitutional provisions,[153] effectively the only type of case to be discussed is that involving nondiscriminatory burdens. When, one might ask, are state regulations likely to impose an undue burden? The answer is, when the state regulation differs markedly from the regulations imposed by its neighboring states, for it is then that those moving in interstate commerce would have to adjust each time they crossed a new state line.[154] But the alternative is virtually parallel state regulation. The obvious cost to a federal system of such federally imposed state regulatory orthodoxy is the loss of the principal advantage of a federal system: the use of the states as small-scale social laboratories, so that other states—or the federal government itself—might benefit by the experience, without incurring all of the possible risks that might result from a similar nationwide experiment.[155]

It might be responded that under the dormant Commerce Clause, such state experimentation is not *inherently* precluded; it is only when the judiciary concludes that the burdens imposed by a particular state regulation outweigh its possible benefits that the regulation falls. The fact remains, however, that judicial invalidation is considerably more likely than congressional invalidation. Thus, the structure adopted by the Constitution's text attempts to foster widespread state experimentation, while simultaneously providing the safety net of congressional preemption in those situations in which the interference with the flow of interstate commerce is truly substantial. Under this constitutional structure, those involved in interstate commerce are put on notice that they may be subjected to different regulations in different states, much as they already must be aware that they may be subjected to differing substantive legal liabilities in different states. This is simply the cost of our having chosen a federal system of government.

Nontextual Justifications for the Dormant Commerce Clause

Several scholars have articulated what can be termed "nontextual" justifications for the dormant Commerce Clause —that is, justifications not based on the Constitution's text, but which nevertheless are thought to legitimize the clause's continued existence in its present form. Examination will be limited to two such justifications. First, I will consider what can be called, for lack of a better term, the "implicit structural" argument for the dormant Commerce Clause. This theory maintains that while there may exist no explicit textual authorization for the dormant Commerce Clause concept, the principle is implicit within the constitutional structure and is therefore valid. I will also consider a "subconstitutional" justification for the dormant Commerce Clause, namely the concept of "constitutional common law." Ultimately, neither of these justifications should be accepted, either because they represent illegitimate constitutional theories, cannot be properly applied to justify the dormant Commerce Clause, or both.

The Dormant Commerce Clause as a Product of the Implicit Constitutional Infrastructure

Professor Regan relies on a "structural argument" to legitimize the Court's use of the dormant Commerce Clause.[156] An important aspect of Professor Regan's structural argument is that it "does not need to be supported by an argument from any single short bit of text (which is what lawyers normally mean by a textual argument), so long as there is no short bit of text that contradicts the structural argument . . . ."[157]

Professor Regan maintains that the dormant Commerce Clause's function is to foster the national interest in avoiding state protectionism.[158] The thrust of his thesis is that under an ideal constitution and in the absence of contrary congressional action, the Court should limit state power to regulate the economy by preventing "the states from engaging in protectionism . . . directed at other states."[159] He suggests three objections to state protectionism that, when taken together, form a structural foundation against such practices, thereby justifying the Court's use of the dormant Commerce

Clause: "[I]t is inconsistent with the very idea of political union";[160] it "cause[s] resentment and invite[s] protectionist retaliation"[161] that "is likely to generate a cycle of escalating animosity and isolation . . . eventually imperiling the political viability of the union itself";[162] and finally it is inefficient because "it diverts business away from presumptively low-cost producers without any colorable justification in terms of a federally cognizable benefit."[163] Based on these objections, Regan concludes that the dormant Commerce Clause's existence can be rationalized, despite the absence of explicit textual authorization.

For reasons of American political theory, one should have a great deal of trouble with any argument that would vest in an unrepresentative judiciary the power to invalidate legislative actions on grounds not even arguably mentioned *somewhere* in the Constitution's text.[164] It is common knowledge that the constitutional text is sufficiently broad to justify numerous modifications of legal doctrine in light of changing social needs and values.[165] One should be properly suspicious, then, of any claims that the Constitution can be found to embody a fundamental—yet implicit—principle, untied to any textual provision or combination of provisions.

Indeed, as Professor Regan's theory aptly illustrates, one making such an argument is likely to be faced with an inherent "Catch 22": presumably only principles that are deemed truly fundamental may be found within the Constitution's implicit structure; yet the more fundamental the principle, the more puzzling is its omission from explicit constitutional text. As to Professor Regan's dormant Commerce Clause argument, for example, since there can be no doubt that the Framers were aware of these grave dangers of state protectionism, one may reasonably wonder why they failed explicitly and directly to prohibit state regulation of interstate commerce if that was in fact their goal, especially when they did just that for certain other forms of state economic regulation. The answer may be that, to the extent the dormant Commerce Clause is thought *solely* to avoid protectionism (a position accepted by Regan[166] but to date rejected by a majority of the Supreme Court),[167] the Framers may well have expressly achieved this goal, at least to a certain degree, in Article IV's Privileges-and-Immunities Clause.[168] This is an issue examined in a later discussion.[169] For present purposes, however, the point to be emphasized is that there is no legitimate basis for reading into the Constitution some *implicit* principle limiting state power to regulate interstate commerce.

More importantly, as already shown, the constitutional text was apparently structured for the very purpose of establishing Congress as the sole overseer of state regulation of interstate commerce—a goal that made political sense at the time of the ratification and remains equally valid to the present day. Even if one were to concede that, in appropriate circumstances, implicit structural principles may be ascertained, surely it would be illegitimate to adopt such a principle when to do so would directly undermine a carefully structured, explicit textual balance.

The Dormant Commerce Clause as Constitutional Common Law

Several constitutional scholars have articulated what can be termed a "sub-constitutional" basis for the dormant Commerce Clause: the concept of constitutional common law. Professor Henry Monaghan is the leading advocate of this concept. He has argued

> that a surprising amount of what passes as authoritative constitutional "interpretation" is best understood as something of a quite different order—a substructure of substantive, procedural, and remedial rules drawing their inspiration and authority from, but not required by, various constitutional provisions; in short, a constitutional common law subject to amendment, modification, or even reversal by Congress. [170]

Monaghan was "driven to conclude that the Court had a common law power" after he examined several cases in which the Court applied a judicially created doctrine designed to deter violations of constitutional rights by prohibiting the use of evidence obtained in violation of the Fourth, Fifth, and Sixth Amendments—the exclusionary rule. [171] He reasoned that either the Court was mistaken in applying the exclusionary rule in these cases or that the Court was exercising a common-law-making power. [172] Unable to recognize the Court's human frailty, he adopted the latter position. [173]

What is interesting about Monaghan's pragmatic explanation of the Court's applications of the exclusionary rule for present purposes is his reference to the dormant Commerce Clause as "one of the most salient illustrations" of constitutional common law. [174] Monaghan noted that the Court had consistently recognized Congress's power to overrule dormant Commerce Clause decisions by appropriate legislation, and quite rightly asked how such a result could obtain if the Court were actually interpreting the Constitution in invoking the dormant Commerce Clause. [175] He rejected the Court's two proffered justifications for the dormant Commerce Clause, [176] asserting that the only "satisfactory" explanation for the dormant Commerce Clause cases was the Supreme Court's development of what he termed constitutional common law, derived from, but not directly based in, the text of the Commerce Clause. [177] This Commerce Clause common law would advance the Commerce Clause's purported "national, free-trade policy," he contended, by negating state-imposed obstructions to free trade. [178]

Before focusing on the specific issue of the dormant Commerce Clause as constitutional common law, it is appropriate to examine the legitimacy of the broad concept of constitutional common law in the first place. The abstract concept of "constitutional common law" is both puzzling and troubling. These issues do not arise except in cases in which a court is considering invalidation of state or federal legislative or executive action—that is, the actions of the representative branches of government. If the court takes such action, it has authority to do so only when it has found the challenged law or activity to violate a provision of the Constitution; in a constitutional democracy, it lacks authority to reach such a result on any other basis. Yet if the court has, in fact, invalidated legislation because of a conflict with a provision of the countermajoritarian Constitution, where does Congress derive authority to overrule that constitutional interpretation?

Constitutional common law, in Monaghan's view, is a species of Judge Friendly's "specialized" federal common law.[179] When it first created federal common law, the Supreme Court had to point to some authoritative text as the source of the substantive law it had just manufactured. Thus, the Court was forced to rely on statutes, treaties and constitutional provisions when it articulated federal common law.[180] Monaghan argues that, because federal courts were recognized as having the power to fashion federal common law where authorized to do so by statute, it follows ipso facto that the Court could fashion constitutional common law.[181] But there is a significant difference between judicial creation of *statutory* common law and *constitutional* common law: the former derives from congressionally created authority and can therefore logically be overriden by Congress, while the latter is super-congressional, and thus not subject to congressional reversal. In a sense, then, the term "constitutional common law" is an oxymoron, since it combines in one phrase authority that is simultaneously beyond yet within congressional power to overrule.

There is no need at this point to provide a detailed analysis of the merits of constitutional common law, however. For present purposes, one need not contest the legitimacy of constitutional common law as an abstract category of Supreme Court jurisprudence. Even if one were to accept the validity of the concept as a general matter, recognition of the dormant Commerce Clause as constitutional common law would be improper.

The federal common law process requires that the Court rely on the relevant authoritative text—in this case the Constitution— for guidance in formulating the appropriate common law rule.[182] But, as Professor Monaghan himself noted, the Court must also consider the "structure of the text, its place, and the need for a uniform national rule of law."[183] This is because federal common law of any sort is designed to play a "gap-filling" role in federal jurisprudence.[184] To be legitimate, then, constitutional common law must at the very least further the policies of a particular constitutional provision and be in accord with the Constitution's structure of government.

If the view adopted here of the delicate structural balance of federalism manifested in the text is accepted,[185] the dormant Commerce Clause does considerably more than play a gap-filling role in constitutional jurisprudence. Under the three-level analysis advocated here, the dormant Commerce Clause is in direct opposition to the Consitution's structure for controlling state power, and thus undermines the constitutional balance of federalism. As such, the dormant Commerce Clause cannot properly be said to further the Commerce Clause's purposes, because those purposes inherently include exclusive congressional oversight of most state regulations of interstate commerce. Nor can it be said to be in accord with the Constitution's structure of government or the constitutional structure of federalism. Characterizing the dormant Commerce Clause as "constitutional common law" therefore does not justify the Court's continued use of the clause.

Postmortem: Life without the Dormant Commerce Clause

If one accepts the rejection of the dormant Commerce Clause advocated here, important questions remain. Must state regulations affecting interstate commerce that unduly burden or discriminate against interstate commerce be deemed constitutional? Could a state, consistent with the Constitution, effectively Balkanize the nation by setting up guards at its borders to collect an entrance tax from out-of-staters? Could it impose custom duties on goods shipped from other states? May it provide economic benefits to its resident businesses while flagrantly denying them to out-of-state competitors? A pragmatist might argue that the dormant Commerce Clause, regardless of its constitutional foundation, is required, if only to invalidate just such state legislation. But even absent the dormant Commerce Clause, the Constitution provides a textual structure for the regulation of commerce that can quite effectively prevent economic armageddon at the hands of the states.

There is no doubt that Congress, pursuant to its commerce power, has authority to preempt all such state legislation, and it is highly likely that it would do just that in the face of such flagrant, indefensible, and harmful state protectionism. Indeed, under my view of the constitutional balance, it was in large part to provide a legislative safety net against state economic Balkanization that Congress was given power in Article I to regulate interstate commerce in the first place. But for much of the potentially most egregious state legislation, it is unlikely that affirmative congressional preemption would even be required. Important elements of the constitutional balance are the provisions prohibiting both specified state action subject to congressional authorization and prohibiting certain activity unconditionally. This section is designed to explore how the textual structure of federalism would—or could—operate, in the absence of the dormant Commerce Clause.

Comparing the Commerce and Privileges-and-Immunities Clauses

Article IV, Section 2, of the Constitution provides that "[t]he citizens of each State shall be entitled to all privileges and immunities of citizens in the several states."[186] While the Court has recognized that the dormant Commerce Clause and Article IV's Privileges-and-Immunities Clause have a "mutually reinforcing relationship" which "stems from their common origin in the Fourth Article of the Articles of Confederation,"[187] there exist notable distinctions, in both interpretation and application.

The Privileges-and-Immunities Clause was purportedly designed to promote interstate harmony and cooperation in order to prevent the dissolution of the Union.[188] Each state was to be constitutionally prohibited from placing out-of-state citizens at a disadvantage under the laws of that state. The text of the Constitution, however, sheds little light on exactly what constitutes the "privileges and immunities of citizens in the several States." The clause has been said to be an abbreviated version of the privileges-and-immunities clause contained in the Articles of Confederation.[189] Thus, examinations of the privileges-and-immunities clause contained in the Articles of Confederation, the development of the parallel clause in the Constitution, and the Court's interpretation of the constitutional clause are required to determine the nature of the constitutional protection afforded by the clause to those engaged in commerce.

The Constitution's predecessor, the Articles of Confederation, contained a similar but more textually elaborate guarantee of interstate comity. Article IV of the Articles of Confederation stated:

> [T]he free inhabitants of each of these states . . . shall be entitled to all privileges and immunities of free citizens in the several states; and the people of each State shall have free ingress and regress to and from any other State, and shall enjoy therein all the privileges of trade and commerce, subject to the same duties, impositions, and restrictions, as the inhabitants thereof respectively . . . .

Note that under the Articles of Confederation, out-of-state residents were *textually* guaranteed that they could engage in commerce in other states "subject to the same duties, impositions, and restrictions, as the inhabitants" of the situs state.

Charles Pinckney, the South Carolina delegate to the Constitutional Convention of 1787 generally recognized as the author of the Constitution's Privileges-and-Immunities Clause,[190] wrote in 1787 that "[t]he 4th article, respecting the extending the rights of the citizens of each State, throughout the United States . . . is formed exactly upon the principles of the 4th article of the present Confederation . . . ."[191] The clause became part of the Constitution with virtually no debate.[192] As Professor Simpson has noted: "[I]t seems reasonable to infer that familar principles—specifically, those spelled out in the provision of the Articles of Confederation on which the clause plainly was based—were widely understood to inform the clause."[193]

If the clause actually had consistently received such an interpretation, it would have been similar in at least certain respects to the operation of the dormant Commerce Clause. Both would have prohibited state economic protectionist action that discriminated against out-of-staters, and therefore to the extent the dormant Commerce Clause was concerned solely with such discrimination, the overlap would be substantial. Even so, significant differences would remain. Initially, the reach of the dormant Commerce Clause has never been limited to discriminatory state regulations. Rather, even regulations neutrally applied to in-staters and out-of-staters alike will be invalidated if they are found to burden unduly interstate commerce.[194] Scholars have debated the theoretical merits of this extension,[195] but there can be little doubt that it remains an accepted element of the Supreme Court's dormant Commerce Clause jurisprudence.[196] There exist no rational means of construing the terms of the Privileges-and-Immunities Clause to extend beyond discriminatory state regulation. Secondly, even as to discriminatory legislation, a major difference exists between the impact of the two clauses. Supreme Court applications of the dormant Commerce Clause may be reversed by congressional legislation;[197] decisions enforcing the Privileges-and-Immunities Clause—much like judicial interpretations of all other constitutional provisions—are beyond congressional reach.

If these were the only differences between the effect of the two clauses, little would be lost, as a practical matter, by abandoning the dormant Commerce Clause. While it is possible that nondiscriminatory state legislation could have a negative impact on national interests, surely such regulation is not nearly as threatening to the goal of national unity as is discriminatory legislation. In the relatively rare instance in which nondiscriminatory legislation is truly harmful, the availability of congressional preemptive power under the Commerce Clause should provide adequate protection. Nor is it clear that the availability of congressional reversal of Supreme Court holdings is either necessary or even wise, since the practice is so strikingly aberrant from traditional constitutional theory.

For reasons that are not entirely clear, however, the Court, at least in modern times, has declined to find all state discriminatory legislation invalid under the Privileges-and-Immunities Clause.[198] Though in the nation's early years the clause often did receive this broad an interpretation,[199] during the early twentieth century the Court shifted its construction of the Privileges-and-Immunities Clause.[200] Instead, it adopted the approach originally taken in the 1823 circuit court case *Corfield v. Coryell*,[201] extending constitutional protection under the Privileges-and-Immunities Clause only if out-of-state residents were discriminated against in the exercise of so-called "fundamental rights."[202] In *Corfield*, Justice Washington had rejected the argument that a citizen of one state could "participate in all the rights which belong exclusively to the citizens of any other state, merely upon the ground that they are enjoyed by those citizens . . . ."[203] He enumerated several general categories of protected privileges and immunities, including the ability "to institute and maintain actions of any kind in the courts of the state; to take, hold and dispose of property, . . .; and an exemption from higher taxes or impositions than are paid by other citizens of the state . . . ."[204]

It is unclear whether more recent interpretations have returned to the earlier broad construction, however,[205] and in any event there appears to be no textual, historical, or policy reason that binds the Court to the "fundamental rights" interpretation. Indeed, if anything, the exact opposite is true: there would seem to be no textual basis for the imposition of such a requirement in the first place.

Nevertheless, advocates of the dormant Commerce Clause have argued that the two clauses may serve different constitutional purposes, and that therefore both clauses are required.[206] These commentators do find some support in modern Supreme Court doctrine. Although at one point the Court noted that there exists a "mutually reinforcing relationship between the Privileges and Immunities Clause of Art. IV, § 2 and the Commerce Clause,"[207] at other times it has declared that the Privileges-and-Immunitites and Commerce Clauses serve different constitutional purposes.[208] In *United Building and Construction Trades Council v. Mayor of Camden*,[209] for example, Chief Justice Rehnquist wrote that "[t]he two clauses have different aims and set different standards for state conduct." He stated that "[t]he Commerce Clause acts as *implied* restraint upon state regulatory powers. Such powers must give way before the superior authority of Congress to legislate on (or leave unregulated) matters involving interstate commerce."[210] Rehnquist distinguished the Privileges-and-Immunities Clause, stating that it "imposes a *direct* restraint on state action in the interests of interstate harmony. . . . It is discrimination against out-of-state residents on matters of fundamental concern which triggers the Clause, not regulation affecting interstate commerce."[211]

Chief Justice Rehnquist's proffered distinctions are unpersuasive, however. Initially, the distinction premised on the implied or direct nature of the regulation has nothing to do with the *purposes* served by the clauses; it merely underscores the lack of any textual support for the dormant Commerce Clause. Similarly, the fact that judicial application of the dormant Commerce Clause "must give way to the superior authority of Congress" also has nothing to do with the purposes of the two clauses; it once again merely underscores the aberrant nature of the dormant Commerce Clause in constitutional theory. Finally, his contention that the Privileges-and-Immunities Clause was designed to foster "interstate harmony" and the avoidance of "discrimination against out-of-state residents" actually underscores the theoretical similarity of the two clauses. While the Court has declared that the rights protected under the Privileges-and-Immunitites Clause are those rights "bearing upon the vitality of the Nation as a single entity that the State must treat all citizens, resident and non-resident, equally,"[212] it has similarly noted that the Commerce Clause was created because of "'the mutual jealousies and aggressions of the states, taking form in customs barriers and other economic retaliation,'"[213] and that "[i]t is . . . beyond doubt that the Commerce Clause itself furthers strong federal interests in preventing economic Balkanization."[214] Moreover, the Court has consistently invalidated discriminatory state regulations of commerce pursuant to the dormant Commerce Clause, because "the peoples of the several states must sink or swim together, and . . . in the long run prosperity and salvation are in union and not division."[215] Thus, it appears that the Court has recognized the same right under both the Privileges-and-Immunities and the dormant Commerce Clauses—the right of an out-of-state resident to be free from discriminatory state regulations of commerce.

The Privileges-and-Immunities Clause and the Corporations Problem

To this point, the analysis has established that, both doctrinally and theoretically, the Privileges-and-Immunities Clause could adequately fulfill at least the primary function now served by the dormant Commerce Clause. However, there remains one current doctrinal aspect of Privileges-and-Immunities Clause jurisprudence that could effectively prevent that clause from serving as an adequate substitute for the dormant Commerce Clause. The Supreme Court has consistently maintained that a corporation is not entitled to the protection granted by the Privileges-and-Immunities Clause, because corporations are not "citizens."[216] The Court's failure to extend the protection of the Privileges-and-Immunities Clause to corporations presents an obvious practical problem, because of the enormous amount of commerce that is conducted by corporations. The scope of the Privileges-and-Immunities Clause is not the primary focus of this chapter and therefore an exhaustive examination of the corporations issue is not included. Nevertheless, it can be reasonably argued that corporations should, in fact, be afforded the protections of Article IV.

From a policy perspective, there can be little doubt that corporations should receive the protections of the Privileges-and-Immunities Clause. A substantial portion of business in the nation—and therefore interstate business as well—is conducted by corporate entities. To the extent the clause is designed to establish interstate harmony, as Chief Justice Rehnquist suggested, the exclusion of corporations from the clause's scope obviously precludes fulfillment of this goal. Thus, the only conceivable basis for the exclusion of corporations is a textual argument: the word "citizens" cannot rationally be defined to include corporations. But in light of the generally liberal interpretations traditionally given constitutional language, such an argument is disingenuous. The term "person" in the Fourteenth Amendment[217] has consistently been interpreted to include corporations,[218] and the term "citizens" in the diversity jurisdictional statute,[219] which in turn is premised on the use of the same term in Article III of the Constitution,[220] has always been assumed to include corporations. Why, then, should we hesitate to treat the same term in Article IV in the same manner? If the right to an abortion can somehow be found within the terms of the Due Process Clause,[221] surely the Court can find it in its heart to include corporations within the scope of the Privileges-and-Immunities Clause.

If, however, corporations cannot, for some unknown reason, be extended rights under the Privileges-and-Immunities Clause, an alternative remains. Congress could, pursuant to the Commerce Clause, prohibit discrimination by the states against out-of-state corporations engaged in interstate commerce. Additionally, Congress could preempt state regulations of commerce that discriminate against corporations by prescribing its own substantive federal regulations. Either of these alternatives would be consistent with the Constitution's text, and would not alter the consitutional balance of federalism.

The "Democratic Process" Model as an Alternative to the Textual Critique

The Nature of the "Democratic Process" Model

In recent years, several commentators have reached an ultimate conclusion similar in many respects to the one reached here: the sole legitimate rationale for judicial invalidation of state legislation burdening interstate commerce is the discriminatory impact of that legislation on out-of-state residents. At least one of those scholars has concluded that that function can adequately be performed by resort to the Privileges-and-Immunities Clause.[222] But while this view and the one advocated here are similar in result, the theoretical analyses leading us to our respective conclusions are quite different. In fact, the reasoning of those scholars who have previously reached this result is fundamentally flawed in several respects. Therefore if one were to rely soley on the arguments of those who wrote prior to this analysis, one would be well justified in rejecting our conclusion. It is therefore important to examine the theory of these earlier scholars, and to explain why the rationale adopted here is preferable.

Earlier commentators have argued that "[t]he time-honored rationales for traditional dormant Commerce Clause jurisprudence have become historical vestiges,"[223] and that "[i]n the end . . . we are left with only a single justification for judicial displacement of state legislative judgments in the commercial area—the process-oriented protection of representational governments."[224] This theory, which can be labeled the "democratic process" model, turns on the fact that the out-of-state citizens affected by a state's commercial regulation are not represented in the legislature that enacted the regulation. Its origins can be found in the opinion of Justice Stone, speaking for the Court in *South Carolina State Highway Department v. Barnwell Brothers, Inc.*[225]

> Underlying the stated rule has been the thought, often expressed in judicial opinion, that when the regulation is of such a character that its burden falls principally upon those without the state, legislative action is not likely to be subjected to those political restraints which are normally exerted on legislation where it affects adversely some interests within the state.

Those who believe this to be the key factor argue that

> [w]hen regulations promulgated by a legislative body fall solely or predominately on a group represented in the legislature there is cause to believe the enactment will be rationally based, efficacious, and no more burdensome than is necessary to achieve the proffered purpose. When the state enacts legislation . . . falling principally on out-of-staters not represented in the regulating body, such a presumption is unwarranted.[226]

As Professor Tushnet has argued, this theory "can be viewed as a political application of the economists' theory of externalities: because a legislative body may underestimate the burdens that its proposals place on people who do not participate in its selection, the resulting statutes may be inefficient."[227]

To reach their ultimate conclusion, advocates of this "democratic process" model as the sole rationale for judicial invalidation of state regulation must establish two points: (1) that the rationale of their model is valid, and (2) that no other conceivable policy rationale justifying a broader-based dormant Commerce Clause is equally valid. While the conclusion reached here, reached through analysis of the textual structure, is coincidentally similar to that of the "democratic process" proponents, their approach—tied purely to policy considerations, rather than a textual anchor—fails to meet either criterion for success.

The Flawed Logic of the ''Democratic Process'' Model

Initially, it should be noted that the democratic process model cannot rationalize a test turning solely on grounds of discrimination, because even if accepted, the model proves too much. Once we agree that the key factor is lack of representation in the legislative process, any state regulation affecting out-of-staters—whether discriminatory or not—is rendered suspect. For even if the regulation does not disproportionately affect out-of-staters, the fact remains that the out-of-staters have had no say in the promulgation of the regulation that affects them. It is the very fact of this representational absence that violates the premise of the "democratic process" model. Moreover, it is at least conceivable that in-state residents may have favored a regulation that out-of-staters might oppose, even though the regulation will affect both equally. It is logically also conceivable that in-staters subjected to the regulation did oppose it, but lacked the political strength to overcome its supporters in the state's legislature. In such an event, if those out-of-staters affected by the regulation had also been represented in the legislature, the regulation might well have failed.[228]

Advocates of the "democratic process" model, however, respond that, in terms of economic efficiency, a regulation equally affecting those represented in the state's legislative process and those unrepresented is much more likely to be efficient and rational, because of the absence of the equivalent of economic externalities. Such an analysis, to borrow a phrase from Professor Regan, smacks of "utopian Coaseism."[229] It is absurd to suggest that the generally nondeliberative legislative process[230] is always—or even often—likely to result in the most rational or efficient result. But even if it did, that fact is largely beside the point. If the key value to be served is representational, as the model's advocates have asserted, the fact remains that whether or not the regulation can ultimately be deemed efficient or rational, those out-of-staters affected by it have had no say in its adoption. This fact would seem to be critical, since by its nature a model premised on notions of democratic theory is concerned with *process* values,[231] rather than the wisdom of a particular outcome. If it were otherwise, a truly wise and benevolent dictator could be as morally acceptable a form of government as democracy, a conclusion rejected by democratic theorists.[232] In short, the interest in economic efficiency as an outgrowth of a concern over adequate representation amounts to a non-sequitur. Thus, acceptance of the "democratic process" model cannot logically stop with invalidation of discriminatory legislation. Even nondiscriminatory legislation affecting out-of-staters suffers from the same process-based defect.

The Rejection of Alternative Values

It is important to recall that advocates of the "democratic process" model base their conclusion not on any analysis of constitutional text, but rather on grounds of reason and political theory.[233] Once the textual anchor is abandoned, advocates of any model for judicial action must of course meet a burden of explaining why their approach is preferable, as a matter of logic and political theory, to any other conceivable model. Under this standard, the "democratic process" model must fall. For even if one were to concede the logic of the "democratic process" model as a basis for invalidation of discriminatory legislation, the model's advocates have failed adequately to dispose of all conceivable alternative values that a reviewing court might reasonably adopt as a rationale for overturning state regulation—values that would not be adequately fostered solely by the prohibition of discriminatory state legislation. Thus, absent a basis in constitutional text to support their conclusion, "democratic process" advocates fail to justify their ultimate solution.

While these advocates attempt to dispose of certain conceivable values that might be served by the dormant Commerce Clause,[234] they neglect to deal with the one value possessing the strongest historical foundation and the most reasonable grounding in American political theory: the avoidance of Balkanization among the states resulting from trade policies that tend to disrupt the union. This was clearly the greatest problem under the Articles of Confederation, and played an important role in the establishment of the congressional commerce power in Article I.[235] While discriminatory state legislation may of course bring about such disunity, even non-discriminatory state regulation that significantly burdens the free flow of commerce from state to state may give rise to this danger. Hence if a reviewing court—freed from all textual restraints—were to conclude that the avoidance of Balkanization, rather than concern over representation, constitutes the primary theoretical focus, it could very easily adhere to the Court's current balancing test for determining the validity of evenhanded, nondiscriminatory state regulation burdening interstate commerce.[236]

The "Democratic Process" Model and Constitutional Text

Perhaps the greatest fallacy of the advocates of the "democratic process" model is their apparent assumption that a reviewing court is authorized to pick and choose among conceivable normative political theories in deciding when to invalidate state legislation.[237] To be sure, there are numerous textual provisions so broadly phrased that a reviewing court—almost by necessity—will be called upon to ascertain and apply specific political or moral values.[238] But as the examination of the textual structure here has shown, limitations on state authority to regulate interstate commerce is not among them.

It so happens that the result reached by these theorists largely comports with the textual structure that is discerned here. However, this fact appears, at most, to be helpful icing on the cake to these theorists, in no way essential to their ultimate conclusion.[239] The analysis here has demonstrated, however, that even if one were to abandon textual constraints in favor of the fundamental normative assumptions made by the "democratic process" theorists, their ultimate conclusion is at best unproven and at worst incorrect. But even if their theoretical assumptions were universally conceded and their logical inferences inescapable, the approach would remain fundamentally flawed. This is because in a constitutional democracy, a reviewing court at the outset must anchor its invalidation of majoritarian action in the language of the Constitution. Absent such a basis in text, all normative issues of political theory remain irrelevant to the exercise of the court's judicial review power.

Conclusion

The dormant Commerce Clause lacks a foundation or justification in either the Constitution's text or history, and, despite the efforts of respected constitutional scholars, the clause cannot be satisfactorily rationalized outside the text of the Constitution. Most importantly, the dormant Commerce Clause alters the delicate balance of federalism clearly manifested in the constitutional text. By vesting initial oversight power in the judiciary, rather than Congress, the dormant Commerce Clause shifts the political inertia against the states in the regulation of interstate commerce, and leaves federal oversight of state regulation in the hands of the governmental body traditionally thought to be least responsive to state concerns.

Moreover, leaving oversight, at least of nondiscriminatory state regulation, exclusively in congressional hands is not likely to be harmful to the interests of the federal system. Indeed, judicial prohibition of such regulation could in many instances stifle individual state experimentation, by requiring orthodoxy in interstate treatment.

If the Court were to overrule its existing doctrine and reject the dormant Commerce Clause, the nation would not be reduced to a Balkanized confederation. On the contrary, as previously demonstrated, the Constitution provides a textual allocation of power designed to prevent just such an occurrence. For example, Article IV's Privileges-and-Immunities Clause can be construed to prohibit the states from discriminating against the citizens of other states who engage in commerce.[240] The power to control nondiscriminatory state regulation, however, is granted to Congress, not the Court. It is Congress that must affirmatively exercise the power to regulate interstate commerce. For those critics who perceive this scheme to be socially or politically inadequate—a conclusion, I should emphasize, that has been rejected here—the only alternative is resort to the amendment process in order to provide textual relief from any perceived inadequacies. It is time to recognize that the dormant Commerce Clause is little more than a figment of the Supreme Court's imagination—hardly a legitimate basis, in a democratic society, upon which to premise judicial invalidations of state legislative action.

4

Pragmatic Formalism and Separation of Powers

While the issues of federalism examined in the preceding chapters are central to the political structure contemplated in the Constitution, by no means do they exhaust that political framework. The structure of federalism contemplated in the Constitution took the preexisting format of state sovereignty and modified it in order to strengthen the federal government without concentrating all policymaking power at that governmental level. In addition, the Framers decided to divide the power of the federal government further, into three separate units that would overlap in their tasks only to the extent necessary to enable one branch to check the potential excesses of the others.

As originally contemplated, the principles of both federalism and separation of powers were designed to reduce the obvious dangers that flow from the concentration of political power. Today, in light of both legal and social developments, the effectiveness of federalism as a means of avoiding such concentration has been undermined. To be sure, the modern judicial interpretation of constitutional federalism could be restructured so that the concept performs its intended role more effectively. Yet it is doubtful—given the practical realities of modern-day life and the corresponding expansion of the concept of interstate commerce—that constitutional federalism could, standing alone, ever work as a truly effective check on the concentration of political power. Thus, the centrality of the separation-of-powers concept to American political theory should be recognized, and as a result the Court's enforcement of that concept needs to become considerably more vigorous than it has been in the recent past.

Even a casual historical inquiry reveals the importance that separation of powers had for the Framers. Of course, unless one is a rigid adherent of originalist thinking,[1] the mere fact that the Framers intended to adopt a particular political structure does not, by itself, automatically establish its modern normative validity. Indeed, several political theorists have challenged the viability of the Constitution's system of separation of powers for modern society.[2] While those of us in constitutional law are presumably not authorized simply to ignore or overrule provisions of the Constitution we now find to be inconvenient or even unwise, it will often be possible for a Court, unhappy with a particular provision, to construe it in a manner that dramatically reduces its impact. This is arguably what the modern Court has done in some of its most recent interpretations of the separation-of-powers provisions.[3] However, the separation-of-powers provisions of the Constitution are tremendously important, not merely because the Framers imposed them, but because the fears of creeping tyranny underlying them are at least as justified today as they were at the time the Framers established them. For as the old adage goes, "Even paranoids have enemies." It should not be that debatable that, throughout history, the concept of representative and accountable government has existed in a constant state of vulnerability. This has been almost as true in the years since the Constitution's ratification as it had been prior to that time. Abandonment or dilution of separation of powers as one of the key methods of reducing the likelihood of undue concentration of political power will dramatically increase that vulnerability. What is called for, then, is an interpretational model that will avoid the diluting impact that recent Supreme Court doctrine has sometimes had on the beneficial protective force of separation of powers. The model recommended here is a type of "formalistic" approach to the interpretation and enforcement of separation of powers—one grounded on the deceptively simple principle that no branch may be permitted to exercise *any* authority definitionally found to fall outside its constitutionally delimited powers.[4]

Any call for a return to "formalism" in constitutional interpretation naturally will expose one to the barrage of ridicule and disdain traditionally reserved by modern scholars for what is almost universally deemed to be such an epistemologically naive methodology.[5] It is important, however, to distinguish "epistemological" formalism from what might oxymoronically be referred to as "pragmatic" formalism. The former represents a commitment to a rigidity and level of abstraction that is quite probably not possible and certainly unwise. "Pragmatic formalism," on the other hand, is a "street-smart" mode of interpretation, growing out of a recognition of the dangers to which a more "functional" or "balancing" analysis in the separation-of-powers context may give rise. It recognizes that once a reviewing court begins down those roads in the enforcement of separation of powers, no meaningful limitations on interbranch usurpation of power remain. More importantly, it recognizes that even if functionalism and balancing could be employed with principled limitation, any such interpretational approach inherently guts the prophylactic nature of the separation-of-powers protections, so essential a part of that system.

The pragmatic nature of the formalistic approach advocated here is manifested in two ways. Initially, pragmatic factors lead to the choice of formalism in the first place: no conceivable alternative adequately guards against the dangers that the system of separation of powers was adopted to avoid. Secondly, pragmatism influences how the differing concepts of branch power are ultimately to be defined. It is important to emphasize that "formalism," as the term is employed here, is not intended to imply imposition of rigid, abstract interpretational formulas, derived from an originalistic perspective.[6] All the term is intended to suggest is that the constitutional validity of a particular branch action, from the perspective of separation of powers, is to be determined not by resort to functional balancing but solely by the use of a definitional analysis. In other words, the Court's role in separation-of-powers cases is to be limited to determining whether the challenged branch action falls within the definition of that branch's constitutionally derived powers—executive, legislative or judicial. If the answer is yes, the branch's action is constitutional; if the answer is no, the action is unconstitutional. No other questions are to be asked; no other countervailing factors are to be taken into account.

Defining those constitutional terms will naturally prove to be no simple task. Yet it should be no more difficult than the tasks facing the Court in defining numerous other constitutional terms[7]—for example, "due process,"[8] "speech,"[9] or "cruel and unusual punishment."[10] It has been argued that the Constitution's separation-of-powers protections are qualitatively different from other constitutional provisions because they are found only in the document's implicit structure rather than its text. Such a distinction, however, is fallacious. The separation-of-powers protections are, in fact, explicitly embodied in the text, in the portions of Articles I, II, and III conveying to each branch a specific type of governmental power. While these provisions do not place explicit *prohibitions* on the exercise of additional power by each branch, such prohibitions are unnecessary, in light of the background understanding, textually confirmed in the Tenth Amendment, that the federal government is one of enumerated powers. Thus, when Article I conveys to Congress the legislative power, it is the failure of the text to delegate executive or judicial power to Congress that imposes the prohibition on congressional authority to exercise those powers. Judicial review of alleged branch usurpations, then, is appropriately deemed to be just as capable of textual construction as is any other constitutional provision.

In fashioning its definitions of branch power, the Court should look to a combination of policy, tradition, precedent, and linguistic analysis. Presumably, within certain linguistic boundaries,[11] the definitions may evolve over time, much as the definitions of other constitutional terms have. The key point, however, is that, no matter how the terms are ultimately defined, the exercise of each branch's power is to be limited to the functions definitionally brought within those concepts. In that sense, the powers of each branch would be "formally" separated from the powers of the other branches.

It might be argued that the inclusion within the definitional analysis of pragmatic factors effectively allows sufficient manipulability to enable the

Supreme Court to employ a form of functional balancing under the guise of a definitional analysis. In a sense, of course, this is correct, since purely as a practical matter the Court—much like the proverbial nine-hundred-pound gorilla—may ultimately say anything it wants. If the Court wishes to assert that a fish is a tree, for example, there is no one to stop it. But the Court's good-faith adoption of the pragmatic formalist model would go far towards confining the unlimited flexibility inherent in a purely functional or balancing model. Though there will no doubt be close cases, both historical tradition and linguistic common sense will impose restrictions on the Court's use of purely pragmatic factors in its separation-of-powers analysis. To be sure, a Court *not* acting in good faith could manipulate the suggested standard into meaninglessness. But that is just as true of any conceivable doctrinal standard, for the interpretation of any constitutional provision. In any event, to do so would impose costs on the Court's institutional capital that open and admitted use of functionalism would not. The Court looks considerably sillier when it stoutly maintains that a fish is a tree than when it explains that, under appropriate constitutional theory, it simply does not matter whether the item in question is a fish or a tree.

The first section of this chapter will examine separation of powers from the perspective of political theory. It will consider the purposes, values, and costs of this system, as well as alternative governmental models recently suggested by theorists unhappy with the confining impact of this governmental form. The second section will make the case for pragmatic formalism as a doctrinal model for separation-of-powers cases. In so doing, it will provide broad definitional guidelines for the scope of the different branches' powers. The section will also test important Supreme Court separation-of-powers decisions by the standard of the "pragmatic formalist" model, indicating how those cases should have been resolved under that structure. The third section will explore the serious problems with four alternative doctrinal structures which have been either employed by the Court or suggested by commentators for resolving separation-of-powers disputes: the "functionalist" model, the "originalist" model, the "conflict of interest" model, and the "ordered liberty" model.[12]

Separation of Powers as Political Theory

Origins and Rationale

It requires neither substantial historical background nor great political insight to recognize the profound mistrust of government reflected in separation-of-powers theory.[13] If one individual or body were trustworthy, presumably that individual or body could be entrusted with total and unreviewable power to check all other organs of government. Instead, under a separation-of-powers scheme each segment of government is simultaneously given its own limited authority and means of checking potential excesses of other governmental units.

Pre-American Theoretical Origins

As a political theory, the concept of separation of powers long predates the American Constitution. In fact, separation of powers as enunciated in our Constitution and understood today is a conglomeration of the ideas of many scholars and the experiences of many governments. Locke and Montesquieu seem to have had the strongest influence in the eighteenth century, for their works were heavily cited throughout the framing period.[14] The impact of their theory on the Framers is hard to gauge, however. Despite their frequent citation to scholarly authority, the individuals who drafted the Constitution seemed always to hark back to pragmatic, common sense evaluations of the Constitution they proposed.[15] Indeed, "when the framers referred to foreign writers such as Montesquieu, they did so to embellish an argument, not to prove it. The argument itself was grounded on what had been learned at home. Theory played a role, but it was always circumscribed and tested by experience."[16] This pragmatic philosophy was summed up by one of the delegates to the Federal Convention: "Experience must be our only guide. Reason may mislead us."[17]

Nonetheless, Montesquieu and Locke apparently played large parts in the theoretical foundation of the Constitution. They, too, however, did not write on a clean slate. The foundations of modern separation of powers theory can be traced to the ancient Greek and Roman theory of mixed government.[18] This concept was based on a "frank recognition of the class basis of society."[19] Each class had its own representative body, which shared in all the decisions of government. The separate departments were not designed to make government more efficient, since each had a part in each decision. Rather, their representativeness enabled them to prevent power from being used to prejudice the interests they represented.[20] Mixed government was designed to prevent absolutism—the arbitrary use of power—by avoiding the concentration of all state power in one body. Separation of powers has the same function, but operates on different assumptions. Two major changes are required to transform mixed government into a government based on separation of powers. First, particular departments must be restricted to certain functions. Second, an independent judiciary must be established.[21]

The transition from mixed government to separation of powers began in the seventeenth century. Although people had long realized the danger of absolute power, the creation of a division of authority not based on class lines took time. As early as 1656, political writers were stressing the importance of the separation between the legislative and executive powers. According to Marchamont Nedham, "[I]n all Kingdoms and States whatsoever, where they have had anything of Freedom among them, the Legislative and Executive Powers have been managed in distinct hands."[22] Nedham warned against allowing the gradual accumulation of power in one branch. Using Rome as an example, Nedham explained that

> their Emperors . . . durst not at first turn both these Powers into the Channel of their own unbounded Will; *but did it by degrees*, that they might

the more insensibly deprive the people of their Liberty, till at length they openly made and executed Laws at their own pleasures . . . and so there was an end of the Roman Liberty.[23]

George Lawson's work formed an important bridge between the theories of mixed government and separation of powers.[24] His two works laid the foundation for Locke's *Second Treatise on Government*.[25] Lawson played a key role in dividing governmental functions into three parts rather than two, and in restricting the power of the executive to its particular functions. Executive power had been perceived as the authority to execute the law through the courts, with the head of state also in command of the courts. But Lawson developed a three-part division of the functions of government: "There is a threefold power civil, or rather three degrees of that power. The first is the legislative. The second judicial. The third executive."[26] It was here that the traditional division between legislation and execution of the laws was initially made. But Lawson divided execution again into "acts of Judgment"—the hearing and decision of causes upon evidence, and "execution."[27] Execution meant the carrying out of judgments, "rather than the carrying into effect of the law as a whole."[28] This division laid the foundation for Locke to move from mixed government to separation of powers.

Locke completed the bridge between the ancient theory of mixed government and the modern doctrine of separation of powers.[29] Although most of the *Second Treatise on Government* sets forth a division of power between two branches of government,[30] Locke did propose a division of power between three branches based on the state of nature. One of his most important contributions to modern political theory was his "reconciliation of legislative supremacy with the ideas of separation of powers."[31] He defined legislative power as the "right *to direct* how *the Force of the Commonwealth* shall be imploy'd for preserving the Community and the Members of it."[32] However, he cautioned that it "may be too great a temptation to human frailty apt to grasp at Power, for the same Persons who have the Power of making Laws, to have also . . . the power to execute them."[33] This pragmatic evaluation of human nature greatly influenced the Framers. Repeated reference is made in *The Federalist*[34] and other writings of the time[35] to the need to guard against such temptation. Locke solved the problem by dispersing the legislators as soon as their task was complete, subjecting them to the laws they had made (thereby ensuring that the laws would be for the public good),[36] and establishing "a *Power always in being*, which should see to the *Execution* of the Laws that are made . . . [a]nd thus the *Legislative* and *Executive Power* come often to be separated."[37]

Locke believed that the legislative power should be supreme "and all other Powers in any Members or parts of the Society, derived from and subordinate to it."[38] This complete legislative supremacy was rejected by the Framers because of their recent experiences with Parliament and their own state governments.[39] Locke also recommended that the executive have a certain residual power since the legislators cannot foresee all events, and because there are many things that "the Law can by no means provide for, and those must necessarily be left to the discretion of him, that has the Executive Power in his hands."[40] Whether and to what extent the Framers adopted this recommendation is still a matter of debate.[41]

Despite Locke's influence, Montesquieu was invoked more often than any other political authority in eighteenth-century America.[42] Perhaps because of the Framers' efforts, his name is most closely associated with separation of powers. But Montesquieu insisted on neither absolute separation nor legislative supremacy. Rather, according to Montesquieu, the branches' powers are supposed to blend and overlap so that they can check one another.[43] Like other eighteenth-century French political writers, Montesquieu lived daily with "the excesses of Bourbon absolutism"[44] and thus recognized the problem of controlling political power.[45] Although he never recommended that the English system be adopted in France, he did express admiration for it.[46] The English system's most attractive elements were the substantial separation of executive, legislative, and judicial power, and the mixture of monarchy, aristocracy, and democracy in Crown, Lords, and Commons.[47] Montesquieu noted that "[i]n every government there are three sorts of power, the legislative; the executive in respect to things dependent on the law of nations; and the executive, in regard to things that depend on the civil laws."[48] The first power is to enact laws, the second is basically a foreign relations power—to make "peace or war, send or receive embassies, . . . and provide[ ] against invasion."[49] The third power is to punish crimes and resolve the disputes that arise between individuals. Montesquieu called this second aspect of executive power the "judiciary power."[50]

Montesquieu was suspicious of governmental power and observed its tendency to encroach on the rights of the citizenry. "Political liberty . . . is there only when there is no abuse of power: but constant experience shows us, that every man invested with power is apt to abuse it; he pushes on till he comes to the utmost limit. . . . To prevent the abuse of power, 'tis necessary that by the very disposition of things power should be a check to power."[51] Thus, Montesquieu thought that the structure of government was the means of preserving liberty. He believed that the English constitution had "political liberty for its direct purpose,"[52] so he took its structure as the ideal.

The Role of Separation of Powers in American Political Theory: "Ambition Must Be Made to Counteract Ambition"[53]

Though the Framers were not satisfied with the structure of the English government, they wholeheartedly concurred with Montesquieu's distrust of governmental power. One of Madison's defenses of the American Constitution was that it had more separation of powers than Montesquieu's ideal.[54] In order to preserve political liberty, which he defined as the "tranquility of mind, arising from the opinion each person has of his safety,"[55] he argued that the legislative and executive powers cannot be united in the same body.

There should be no union because the tranquility of the subject would be disturbed by the apprehension that the "same monarch or senate should enact tyrannical laws, to execute them in a tyrannical manner."[56]

"If men were angels," Madison wrote in *The Federalist* No. 51, "no government would be necessary. If angels were to govern men neither external nor internal control of government would be necessary."[57] Since experience had taught that neither option was available, the Framers sought to institutionalize methods for controlling government. Montesquieu's suspicion of governmental power struck a sympathetic chord in the minds of the Framers. In fact, there was little debate about whether or not Montesquieu was correct in his theories as to how government should be designed. Instead, much of the argument over the proposed Constitution concerned whether it was faithful to his theories.[58] The argument arose, because the severe mistrust of governmental power that motivated the Framers[59] actually forced them to modify rigid separation in the sense of the mutually exclusive exercise of branch power, so that each branch could in some way check the others. It was in this manner that the Framers blended the seemingly conflicting theories of separation of powers and checks and balances—a blending that Madison was forced to explain and defend.[60]

Two methodological insights may be drawn from the Framers' virtual obsession with the concentration of power. First, to be meaningful, the separation of powers must be institutionalized in a manner that provides each branch with the formal tools necessary to limit the excesses of its rivals.[61] Second, and of greater importance for modern doctrinal purposes,[62] the separation of powers must operate in a prophylactic manner—in other words, as a means of *preventing* a situation in which one branch has acquired a level of power sufficient to allow it to subvert popular sovereignty and individual liberty.

This, of course, was by no means the only conceivable method one might have chosen to deal with the undue accumulation of power, even under a separation-of-powers structure. Presumably, the Framers could have established a system in which each branch could exercise any form of governmental power, unless its exercise of that power was found to reach a level that enabled that branch to impose tyranny—what might be labeled the "undue accretion" model of separation-of-powers theory. Alternatively, they could have chosen a slightly more protective format, in which each branch would be allowed to exercise any form of governmental power until it was determined (by whom, could be subject to debate) that that branch's power had reached a level at which the *potential* for undue accretion was evident—what might be labeled the "clear-and-present danger" model. Yet a third alternative, of course, would have been to reject separation of powers completely—to impose no prophylactic barriers to the undue accretion of power—but instead simply to prohibit the tyrannical misuse of that power in its particular exercise.

Given their recent experience with the usurpations of power under state constitutions,[63] not to mention the generally poor survival rate of republican governments throughout history, it should not be surprising that the Framers chose none of these alternatives. The last alternative was rejected, almost as a definitional matter: Madison described the very accumulation of all power in the hands of one body or individual as the essence of tyranny.[64] Note that under his definitional structure, "tyranny" is not limited to the *misuse* of this power, or even its exercise. Rather, it is the very fact of its accumulation that Madison equated with tyranny. This might have resulted from his assumption that the very fact of accumulation would so undermine the individual's sense of security that the benefits of free government would automatically be lost. On the other hand, it could have stemmed from the assumption that the likelihood of the abuse of such accumulated power is so inevitable and imminent that the accumulation itself, is, both conceptually and temporally, tantamount to its abuse.

One could possibly define "tyranny"—assumed to be an unacceptable result—as the undue accumulation of political power, yet nevertheless adopt either the "undue accretion" or "clear-and-present danger" modifications of separation of powers as the best means to avoid such a danger. Closer examination reveals, however, that neither is acceptable. The reason for rejection of the "undue accretion" model derives from the same type of pragmatic, experiential, common sense analysis that led the Framers to adopt a separation-of-powers structure in the first place. As Jefferson recognized, once the power is accreted, it will, as a practical matter, be virtually impossible to remove it:

> The time to guard against corruption and tyranny, is before they shall have gotten hold on us. It is better to keep the wolf out of the fold than to trust drawing his teeth and talons after he shall have entered.[65]

The far wiser methodology, then, would be to focus on means of preventing the accretion in the first place. It is this reasoning that renders the prophylactic nature of separation-of-powers protections so essential an element of that concept.

Arguably, the "clear-and-present danger" model does not directly suffer from the same flaw as the "undue accretion" model, yet it, too, is inconsistent with the prophylactic goals of the Framers' separation-of-powers theory. Because, in Madison's words, "power is of an encroaching nature,"[66] its accretion is likely to lead to more accretion. However, short of an overt coup, such accretion need not be—indeed, is unlikely to be —of a dramatic form. Rather, it may be almost microscopic, to the point that the naked eye will be unable to perceive its occurrence. It is certainly conceivable, then, that the accretion will proceed in a manner that effectively circumvents the warning system sought to be established by the clear-and-present danger model. Moreover, unless one can establish some generalizable criteria by which one may test whether a particular accretion of power is "undue," it would be impossible for any monitoring organ to determine exactly when a "clear and present danger" had actually been established. To date, no such criteria have been suggested,[67] and it is doubtful that any exist. The problem—one that arguably does not plague the free speech area, where "clear and present danger" has received its widest use—is that it is all but impossible to ascertain the concrete likelihood of the danger occurring, until it has actually occurred, and that point will be too late for effective remedial action.[68]

We are, then, left with the prophylactic structure adopted by the Framers in the Constitution's text: each branch is limited to the exercise of the power given to it, which, in turn is largely exclusive of the power exercised by the other branches[69] (with the limited exceptions explicitly provided in the text that allow one branch to check another).[70] Under this structure, no case-by-case inquiry is made into the likelihood that tyranny will be threatened by a breach of branch separation, for the simple reason that no effective method of making that inquiry—at least until it is too late to avoid the danger—exists.

Separation of Powers as a Zero-Sum Game: The Modern Theoretical Assault

It might reasonably be suggested that in this country it is too late in the day— except in the highly unlikely context of a movement for wholesale constitutional amendment—to mount a frontal assault on our system of separation of powers. The question of its normative validity has been overwhelmed by the Constitution's force, both as positive law and moral tradition. One need not rely on this fallback position, however. A comparison of separation of powers to the alternative models that have been suggested to replace it reveals that, whatever its faults, separation of powers provides the optimum methodology for attaining the goal of assuring the maintenance of popular sovereignty and individual liberty.

The Radical Attack

Some of the most strident criticisms of separation of powers have come from those who argue that it deadlocks government.[71] These arguments rest on the proposition that modern governments need to be able to act more quickly than a separation-of-powers system permits. Lloyd Cutler, for example, has argued that the major shortcoming of our government is its inability to propose, legislate, and administer a balanced program for governing.[72] Separation of powers is the culprit, he believes, because Congress will not support presidential programs, but since the opposition is not unified, its programs are not implemented, either.[73] Moreover, neither the president nor Congress can be held accountable by the voters for the failure to implement new programs, because each can blame the other. Another commentator echoes Cutler's objections: "Separation of powers inhibits the capacity of government, especially the President, to enact policies that are bold, timely, and comprehensive and reduces the ability of the citizenry to hold government . . . accountable for those policies."[74] Finally, another commentator complains:

[T]here is growing evidence that the problems confronting the American constitutional system are outstripping its capacity. . . . A government is an organism with work to do. It must be judged according to its fitness to perform the tasks we assign to it. When the Constitution was framed two centuries ago, only a few crucial tasks required a national government. . . . [But times have changed and] [t]he system no longer operates as intended. [75]

The solutions these critics offer vary. Cutler proposes that we adopt a parliamentary system similar to the one employed in England. Professor Wilson suggests that the crumbling two party system be reforged and strengthened in order to "overcome the separation of powers by bringing together under informal arrangements what the founders were at pains to divide by formal ones."[76] Professor Robinson suggests that bicameralism be abolished, power to call new elections be given to the majority of Congress and the president, terms of office be limited to five years, and that a national council of about one hundred persons be established to manage the new election system and to advise the president.[77]

One difficulty with these solutions is the underlying assumption that more federal governmental action is necessarily better than less. Making innovation difficult ensures that "foolish or sinister schemes [are] . . . exposed and defeated" and that there is "deep and broad consensus about proposed changes."[78] Cutler's system would require a citizen to vote for a trio of candidates—each district would have teams of president, vice president and member of Congress for each party.[79] The purpose of this team voting is to join the political fortunes of the party's presidential and congressional candidates. These officers would all be elected to simultaneous six-year terms. Once per term the president could dissolve Congress and call for new elections. But within 30 days, Congress by majority vote could call for a new presidential election. The elections would be held within 120 days of the call, while Congress, even if dissolved, would remain in session during this period. Presidents would be permitted only one six-year term.[80] According to Cutler, limiting presidents to a single term "would enhance objectivity and public acceptance"[81] of their programs. Their ability to dissolve Congress would avoid the lame duck problem and prevent impasse.[82]

Perhaps the biggest problem with Cutler's proposed system is that it would sharply limit voters' ability to choose their representatives. For example, a voter who approves of one party's congressional candidate, but opposes that party's presidential candidate, is placed in a serious dilemma. Moreover, Cutler's proposal assumes that there are few (probably two) strong, cohesive parties that can represent all voter's interests. Cutler's proposal thus seems to threaten the concept of popular sovereignty, by reducing the electorate's ability to express its true wishes.

Under the parliamentary system, the president would have the potential to become quasidictatorial. It would simultaneously make a president more powerful and less accountable. The reason Parliament generally accepts executive programs is because it lacks the strength to object.[83] Moreover, it seems unlikely that Congress (if it even retained the power) would be ready to impeach the president or any key officers, since in response the president could simply dissolve it. The British themselves have made this point.[84]

The disruption caused by the threat of dissolution would create a more serious problem than the deadlock it seeks to avoid. The new check would weld Congress to the president in all but the most egregious situations. Moreover, these are probably situations of national crisis, when it is least desirable to put government on hold for 120 days. Indeed, "[t]he no-confidence vote is so drastic an alternative that in Britain . . . it succeeds in forcing a new general election only two or three times a century."[85] Further, the valuable deliberative powers of Congress might well be lost, since the executive has no need to consult it. After the president uses the once-per-term dissolution power, impasse, as Cutler calls it, could occur again. Such a system might also destroy limited government because an effective control of executive power no longer exists.[86]

Finally, the parliamentary system proposal depends upon the existence of cohesive political parties. The British system operates successfully because Britain, for the most part, has a relatively small, homogeneous culture. The problems the British have faced in Ireland[87] illustrate the difficulty the system has in accommodating disparate interests. Although our system has been far from perfect in this regard, even Cutler acknowledges that more representation is permitted by a system of separation of powers.[88]

The political heritage of Britain's parliamentary system is also far different from our own constitutional tradition. The British have a history of parliamentary action by consensus.[89] Until 1646, the British Parliament had made more than half of its decisions without voting.[90] In contrast, the United States, from the beginning, has struggled to accommodate regional and ethnic differences.[91]

The extreme differences between the systems in the United States and Great Britain arise not only from the different view of class in the two societies,[92] but also from the fact that the United States has a considerably more diverse political and social culture. One result of these differences is the existence of a federal system of states. Because of vast differences from region to region (climate, ethnicity, and industry), it is unrealistic to expect all the citizens to possess the same goals and interests. We cannot transplant a governmental system designed to serve a small, homogeneous nation into our vast, heterogeneous one. It is both inevitable and desirable that the electorate in a system as large and diverse as ours will hesitate to embrace a tightly unified system.[93] They will require more control over governmental power than a mere choice between two political parties. The political elite is always tempted to "distort its perception of national policy . . . to maintain its own profit and power."[94] The United States is simply too big and its population too heterogeneous for a single set of policies to accommodate.

The Moderate Attack

Other, less radical solutions to the problems of separation of powers do not require constitutional amendment, as Cutler's obviously would. They call for informal measures to combat the perceived inefficiency of separation of powers. One commentator, for example, suggests that we reforge the party system and rely on it to overcome legislative-executive deadlock.[95] This solution, however, shares the weaknesses of the parliamentary proposal. Strong parties require both a single set of policies and strict adherence to party lines in voting. But the same diverse population that prevents accommodation of many interests in a parliamentary system would also prevent them in a strong party system. The crumbling of the party system was due in large measure to the need to satisfy the broadening field of constituents.[96] Thus, even if it were possible to reunite the parties or to form new strong ones, they would still leave many effectively unrepresented.

A less drastic method proposed to alleviate the fragmenting of federal power is make changes in our "unwritten constitution."[97] "The first step in the right direction," according to one commentator, would be to "quit talking about constitutional separation of powers."[98] The proponent of this solution first suggests modifications in Congress's informal checks on the executive. Congress should be permitted to act only "on what the President actually decides and recommends publicly."[99] Presidents should have the ability to manage the preliminary processes and procedures at their discretion.[100] Structural values are to be balanced against political ones.[101] Although the plan urges that "we must pay at least as much attention to ensuring the accountability of our executive institutions as to improving their efficiency and economy,"[102] it is not clear that it preserves executive accountability. Initially, ensuring executive efficiency by imposing informal (that is, non-statutory, nonconstitutional) restraints on Congress seems naive at best. If the restraints are not enforceable, what will keep self-interested[103] members of Congress from encroaching on the executive sphere? Moreover, if the "unwritten constitution" can modify the tenets of the written one, this proposal is effectively advocating a circumvention of the amendment process. These modifications and the precedent they set actually present greater dangers than the radical parliamentary proposals, because their subtlety might prevent them from being held up to public scrutiny, as they would be if the Constitution were sought to be formally amended.

The Costs of Abandoning Separation of Powers

The most significant problem with the modern attacks on separation of powers is that they completely ignore the very real fears that led to adoption of the system in the first place. No critic has adequately demonstrated either that the fears of undue concentrations of political power that caused the Framers to impose separation of powers are unjustified, or that separation of powers is not an important means of deterring those concentrations.

It might be argued that the dangers of tyranny thought to be prevented by the use of separation of powers are at best speculative. After all, no one can predict with certainty that, but for the formal separation of branch power, the nation would be likely to sink into a state of tyranny. It is, then, conceivable that all of the Framers' efforts to separate and check powers have been wasted. But that is a risk inherent in the use of any form of prophylactic protection: we cannot be sure that, but for the use of the protection, the harm we fear would result.

The decision regarding whether to employ a particular prophylactic device, then, must come down to a comparison of the costs incurred as a result of the device's use with an estimate of both the likelihood and severity of the feared harm.[104] Although some undoubtedly believe that separation of powers imposes severe costs on the achievement of substantive governmental goals, it would be inaccurate to suggest that government has been paralyzed as a result of separation of powers. Too much legislation is enacted by Congress to accept such a criticism. More importantly, in critiquing the failure of the federal government to act, one must do so behind a Rawlsian "veil of ignorance":[105] Assuming that abolition of separation of powers would result in an increase in governmental action, we cannot know whether those actions will be ones with which we agree. Moreover, the facilitation of governmental programs could just as easily lead to a withdrawal of existing governmental programs that we deem to be wise and just. For example, but for separation of powers, election of Ronald Reagan could have easily led to the abolition of social welfare programs that had been instituted in previous Democratic administrations. Political liberals who criticize separation of powers for the constraints it imposes on governmental action should therefore recognize how removal of separation of powers could turn into a double-edged sword.

Thus, the costs imposed by maintenance of separation of powers are probably nowhere near as great as critics have suggested. Whether the costs that we actually do incur are justified by the system's benefits requires us to examine the likelihood and severity of harm that could result if separation of powers were removed. As previously noted, some might question the likelihood of tyrannical abuse of power if separation of powers were abolished. After all, Britain lacks our system of formalistic separation of powers, and democracy still flourishes. Why, then, could we not do the same here? The same could, however, be said of the First Amendment rights of free speech and press: In Britain, speech and press receive no countermajoritarian constitutional protection, yet it is probably reasonable to believe that for the most part those institutions flourish there. Yet undoubtedly, few would feel comfortable with the repeal of the First Amendment.

If we have begun to take the value of separation of powers for granted, we need only look to modern American history to remind ourselves about both the general vulnerability of representative government and the direct correlation between the concentration of political power and the threat to individual liberty.[106] The widespread violations of individual rights that took place when President Lincoln assumed an inordinate level of power, for example, are well documented.[107] Arguably as egregious were the threats to basic freedoms that arose during the Nixon administration, when the power of the executive branch reached what are widely deemed to have been intolerable levels.[108] Though in neither instance did the executive's usurpations of power ultimately degenerate into complete and irreversible tyranny, the reason for that may well have been the resilience of our political traditions, among the most important of which is separation of powers itself. In any event, it would be political folly to be overly smug about the security of either representative government or individual liberty. Although it would be all but impossible to create an empirical proof to demonstrate that our constitutional tradition of separation of powers has been an essential catalyst in the avoidance of tyranny, common sense should tell us that the simultaneous division of power and the creation of interbranch checking play important roles toward that end.

To underscore the point, one need imagine only a limited modification of the actual scenario surrounding the recent Gulf War. In actuality, the war was an extremely popular endeavor, thought by many to be a politically and morally justified exercise. But imagine a situation in which a president, concerned about his failure to resolve significant social and economic problems at home, has callously decided to engage the nation in war, simply to defer public attention from his domestic failures. To be sure, the president was presumably elected by a majority of the electorate, and may have to stand for reelection in the future. However, at this particular point in time, but for the system established by separation of powers, his authority as commander in chief[109] to engage the nation in war would be effectively dictatorial. Because the Constitution reserves to the arguably even more representative and accountable Congress the authority to declare war,[110] the Constitution has attempted to prevent such misuses of power by the executive.[111] It remains unproven whether any governmental structure other than one based on a system of separation of powers could avoid such harmful results.

Pragmatic Formalism as an Analytical Model in Separation-of-Powers Cases

The Case for Pragmatic Formalism

Once one accepts that separation of powers is an essential means of preserving both individual liberty and representative government, the next task is to find the most effective doctrinal model for preserving those protections. The answer to that problem is "pragmatic formalism"—an approach which requires a "formal" separation of branch power, to be determined by means of a pragmatically based definitional analysis of the concepts of "executive," "legislative," and "judicial" power. The primary rationale for the choice of pragmatic formalism is the relative inadequacy of every conceivable doctrinal alternative as a means of ensuring the effectiveness of separation of powers.[112] In this sense, the argument is not that pragmatic formalism is free from doubt or difficulty but rather—much like Churchill's defense of democracy as a form of government[113]—that it is a preferable to any of its competitors.

Before exploring the fatal defects in those alternatives, however, it is necessary to flesh out the concept of pragmatic formalism, and in so doing alter widespread—but unjustified or misleading—perceptions. Professor Thomas Sargentich, for example, has characterized "formalism" as "a range of possible legal theories stressing the centrality of rules or principles as guide posts of analysis. . . . The key idea is that legal norms are distinct from moral and political discourse, and that the former have guiding force of their own."[114] Having so characterized "formalism" as an abstract matter, Sargentich criticizes the concept's application to separation-of-powers doctrine as "simplistic," and representative of an "inflexible and unrealistic attitude."[115] Sargentich's description of the place of formalism in the spectrum of legal thought represents, for the most part, an accurate characterization.[116] To the extent that the term is thought necessarily to imply a rigid separation of law and morality, or the use of abstract and unbending legal principles, it should naturally be rejected. A reasonably competent first-year law student knows that that is not how law evolves. In the sense the term is employed here, "formalism" implies merely the formal separation of "executive," "legislative," and "judicial" power, without either an attempt to discern whether a breach of those barriers presents a danger of "undue" accretion of power in a particular instance or any discounting for countervailing political or social interests—an approach chosen because of the pragmatic assessment that it is far and away the best means of ensuring the viability of separation of powers, which is itself designed to foster broader social and political values.[117] Thus, far from representing a formal separation of law on the one hand and politics and morality on the other, the brand of formalism advocated here is adopted for the very purpose of implementing carefully reasoned political values.

The justification for the use of pragmatic formalism flows from recognition of the purposes served by separation of powers in the first place.[118] Central to that concept are the simultaneous insights that (1) the very fact of the concentration of political power in the hands of one governmental organ is unacceptable, even absent a showing of misuse of that power, (2) it will, as a practical matter, be all but impossible to determine when the level of the concentration of political power has reached the danger point, and (3) the point at which such an unacceptable concentration is actually reached is too late for the situation to be remedied.[119] Separation-of-powers guarantees are, then, prophylactic in nature. They are designed to avoid a situation in which one might even debate whether an undue accretion of power has taken place. In short, the idea is to provide a buffer zone between government and the accretion of even potentially abusive power.

No doctrinal model other than a formalistic approach can assure that a system of separation of powers will perform its prophylactic function. The key advantage of a formalistic analysis is that it frees a reviewing court from the impossible task of determining whether a particular usurpation of branch power presents a serious step toward tyranny. Indeed, avoidance of the need for such a subjective case-by-case analysis is undoubtedly the very reason that those who drafted the Constitution chose to impose a non-fact-based standard for separation of powers.

The intellectual bankruptcy of a doctrinal approach that measures the validity of branch usurpations in terms of the particular threat of undue concentration of power posed in each case is well illustrated by the Court's most recent use of such a standard in *Morrison v. Olson*.[120] Title VI of the Ethics in Government Act of 1978[121] allowed for appointment of an independent counsel to investigate and possibly prosecute certain government officials. The act provided substantial authority to a specially created Article III court, the "Special Division," both to appoint and supervise the independent counsel.[122] "It is undeniable," said the Court, "that the Act reduces the amount of control or supervision that the Attorney General and, through him, the President exercises over the investigation and prosecution of a certain class of alleged criminal activity."[123] However, noting that the act nevertheless "gives the Executive a degree of control" over the counsel's actions,[124] the Court concluded that "these features of the Act give the Executive Branch sufficient control over the independent counsel to ensure that the President is able to perform his constitutionally assigned duties."[125] But at no point does the Court even attempt to tell us how one can begin to know whether a particular usurpation of branch power leaves "sufficient" power in the hands of the undermined branch, or what would constitute an undue accretion of power to the undermining branch. Such an "analysis" not only represents a total failure of the judicial function, but also constitutes an effective abandonment of the inherently prophylactic nature of separation of powers.

Resort to formalism in the shaping of separation-of-powers doctrine has been severely criticized. The use of formalism in separation-of-powers doctrine, one commentator has alleged, "tends to produce excessively mechanical results,"[126] and "to straitjacket the government's ability to respond to new needs in creative ways, even if those ways pose no threat to whatever might be posited as the basic purposes of the constitutional structure."[127] Another has charged that "[t]o insist upon the maintenance of an absolute separation of powers merely for the sake of doctrinal purity could severely hinder the quest for 'a workable government' with no appreciable gain for the cause of liberty or efficiency."[128] But such criticisms fail to recognize the manner in which formalism uniquely fosters one of the central structural elements of separation-of-powers theory: its inherently prophylactic nature. The concept of a prophylactic is that it prevents the creation of a critical situation, by proceeding on the assumption that it will be impossible to determine, in the individual instance, the existence of a real threat to the values sought to be fostered. This assumption appears grounded in both logic and experience, in the case of separation of powers. Moreover, it is one upon which the Constitution's text clearly proceeds. Thus, to criticize formalism for producing overly mechanical results or for failing to produce recognizable gains misses the point of the preventive methodology inherent in our separation-of-powers theory.

Criticism of formalism for imposing an unrealistic "straitjacket" on governmental innovation likewise misses the point. Quite obviously, separation-of-powers protections, like many other structural elements of the Constitution,[129] were inserted for the very purpose of preventing precipitant governmental action. If one believes that the use of such "speed bumps" to action are unwise, presumably one would concur with one or more of the proposals for radically reshaping our governmental structure—proposals which are extremely dangerous to the values of liberty and representational-ism central to our nation's political theory.[130] To shape modern separation-of-powers doctrine on the basis of a hostility towards the very purposes sought to be served by that governmental structure, however, would ignore the limited role the judiciary was designed to play within our constitutional system.[131] In any event, as long as one employs a "pragmatic" brand of formalism in the shaping of branch power, the constraints imposed on governmental action by a formalistic approach to separation-of-powers doctrine should not prove to be wildly impractical.[132]

The Problem of Definition

The Issue of Linguistic Skepticism

One who is skeptical about the meaning of text[133] might well respond to the defense of pragmatic formalism that this doctrinal model provides no more protection against undue accretions of power than would a case-by-case standard, because of the inherently vague and manipulable nature of the constitutional terms to be defined.[134] If the terms, "executive," "legislative," and "judicial" are incapable of any meaningful distinction, then reliance on the definitional analysis inherent in the pragmatic formalist model would actually prove to be counterproductive: it would force a reviewing court to engage in a meaningless abstract linguistic analysis, instead of attempting to deal with cold, hard political realities.

Concededly, one who believes that words are inherently capable of infinite, equally acceptable meanings will not likely be impressed with this interpretational model. However, this analysis proceeds on the assumption—previously both articulated and defended[135]—that the words in constitutional text are not so easily manipulable. To be sure, it would be equally unwise to posit that constitutional terms are to receive rigid, unbending, and abstract definitions. But surely, there exists a happy medium in constitutional interpretation, between these two hermeneutical extremes. Words in the text of the Constitution are, for the most part, sufficiently broad-based that they may evolve over time, in order to take into account pragmatic and social concerns, yet not simultaneously descend into a pit of linguistic anarchy.[136]

Defining Branch Power

Construction of the terms "legislative," "executive," and "judicial," as employed in Articles I, II, and III, respectively, provides a classic illustration of this mode of textual interpretation.[137] With relatively narrow, historically based exceptions,[138] "legislative" power includes only the authority to promulgate generalized standards and requirements of citizen behavior or to dispense benefits, for the purpose of achieving, maintaining, or avoiding particular social policy results. So broadly phrased, of course, such a standard could conceivably be employed to describe the functions performed by the judicial and executive branches, as well. However, the difference is the structural "baggage" that the exercise of the judicial and executive powers are required to carry—baggage which does not affix itself to the exercise of the legislative power. The judicial branch may establish such rules of behavior only in the context of the performance of the "traditional" judicial function of the adjudication of live cases or controversies.[139] Indeed, that it is, at least to a large extent, the procedural and structural context in which a policy choice is made—rather than the substance of that choice—that distinguishes the legislative and judicial functions is demonstrated by the fact that, on nonconstitutional issues, Congress may overrule judicially created substantive rules that have been fashioned in the context of case adjudication.[140]

The executive branch, on the other hand (with exceptions specified by the Constitution),[141] is confined to the function of "executing" the law. Such a function inherently presupposes a preexisting "law" to be executed. Thus, the executive branch is, in the exercise of its "executive" power, confined to the development of means for enforcing legislation already in existence.[142] Hence, every exercise of executive power not grounded in another of the executive's enumerated powers must be properly characterized as enforcement of existing legislation.[143]

It should be emphasized that this requirement in no way implies that the executive branch's power should somehow be confined to the performance of "ministerial" functions, bereft of any room for the exercise of creativity, judgment, or discretion. All it means is that, unless some other specifically delegated executive branch power applies,[144] the executive branch must be exercising that creativity, judgment, or discretion in an "implementational" context. In other words, the executive branch must be interpreting and/or enforcing a legislative choice or judgment; its actions cannot amount to the exercise of free-standing legislative power.

A helpful doctrinal illustration of the point—though not normally thought of in this vein—is *United States v. Curtiss-Wright Export Corp.*[145] There a joint resolution of Congress had provided

> [t]hat if the President finds that the prohibition of the sales of arms and munitions of war in the United States to those countries now engaged in

armed conflict in the Chaco may contribute to the reestablishment of peace
between those countries, and if he makes proclamation to that effect, it shall
be unlawful to sell [any arms], except under such limitations and exceptions
as the President prescribes. [146]

The issue before the Court was whether the resolution constituted an impermissible delegation of "legislative" power to the executive.

Under this analysis, if the power given to the president was, in fact,
properly characterized as "legislative" rather than "executive," the resolution should have been found unconstitutional. Justice Sutherland, speaking
for the Court, did not reach that conclusion, reasoning—in a highly tenuous
and convoluted opinion[147]—that the power to control foreign policy was
inherently an executive function. [148] For reasons discussed in a later section,
Justice Sutherland's logic in reaching this conclusion should be rejected.
However, the Court's ultimate conclusion in *Curtiss-Wright* that the resolution was constitutional was correct, for the simple reason that the power to be
exercised by the president should properly have been classified as "executive," rather than "legislative." To be sure, the president's performance of
the task dictated by the resolution would require the exercise of a substantial
degree of judgment and discretion. But in so doing, the president would
nevertheless be "implementing" a preexisting legislative policy choice. By its
resolution, Congress had determined that "the reestablishment of peace" in
that area of the world was the policy choice of the United States. This was a
decision that the president was neither authorized nor permitted to reject. [149]
All the president was authorized to do was to make the decision whether a
prohibition on the sale of arms would "contribute" to attainment of that goal.

Characterization of the president's power under the resolution as "executive" illustrates the appropriately pragmatic nature of the definitional process. [150] Presumably, Congress could reasonably conclude that political conditions in the area were so volatile that they required the potential for flexible
and immediate response, the kind of response for which the cumbersome
legislative process is ill suited. It was therefore necessary for Congress to be
able to vest in the president the authority to make this judgment, the very
type of judgment that the executive branch is best suited to make. As long as
such pragmatic considerations are not allowed to consume all other relevant
factors, such as accepted tradition and language, their influence is no more
inappropriate in the fashioning of separation-of-powers than in any other area
of constitutional interpretation. This is especially true, in light of the fact that
pragmatic considerations, learned the hard way during the tumultuous period without an executive under the Articles of Confederation, [151] led to the
recognition of the need for the presence of an executive in the first place.

Presumably, the decision to prohibit the sale of arms could, in the abstract, also be classified as legislative power. Had Congress itself chosen to
prohibit such sales, it could hardly be doubted that this action would properly fall within Congress's legislative power. But this fact does not imply a

fungibility of executive and legislative power. It merely underscores that the distinctions between branch powers will often turn not on the abstract nature of the substantive decision but rather on the surrounding political and structural context. In *Curtiss-Wright*, for example, the president's authority to ban arms sales is appropriately characterized as "executive," because under the circumstances, it constituted a means of implementing Congress's previously expressed legislative goal. Had the president decided to ban arms sales as a free-standing decision, however, it could not properly be viewed as an exercise of "executive" power, for the obvious reason that it would have failed to implement a specific congressional policy judgment. Only Congress, in the exercise of its legislative power, could have made this free-standing choice.

One other illustration of the pragmatic nature of the definitional process appeared in *Youngstown Sheet & Tube Co. v. Sawyer*,[152] the "steel seizure" case. There the Court had to decide whether the president was acting within his constitutional power when he issued an order directing the secretary of commerce to take possession of and to operate the majority of the country's steel mills. The opinion of the Court, over the dissent of Chief Justice Vinson,[153] refused to find that this authority could be grounded in the president's Article II power as commander in chief: "Even though 'theater of war' be an expanding concept, we cannot with faithfulness to our constitutional system hold that the Commander in Chief of the armed Forces had the ultimate power as such to take possession of private property in order to keep labor disputes from stopping production. This is a job for the Nation's lawmakers, not for its military authorities."[154] Linguistically, it probably would not be irrational to construe the commander-in chief power to cover a domestic situation arguably so closely tied to the success or failure of the nation's war effort. However, because of an obvious concern over the dangers of extending military power over domestic matters, a majority of the Court declined to do so.

Adding a Functionalist Perspective:
"Supplemental Functionalism"

Under pragmatic formalism, each branch is confined to the exercise of only those powers that definitionally fall within the concept of power textually allocated to that branch. It is possible to hypothesize situations, however, in which the definitional approach of the formalist model is technically satisfied by a particular exercise of branch power, yet a significant threat to the values of separation of powers nevertheless results. For example, the congressional exercise of what is appropriately characterized as "legislative" power under Article I may still undermine executive power, as when Congress enacts a law, technically constituting the proper exercise of legislative power, that creates an enforcement mechanism beyond the control of the president, thereby undermining the president's exercise of the executive power vested in him by Article II. Thus, it is appropriate to add to the definitional approach of pragmatic formalism a "supplemental functionalist" model, which posits that even where a branch acts within the scope of its delegated powers (as required by a formalist model), such action may nevertheless be unconstitutional if it is found to interfere with the proper operation of another branch.

For reasons already discussed, *exclusive* reliance on a functionalist model as the basis for deciding separation-of-powers challenges provides an inadequate means of assuring adherence to constitutionalized values. It is often difficult to determine whether one branch's actions have "unduly" invaded the province of another branch. Functionalism thus leaves too shaky a foundation to assure the protection of separation of powers. However, in its supplemental form, functionalism can fill certain gaps left by exclusive use of a definitional formalist approach. Hence, consistent with the practical perspective of the pragmatic formalist model, it is appropriate to add to a definitional formalish approach a form of supplemental functionalsim. Under such a combined approach, the dangers presented by exclusive use of a functionalist model would be avoided because of the floor provided by the definitional formalist approach. Moreover, the combined approach would have the benefit of assuring that threats to separation of powers that do fall within the definitions of branch power are nevertheless avoided.

The "Inherent Executive Power" Theory

Certain scholars have suggested that the president's authority is not limited to those powers specifically enumerated in Article II, but rather includes an ill-defined group of "inherent" powers not explicitly embodied in the Constitution's text.[155] If this theory were accepted, the preceding effort to define the meaning of "executive" power would be pointless: any exercise of power by the president not found to fall within the terms of Article II could simply be justified as falling within the "inherent" authority of the office. But while such a theory actually does find support on some levels in Supreme Court doctrine,[156] it represents a highly dubious—and possibly very dangerous—construction of constitutional power.

The textual argument supporting so broad a construction of executive power could be charitably described as strained. It is premised on the theory that Article II's Vestiture Clause, providing that "the executive power shall be vested in a President," constitutes an independent grant of unspecified authority, above and beyond the specific powers subsequently enumerated in the body of Article II.[157] Though supporters of this construction readily concede that the comparable provision concerning congressional power in Article I[158] implies no such expansive power, they point to the presence in Article I of the words, "herein granted" following the words "all legislative powers," and the simultaneous absence of this wording in Article II.[159] At best dispositive of nothing, this textual argument's fatal flaw becomes evident when one points to a similar absence of such wording in Article III, concerning the judicial power, despite the fact that the well-accepted view is that this fails to imply the existence of judicial powers not expressly outlined in Article

III.[160] Moreover, it is by no means clear that even the broadest reading of the Vestiture Clause provides significant support to the "inherent power" theory. Even if viewed as an independent grant of authority, all the clause vests in the president is "executive" power, that is, power to "execute" the laws, an obligation subsequently imposed on the president by Article II in any event.[161]

Most damning to the inherent executive power theory, however, is its inescapable inconsistency with the fundamental "horizontal" and "vertical" tenets of American political theory. In the "horizontal" sense, that is, with regard to relations among the coordinate branches of the federal government, it would make little sense, given the deeply ingrained mistrust of the concentration of political power in general[162] and the mistrust of executive power in particular[163] that prevailed at the time, to tie two of the branches to specifically enumerated authority, yet simultaneously vest in the executive branch what amounts to unlimited political authority. Such a construction of Article II would effectively circumvent the separation-of-powers structure the Framers had so carefully embodied in the Constitution's text.

So broad a reading of executive power would also seriously disrupt the intended "vertical" relationship between the state and federal governments. It was clearly understood by all involved that, under the Constitution, the federal government was one of enumerated, and therefore limited, powers.[164] In the event that anyone might have doubted this fact, the states demanded enactment of the Tenth Amendment[165]—expressly declaring the limited nature of federal power—as one of the conditions for ratification.[166] Yet the "inherent authority" model of executive power automatically extends the power of one branch of the federal government beyond any constitutionally described limits. Such a model therefore undermines the carefully crafted structure of constitutional federalism.[167] In light of the tenuous textual basis for the "inherent authority" model of executive power, as well as its extremely detrimental impact on the core premises of American constitutional and political theory, it should be clear that it has no place in a proper definitional analysis of branch power.

The "Cumulative Effects" Approach

One other important issue to be examined from the perspective of the definitional analysis of the pragmatic formalist model is what might be labeled the "cumulative effects" approach to separation of powers.[168] This approach is most often associated with Justice Jackson's famed concurrence in *Youngstown Sheet & Tube Co. v. Sawyer*,[169] the so-called steel seizure case.[170] In that opinion, Justice Jackson posited a tripartite approach to the validity of presidential power:

1. When the President acts pursuant to an express or implied authorization of Congress, his authority is at its maximum, for it includes all that he possesses in his own right and all that Congress can delegate. . . .

2. When the President acts in absence of either a congressional grant or denial of authority, he can only rely upon his own independent powers, but

there is a zone of twilight in which he and Congress may have concurrent authority, or in which its distribution is uncertain. Therefore, congressional inertia, indifference or quiescence may sometimes, at least as a practical matter, enable, if not invite, measures of independent presidential responsibility. . . .

3. When the President takes measures incompatible with the expressed or implied will of Congress, his power is at its lowest ebb, for then he can rely only upon his own constitutional powers minus any constitutional powers of Congress over the matter.[171]

In key respects, such an approach is fundamentally inconsistent with the definitional analysis associated with the pragmatic formalist model. Although Justice Jackson's analysis appears consistent with some form of a definitional approach to separation of powers,[172] by positing a principle of transferability of branch power (at least for the executive and legislative branches) he has largely rejected the premise underlying the pragmatic formalist model.

Jackson's assumption that the executive branch's power may be either augmented or decreased by congressional addition or subtraction—a type of congressional additur and remittitur—is valid in the narrow sense that if Congress has exercised its legislative power directing or authorizing implementation or enforcement, the president is expressly obligated by Article II to "execute" those laws, a power to act that the president would lack in the absence of such legislation. Beyond that limited usage, however, Justice Jackson's "cumulative effects" theory makes neither textual nor theoretical sense.

Jackson's first category[173] assumes a situation in which the president's actions, if premised exclusively on his Article II power, might be subjected to legitimate constitutional challenge. However, because Congress has, hypothetically, approved or authorized the president's actions, Jackson believes that the president's questionable power under Article II is somehow strengthened by an infusion of Congress's Article I power. Other than in the narrow sense already described,[174] such an approach effectively destroys the "separation" of branch powers: one branch would be exercising power clearly marked for another branch.

It might be argued, however, that as long as Congress has voluntarily chosen to convey its power to the executive branch (an assumption of Justice Jackson's first category), no separation-of-powers violation has occurred: Congress has effectively waived that protection, deciding that separation-of-powers concerns are outweighed by the competing need for an increase in executive authority. Separation-of-powers values are preserved, the argument proceeds, as long as Congress retains the option of curbing executive usurpation.[175] But both theoretically and practically, this waiver analysis is unacceptable. From the perspective of American political theory, the concept of congressional waiver ignores the fact that separation of powers protections were not inserted to protect the other branches but rather to protect the populace. Thus, just as a litigant is not permitted to waive limitations on a court's subject matter jurisdiction because such limitations are imposed to protect the system rather than the litigant,[176] so too should Congress not be authorized to waive systemic protections of the electorate.[177] From a practical perspective, the waiver theory ignores the obvious possibility that Congress may be controlled by the same party as the executive branch, effectively reducing Congress's check on the president. In such a situation, the only means of assuring the prevention of branch usurpation is by judicial enforcement of separation of powers.

In Justice Jackson's third category, negative action by Congress may detract from what would otherwise be a valid exercise of executive power. This principle ignores the fact that if presidents may properly ground their actions in the enumerated powers described in Article II, those actions stand on their own bottom: to allow Congress to undermine them would defeat the purposes of separation of powers, by enabling Congress to interfere with the exercise of constitutionally authorized executive power. Thus, if separation-of-powers principles are to remain as meaningful limitations on the exercise of political power, Justice Jackson's "cumulative effects" analysis must be rejected.

Applying the Pragmatic Formalist Model

Examination of two modern Supreme Court decisions will increase understanding of the pragmatic formalist model. In *Bowsher v. Synar*,[178] the Court held unconstitutional the provision of the Gramm-Rudman Act[179] assigning to the comptroller general the authority to specify spending reductions binding on the president. The act set a maximum deficit amount for each fiscal year between 1986 and 1991. It provided that if in any fiscal year the budget exceeds the maximum amount, across-the-board cuts were required in order to reach the target deficit.[180] Under the act, the comptroller general, after reviewing the recommendations of the directors of the Office of Management and Budget and the Congressional Budget Office, was to report his or her conclusions to the president, who would then issue a "sequestration" order mandating the spending reductions specified by the comptroller.[181] Congress could then reduce spending in order to avoid the need for the sequestration order.[182]

The Court, in an opinion by Chief Justice Burger, held that the act unconstitutionally vested executive functions in the comptroller general, who, as an officer subject to congressional removal, was deemed to be part of the legislative branch.[183] "The Constitution," he reasoned, "does not contemplate an active role for Congress in the supervision of officers charged with the execution of the laws it enacts. . . . To permit the execution of the laws to be vested in an officer answerable only to Congress would, in practical terms, reserve in Congress control over the execution of the laws."[184]

In terms of its broad methodology, the Court's approach in *Bowsher* is entirely consistent with the pragmatic formalist model. Under that model, in a case such as *Bowsher* the Court is directed to make two inquiries: what type of power is being exercised, and which branch is exercising it? The Court in *Bowsher* decided that the comptroller general is part of the legislative branch, and, under the act, was improperly exercising executive power.[185] While the former conclusion appears reasonable,[186] the latter is subject to debate. Justice Stevens, in his separate concurrence, argued that "the powers assigned to [the comptroller general] under [the act] require him to make policy that will bind the Nation. . . ."[187] In this sense, as Justice White noted in dissent,[188] the decision as to which programs are to be funded and which are not are fundamentally congressional appropriations decisions, pursuant to Article I, Section 9, Clause 7. They are in no way properly viewed as "executive," he reasoned, because they implement no preexisting legislative decision. Rather, they are nothing less than free-standing, legislatively unguided policy choices. Yet the comptroller general, under the act, did not possess discretion to pick and choose which programs were to be cut. In this sense, the majority's characterization of the comptroller general's power as executive is plausible. *Bowsher* thus demonstrates that a definitional approach will occasionally have to be applied to situations in which the answer is not automatically obvious. Since no other approach would be able to avoid such complexities, however, this fact should not disqualify pragmatic formalism.

Even if one were to conclude that the power exercised by the comptroller general pursuant to the Gramm-Rudman Act is legislative in character, however, it would not necessarily follow that the act should have been upheld. As Justice Stevens argued,[189] for legislative power to be properly exercised, it must meet the bicameralism and presentment requirements imposed by the Constitution, presumably for many of the same reasons that the Framers adopted interbranch separation of powers, namely, to encourage deliberation and to avoid the concentration of political power in only a few hands.[190] In this sense, the bicameralism and presentment requirements foster each of the three instrumental values upon which our system is based: diversity, accountability, and checking.[191] To vest unchecked authority to make basic policy choices in a single individual, such as the comptroller general, who is not directly accountable to the electorate, would simultaneously undermine each of these goals. Thus, even in those cases in which a conceptual characterization of governmental power is not clear, use of a pragmatic formalist model may nevertheless provide a resolution.

In the second decision, *Morrison v. Olson*,[192] the Court upheld the power of Congress to establish an independent counsel, supervised by a unit of the judicial branch and not part of the executive branch, to investigate and prosecute high government officials for certain criminal activity.[193] The Court did so, despite its express concession that the powers to investigate and prosecute crime were definitionally characterizable as "executive" power.[194] Under the pragmatic formalist model, this concession would of course have ended the inquiry: it is unconstitutional for the legislative branch to vest executive power in the judicial branch.

Some might suggest that such an apparently simplistic analytical model ignores the inherent complexities of the situation, where competing interests must be carefully reconciled.[195] It might further be charged that reliance on simple-minded definitional approaches to constitutional interpretation, without any regard for the specific social and political consequences of those decisions, ignores the vital political role that the judiciary must exercise in constitutional adjudication. But as has already been demonstrated, such a characterization of pragmatic formalism unfairly sees only the tip of the iceberg. The judiciary's role in separation-of-powers analysis should be narrow (albeit in many cases anything but simple), not because of the dictates of rigid and abstract principle of legal formalism, but because the Constitution's drafters wisely concluded that a case-by-case analysis to determine "undue accretions" of power was simply too speculative a method to provide effective protection against the incremental development of a threat of tyranny.

The Defects in Alternative Analytical Models

The "Functionalist" Model

The flaws in a functional model of separation-of-powers analysis—the leading competitor to pragmatic formalism—have to a great extent already been catalogued earlier in this chapter, because much of the case for the pragmatic formalist model is the woeful inadequacy of its chief rival. Functionalism, in the separation-of-powers context, actually divides into two submodels.[196] Under one, the reviewing court invalidates branch usurpation only if it is found to reach some unspecified quantitative level of intensity—in other words, if it is found to undermine another branch's performance of its essential function or to accrete "too much" power to the usurping branch. Under the other, branch usurpation may be justified by a sufficiently strong competing social interest—in other words, an application of an ad hoc balancing approach.

One important problem with both categories of functionalism is that neither provides any comprehensible standard by which to judge particular incursions on the separation of powers. As the Court's decision in *Morrison* demonstrated, the "undue accretion" standard ultimately degenerates into little more than the statement of a wholly subjective conclusion. The ad hoc balancing approach, on the other hand, effectively attempts to measure apples against oranges: how can one reasonably quantify the harm to separation-of-powers interests, and weigh that against an equally unquantifiable—and totally different—interest in governmental efficiency? Equally important, both types of functionalism undermine the key structural assumption of separation-of-powers theory—that it will be impossible (at least until it is too late) to determine whether or not a particular breach of branch separation will seriously threaten the core political values of accountability, diversity, and checking.[197] Thus, functionalism, as the basis for the design of a doctrinal model of separation of powers, fails to fulfill the goals intended by the choice of a governmental system premised on separation of powers.

The "Originalist" Model

Yet another suggested means of dealing with separation-of-powers controversies, one associated with Professor Stephen Carter,[198] is through resort to a selective form of originalism. At the risk of oversimplification, originalism attempts to maintain the legitimacy of the antimajoritarian Court by confining it to the ascertainment of the Framers' original intent as a means of constraining constitutional interpretation.[199] Rather than accept a generic form of originalism, however, Professor Carter divides the Constitution into two parts: the political Constitution, which establishes the governmental structure in general and the system of checks and balances in particular,[200] and what he deems to be the less precise provisions protecting individual rights.[201] Carter believes that because important parts of the text are indeterminate, the definite portions setting out the system of checks and balances are "of crucial importance"[202] as a means of providing limits on the governmental transformation of values into policy.[203] He argues that since the Framers were careful clearly to describe their institutional design, "the interpretive task is simply to discover what they meant."[204] As Carter articulates his selective resort to originalism,

> When . . . the language or structure of a clause makes plain that its authors had in mind a specific conception, the purpose of the interpretive rules is plain. In that case, the task of the theorist is to discover precisely what that something is. . . . The purpose of the rules for interpreting the more determinate clauses ought to be to discover the objectives of the drafter.[205]

In one sense, Professor Carter's use of originalism is conceptually aligned with pragmatic formalism. In contrast to all other analytical models, both originalism and pragmatic formalism approach separation of powers from a conceptual-definitional framework: both limit the judiciary's role in separation-of-powers disputes to an ascertainment of the meaning of the terms employed in the constitutional text to describe branch authority. It is there, however, that the similarity ends. For unlike Carter's originalist model, pragmatic formalism (as the name implies) posits that a reviewing court is not tied to particular conceptions of branch power found to be held by the Framers, but rather may treat those concepts—much as other constitutional provisions are construed—as part of an evolutionary, pragmatically based definitional process.

Serious questions may be raised about the validity of Professor Carter's use of selective originalism. Carter's resort to originalism in the structural context is plagued by all of the difficulties that plague generic originalism as a model of constitutional theory. Chief among them are the many variations in opinions among the Framers and the difficulty of extrapolating how the Framers would approach unforeseen problems or take into account modern developments.[206] Professor Carter asserts that the best evidence of original understanding will be obtained from comprehensive review of the political theory and practical concerns that motivated the founders; the second best is a study of the ratification debates, including pamphlets and newspaper articles; and the third best evidence is Madison's notes of the Convention.[207] But it is unclear why these inquiries are likely to be more successful in the context of the separation-of-powers provisions than they have been generally in constitutional interpretation.

Carter's resort to the political question doctrine casts further doubt on the usefulness of his theory. Whenever resort to original intent leaves the matter indeterminate, Carter asserts, the judge must defer to the determination of the political branches.[208] Judges are to invoke the political question doctrine whenever they "will have trouble applying" their originalistic interpretation to the case at hand.[209] Considering the vast differences in the nature of government since the Constitution's framing, a firm commitment to this rule would quite probably require the Court to abstain in most cases. Carter's approach, then, simultaneously over- and underregulates majoritarian power.

Carter is forced to resort to an originalist approach to separation of powers, because he incorrectly views the conceivable interpretational models from an all-or-nothing perspective. He sees the choice as one between "evolutionary" and "de-evolutionary" models. In Carter's framework, the evolutionary tradition "emphasizes the need to adapt the powers of the federal government to the perceived demands of a changing society."[210] It "is highlighted by a deference to the congressional judgment on the most effective means to deploying its authority."[211] The extreme flexibility of the evolutionary approach is underscored by Carter's reference to Justice White's deferential use of functionalism in his *Bowsher* dissent as an illustration of such a model.[212] The "de-evolutionary" tradition, in contrast, "actively seeks return to a system of balanced and separated powers modeled closely on the governmental design that the Framers had in mind when they established a constitutional government."[213] It "rejects the view that evolution in the larger society requires a concomitant evolution in the manner in which the federal government organizes itself for the exercise of power."[214]

While Carter sees dangers in both interpretive traditions,[215] he ultimately feels forced to conclude that a modified de-evolutionary model is required for interpretation of the separation-of-powers provisions,[216] because "the structural clauses . . . are concerned with *authority* as well as power. . . . [U]nless the jurisprudence regarding the structure of the government, including the system of balanced and separated powers, relies for its force on disciplining interpretive rules capable of generating answers that are in most cases relatively determinate, the legitimacy of the entire project of constitutionalism, and of judicial review in particular, is set seriously at risk."[217]

One could debate whether or not Carter has adequately defended his assertion that the need for determinate rules is more compelling in the case of the structural provisions than in that of the individual rights provisions. The key problem is that, as Carter to some extent acknowledges,[218] a historical inquiry will often reveal preciously few answers. Of course, if the only conceivable alternative to such a historically based inquiry were the intellectual chaos associated with Carter's version of the "evolutionary" model, one might sympathize with his desire to escape his interpretational dilemma. But as the discussion of pragmatic formalism has demonstrated, there exists a middle course between the extremes of a fruitless search for rigid historical answers on the one hand and chaotic, unlimiting judicial deference on the other. That course is to recognize that while constitutional terminology was usually chosen—quite consciously—for the purpose of allowing evolutionary change over time,[219] it does not follow that the chosen wording imposes no constraints at all. Thus, the terms, "executive," "legislative," and "judicial" are to be construed in an appropriately flexible manner in order to allow, within a certain range, examination of pragmatic factors. However, linguistic meaning, shaped in part by tradition, imposes restrictions that cannot rationally be circumvented simply to meet what are perceived to be countervailing social needs.

The "Conflict of Interest" Model

Paul Verkuil has offered still another solution to the separation-of-powers controversy.[220] His "conflict-of-interest" model is offered as a "tie breaking rationale," "to extract the separation of powers debate from the realm of maxim."[221] Verkuil contends that current separation-of-powers doctrine is deadlocked between two competing theoretical goals: preventing tyranny (at the cost of slowing the wheels of government) and ensuring that government function efficiently. He observes that originally, governmental powers were separated to make government more efficient.[222] The Framers emphasized the ability of separated powers to check governmental power. "The exclusive focus on the checks and balances aspect," Verkuil asserts, "turned the original purpose for separation of powers on its head."[223] He concedes, however, that "both the efficiency and the counter-efficiency, or tyranny rationales are correct."[224]

Verkuil posits that a way out of this deadlock is to recognize another purpose for separating the branches—to neutralize conflicts of interest.[225] This model sees as the premise of separation of powers the maxim that no one can be above the law or judge his own case.[226] Conflicts can occur at three levels: between branches, within a particular branch, and where an individual has a personal stake in the outcome of a particular proceeding.[227] These conflicts, Verkuil contends, are inherent in the governmental process.[228] One example of a personal conflict is a congressman second-guessing an agency's application of a statute in the face of pressure from a constituent. Verkuil asserts that a conflict of interest always exists when the same authority that makes the law executes it.[229] Conflicts of interest also occur when a decision maker is dependent upon a person affected by the decision for some benefit. For example, the comptroller general in *Bowsher* faced a conflict of interest because he was dependent on Congress for his position.

A recurrent theme in Verkuil's analysis is the intertwining of separation of powers and other constitutional provisions. In other words, to avoid the problems inherent in the application of the Constitution's structural provisions, Verkuil argues that the Court should employ the Constitution's individual rights protections as a measuring rod for separation of powers. He suggests, for example, that if due process is not offended by a delegation of Article III power to an Article I court, where arguably due process and separation of powers serve congruent interests, "why should the latter be offended if the former is satisified?"[230]

The conflict-of-interest model focuses on the need for independent decisionmakers. Thus, it exerts pressure on the system to depoliticize the administrative process.[231] Under Verkuil's model, then, the role of separation of powers as a check upon government is deemphasized, and the need for independence and professionalism in governmental decisionmaking becomes the central focus. To achieve this professionalism, Verkuil reasons that very few executive officials should be removable at will by the president; only the secretaries of state and defense and other "inner-circle" officers should be subject to the will of the president.[232] This model thus permits Congress to insulate every other executive officer from plenary presidential control.[233]

Verkuil's model was largely "designed to answer the independent counsel inquiry."[234] Verkuil frames the issue thus: "Can Congress cure intrabranch conflicts of interest without causing an interbranch separation of powers crisis in the process?"[235] Rather than weigh the values and explicitly conclude that independent prosecutions are more important than executive freedom from congressional intrusions, he adopts the "least restrictive alternative" analysis. This analysis, derived from First Amendment doctrine,[236] asks whether the restrictions upon executive prerogatives "advance some vital government interest, and are they the least restrictive means of achieving that end?"[237] Since most would agree that controlling criminal behavior in the executive branch is vital, separation of powers concerns are, not surprisingly, trumped.

At best, Verkuil's conflict-of-interest model artificially truncates the values designed to be fostered by separation of powers, rendering its protections dangerously incomplete. At worst, the model could be said to completely miss both the theoretical and methodological essence of the American system of separation of powers. It is not incorrect to see the concern over biased decisionmaking as an important theme in separation-of-powers theory. The logic behind separation of the power of legislation and of execution, for example, is to assure that those who make society's basic policy choices (the legislators) are not in a position secretly to exempt themselves or those close to them from the consequences of those decisions.[238] But surely it is incorrect to assume that separation-of-powers concerns are exhausted when the independence interest is satisfied.[239] Generally, the constitutional concern for decisionmaking independence is adequately handled through resort to the protections of due process.[240] To a certain extent, particularly in the preservation of judicial independence from the political branches, this concern overlaps both due process and separation of powers.[241] But completely to collapse the two concepts, so that meeting the requirements of one will automatically satisfy the requirements of the other, renders the separation-of-powers protections largely superfluous. More importantly, it ignores the interlocking backup systems employed by the Framers to avoid the threat of tyranny.[242]

When placed in a separation-of-powers context, then, the independence concern can be seen as merely one small portion of a broader checking concern. For example, by requiring that those who make the laws cannot be charged with the responsibility for executing them, separation of powers does, of course, preserve the independence of both decisionmakers. However, in doing so separation of powers simultaneously prevents the concentration of political power in one governmental organ and enables one branch to check the other. The same is true when an independent judiciary is given final say on the constitutionality of the actions of the political branches.[243] But it would be incorrect to conclude that independent decisionmaking is all that separation of powers is about. It should not be difficult to imagine situations in which interbranch usurpation of power poses no immediate threat to independent decisionmaking, yet may well present the very dangers of the concentration of political power which separation of powers was designed to prevent.[244] Thus, Professor Verkuil's model does not go nearly far enough in protecting the values sought to be fostered by separation of powers.

At the same time, the conflict-of-interest model could, paradoxically, be said to go much too far. By focusing so much constitutional energy on the preservation of independent decisionmaking, it actually poses a serious threat to branch separation. The conflict-of-interest model emphasizes decisionmaking independence as an abstract and unwavering value, ignoring the surrounding political context which, in certain instances, may render an exclusive focus on the independence concern nonsensical. For example, while it is wise to have a decisionmaker in an adjudicatory context independent of the parties appearing before her, the interests are quite different when one considers the need of a subordinate official in the executive branch to act independently of the president. *Interbranch* checking, in the manner set out in the Constitution, is a necessary part of an effective separation-of-powers scheme. *Intrabranch* checking, on the other hand, only weakens one of the branches in the performance of its constitutionally assigned duties, and thus undermines both the balance of constitutionally prescribed power among the branches and the political value of accountability.[245] It is, after all, the president who was elected by and is accountable to the public. Thus, to establish an unelected subordinate executive officer, independent of the president, does no service to the values sought to be fostered by separation of powers. Though decisionmaking independence plays an important role in separation of powers theory, it is necessary to understand its limits. Independence of the executive from the legislative branch assures an absence of conflict of interest in translating policy into action. Independence of the judiciary from the political branches assures a countermajoritarian constitutional check on majoritarian institutions. But rendering subordinate executive officers independent of the one representative official in the executive branch is only counterproductive to the goals of separation of powers.

The "Ordered Liberty" Model

In a provocative article,[246] Professor Rebecca Brown posited what she labels the "ordered liberty" approach to separation-of-powers doctrine. "Ordered liberty," she suggests, "has come to represent a counter-majoritarian protection of the rights of the individual against arbitrary or unfair treatment at the hands of the government, rights now embodied in the due process clauses of the fifth and fourteenth amendment."[247]

Proceeding from the premise "that the structure of the government is a vital part of a constitutional organism whose final cause is the protection of individual rights,"[248] Professor Brown argues "that the Madisonian goal of avoiding tyranny through the preservation of separated powers should inform the Supreme Court's analysis in cases raising constitutional issues involving the structure of government."[249] Put in other words, "when government action is challenged on separation-of-powers grounds, the Court should consider the potential effect of the arrangement on individual due-process interests."[250] Professor Brown contrasts her suggested model with an approach that focuses on "the aim of preserving the government for its own sake"[251]—an approach she criticizes because "it does not look beyond any specific cases to a higher objective that the separation of powers may serve."[252]

While Professor's Brown's suggested model admirably rejects the false dichotomy thought to exist by certain commentators between issues of constitutional structure and individual rights,[253] she goes too far to the other extreme and in so doing confuses the *goals* of separation of powers with the *instrumental methodology* chosen to implement those goals. This confusion is revealed in her contrast of separation of powers to interpretation of the Eighth Amendment's cruel-and-unusual punishment prohibition. In commenting on the Supreme Court's doctrinal approach to the Eighth Amendment, Professor Brown notes that "the Court . . . relies on a vision of the amendment's underlying goal and spirit in the process of deciding cases"[254]—an approach that she deems far preferable to a doctrinal analysis of separation of powers that "does not look beyond any specific case to a higher objective that the separation of powers may serve."[255] Under such an approach, she argues, "it is easy to lose sight of the big picture."[256]

Although Professor Brown's critique possesses a superficial appeal, it ignores important differences in the wording of the Eighth Amendment on the one hand and the separation-of-powers provisions on the other—differences that reveal a significant distinction in the methodology chosen to implement the respective provisions' underlying goals. By its terms, the Eight Amendment imposes what might be called a "conditional" standard—

that is, rather than prohibiting all punishments, it prohibits only those that the Court classifies as "cruel" or "unusual." It does this, because its goal is not to prevent all forms of punishment, but only those that exhibit certain elements deemed to be offensive, and there is no fear of a risk that an enforcing court will be unable to distinguish those punishments that exhibit the relevant characteristics from those that do not. Thus, the drafters collapsed the amendment's goal and methodology into a single standard.

The separation-of-powers provisions (that is, the vesting of only a certain type of power in each branch) may arguably have an equally conditional goal—to prohibit only those interbranch usurpations of power that may, at some future point, evolve into tyranny. However, a casual examination of the constitutional language reveals that, unlike the Eighth Amendment, the provisions protecting separation of powers do not collapse goal and methodology. By their terms, they do not limit the branches only to usurpations that do not present a threat of tyranny. Rather, when read in light of the understanding that the federal government possesses only those powers delegated to it by the Constitution,[257] the separation-of-powers provisions clearly impose an absolute, rather than a conditional standard of implementation.

It should be emphasized that the primary point is not a textual one (though the relevance of the textual argument against the use of a conditional standard in separation-of-powers cases should not be underestimated). The argument, rather, is that an absolute standard of implementation was employed in the separation-of-powers area because of the fully justified fear that an enforcing court would be unable, on a case-by-case basis, to distinguish between those interbranch usurpations that presented a threat of tyranny and those that did not—at least until it would be too late to avoid that tyranny. This dichotomy between constitutional goal and constitutional methodology reflects the inherently prophylactic nature of our separation-of-powers structure.

To put the point in terms familiar to all, the difference in the nature of the Eighth Amendment on the one hand and the separation-of-powers provisions on the other is analogous to the difference between a yield sign and a stop sign. Like the Eighth Amendment, a yield sign imposes a conditional behavior restriction: one must come to a full stop only if vehicles with the right of way are present. A stop sign, on the other hand, imposes an absolute behavioral requirement: one must come to a full stop, whether or not other vehicles are present in the intersection at the time. Presumably, the purpose served by both types of signs is to prevent collisions (there is, after all, no inherent social benefit to be derived from stopping for its own sake). Yet it surely is no defense to a charge of failing to stop at a stop sign that no other vehicles were present in the intersection at the time. A stop sign is employed, rather than a yield sign, presumably at locations where we do not wish to risk the consequences of an incorrect judgment as to the presence of the specific danger sought to be avoided. Hence, we impose a restriction upon action, even in specific instances in which it can be established that the danger sought to be avoided did not exist. Similarly, the Framers chose to provide a buffer zone of protection in their separation-of-powers structure that they did not deem necessary in the prohibition of cruel or unusual punishments.

What Professor Brown urges, then, amounts to a wholesale abandonment of the carefully reasoned method of implementation chosen by those who established our constitutional system of separation of powers. The fact that in doing so she may preserve the ultimate political goals sought to be fostered by separation of powers[258] is of only minimal consolation, since without use of the instrumental methodology employed to achieve that goal, she has done more than simply ignore a clear textual directive. By collapsing separation of powers into the goal of preserving "ordered liberty," she has effectively undermined both the inherently prophylactic nature of separation of powers and the use of multibarrier "safety nets" against tyranny, which the Framers so wisely inserted into our intricate constitutional structure. The net result is an abandonment of the entire separation-of-powers structure, despite her obvious desire to do no such thing.

Conclusion

Professor Brown's critique of the reliance on formalism in separation-of-powers analysis[259] underscores the problems facing anyone who urges resort to a formalistic analytical model. Those of us trained in the law in the post-realist period[260] quite naturally feel uncomfortable with any doctrinal structure that appears to interpret and enforce governing text in a mechanical manner, untied to the discernible social and political purposes that the relevant provision was designed to achieve. The pragmatic brand of formalism advocated here, however, grows not out of a rejection of an inquiry into the social and political purposes underlying text, but out of a careful search for them. While it is probably correct to discern the goal of avoiding tyranny from the Constitution's separation-of-powers structure, any interpretational inquiry that ends at that point is fatally incomplete.

The Constitution's drafters knew all too well—from a study of history as well as from their own experience—that those who govern are anything but angels. The danger of tyranny is always present, yet it may develop in forms so insidiously subtle that its recognition will come at a point too late to avoid the ultimate danger. For this reason, power must be divided, not only in those instances in which a threat to liberty is discerned. Additional constitutional enclaves of liberty have been inserted to deal with such individualized threats. Rather, it must be divided always and for all time. To be sure, the limited definitional flexibility traditionally associated with constitutional terminology may provide a reviewing court some degree of pragmatically based maneuverability. But, for pragmatic reasons of the most compelling sort, the judicial inquiry must still be limited to defining the scope of each branch's delegated authority. Such an inquiry must be untied to any investigation of whether the ultimate political goal of separation of powers is threatened by interbranch usurpation in the particular case or whether harm to competing social or political interests would result from enforcement of separation of powers. Analytical models that do any less give rise to all of the dangers which those who established our system correctly sought to avoid.

5

Legislative Delegation, Pragmatic Formalism, and the Values of Democracy

The Dilemma of Legislative Delegation

One of the key constitutional strategies of the New Deal—along with abandonment of both substantive due process[1] and the concept of constitutionally reserved state power[2]—was a dramatic relaxation of the so-called nondelegation doctrine.[3] Under that doctrine, the Supreme Court had invalidated congressional delegations of its legislative power to other branches of the federal government.[4] Such a relaxation was dictated by the social goals and political philosophy of the New Deal, which focused on the need for efficiency and expertise in the administration of governmental programs and which therefore called for substantial administrative discretion in substantive policymaking.[5] The post–New Deal Supreme Court for the most part complied by substantially relaxing the constitutional limits on legislative delegation.

Purely as a matter of constitutional theory, it is difficult to understand the Court's abandonment of the limits on delegation. While advocates of a strong federal government have often expressed impatience with the constraints that separation of powers principles impose on that end,[6] few have attempted to explain how these constraints may legitimately be ignored within the confines of the constitutional system under which we operate.

On a purely textual level, critics of the nondelegation doctrine must deal with the simple directive of Article I, Section 1, that the legislative power shall be vested in Congress. No other branch of government is given power to "legislate." While definitional questions will arise as to whether specific action may properly be characterized purely as "legislative power" rather than executive power,[7] there can be little doubt that judicial abandonment of the nondelegation doctrine has authorized breaches of the definitional limitations. Although textual limitations have often failed to confine the scope of modern constitutional doctrine,[8] this deceptively simple textual directive embodies fundamental elements of American political theory—namely accountability and checking —which are seriously undermined by its abandonment.[9] Careful examination of all of the asserted theoretical justifications for abandonment of the nondelegation doctrine demonstrates that none is sufficiently compelling to outweigh the serious harm caused by such abandonment to the infrastructure of American political theory.

The most difficult challenge for a modern defender of the nondelegation doctrine is to devise a method for determining exactly which investments of authority in the executive branch by Congress are constitutionally permissible and which are not. If one begins the analysis with the assumption that only Congress may exercise "legislative" power, one is then faced with the burden of providing a coherent and workable definition of that concept. The line between legislation and execution will often be a difficult one to draw. Surely, in drafting a statute a legislature cannot be expected to foresee every conceivable set of factual circumstances that will arise; it therefore must draft the statute in at least minimally general terms. Hence, those in charge of enforcement of a statute will necessarily have to exercise a certain degree of latitude and discretion in deciding exactly when and how to apply the broader legislative directive to a specific set of circumstances. At what point that latitude unconstitutionally spills over into the category of legislation, rather than merely execution, will not always be obvious.

As was true of general separation-of-powers questions, however, these difficulties should be no greater than those facing the Court in attempting to delineate the scope of numerous other constitutional concepts.[10] Under the "pragmatic formalist" model,[11] workable distinctions may be drawn between legislative and executive power, premised largely on an understanding of the role which the two branches of government were designed to play within our political structure.[12] Based upon this understanding, a guiding principle can be fashioned for unconstitutional legislative delegation by examining the composite of political values that underlie the functioning of the two branches.

The legislative branch was established on the basis of an intricate structure of localized accountability—an accountability that was expanded with adoption of the Seventeenth Amendment, mandating the direct election of senators.[13] Such accountability for lawmakers constitutes the sine qua non of a representative democracy.[14] It therefore seems reasonable to demand as the prerequisite for legislative action some meaningful level of normative political commitment by the enacting legislators, thus enabling the electorate to judge its representatives. If this commitment is present in a statute, the electorate will become more informed about their representatives by learning whether they voted for or against the law in question, thereby facilitating the accountability that inheres in a representative democracy.

Statutes that fail to make such a commitment, instead effectively amounting to nothing more than a mandate to an executive agency to create policy, should be deemed unconstitutional delegations of legislative power. A reviewing court will be able to determine whether the necessary political commitment has been made by deciding whether the voters would be better informed about their representatives' positions by learning how their representatives voted on the statute. A statute which did nothing more than delegate substantive policymaking authority to an executive agency would not meet this standard. From the perspective of the executive branch, an important question to be asked by the reviewing court is whether the task to be performed pursuant to the legislation is "implementational" or "interpretive" on the one hand, or wholly creative and discretionary on the other. Unless the executive tasks authorized by legislation fall into the former category, they cannot properly be characterized as "executive."

Use of such a guiding principle would likely lead to neither widespread enactment of detailed legislative codes nor the relegation of administrative agencies to little more than the performance of mechanistic or ministerial functions. Nor would the requirement that Congress make difficult social choices necessarily lead to the denial of substantial discretion in the implementation of legislative directives. Indeed, advocates of a rigorous nondelegation doctrine might well criticize the political commitment principle for leaving administrators unduly expansive implementation authority. But the political commitment principle is suggested here as a compromise between those who demand the excision of virtually all administrative discretion and those who argue that any return to a meaningful nondelegation doctrine will lead to confusion in judicial enforcement, the required creation of unwieldy statutes, or both. The impact of adoption of the political commitment principle would be to preclude the most egregious of the statutory violations of the nondelegation limitation: those laws that effectively do nothing more than authorize executive lawmaking in a particular area—a category of statutes by no means insignificant in size or importance. Because in the enactment of such laws Congress fails to fulfill its constitutionally dictated role in a representative form of government, these statutes should be held unconstitutional.

Admittedly, it would be absurd to suggest that invocation of the political commitment principle would magically end all uncertainty and unpredictability in the measurement of statutes' constitutionality. It would be equally absurd, however, to demand such certainty from constitutional doctrine. Few, if any, of the Supreme Court's modern constitutional doctrines meet such a standard, yet somehow our system of judicial review manages to function. One may reasonably demand no more from the doctrinal standard by which we measure the constitutionality of legislative delegation.

The nature of permissible delegation should differ dramatically, however, when the recipient of the delegation is not the executive, but rather the judicial branch. A congressional delegation of lawmaking authority to the federal judiciary, as long as that delegation is confined to the adjudication of live cases or controversies,[15] is properly viewed merely as a limited repeal of Congress's preexisting statutory prohibition on federal judicial creation of common law, embodied in the Rules of Decision Act.[16]

This chapter begins with a brief description of the nondelegation principle's doctrinal development in the Supreme Court, from the Court's aggressive use of the doctrine in the early years of the New Deal[17] to the doctrine's general retreat in later years.[18] The following section will consider possible grounds for distinguishing between delegations of lawmaking power to the executive and judicial branches. The chapter will then explore the role that the nondelegation doctrine should play in American political theory in general and in our nation's system of separation of powers in particular. It proceeds to explore the theoretical and pragmatic attacks which have been made on the nondelegation doctrine, pointing out the serious flaws in each of them. It then explains the political commitment principle, and indicates how its application would affect the constitutional status of several important statutes. Finally, the chapter will consider the practical implications that adoption of the political commitment principle would have on an ancillary constitutional doctrine, the constitutional prohibition of the legislative veto.

The Nondelegation Doctrine in the Supreme Court: A Brief History

Any doctrinal examination of nondelegation should begin by emphasizing the principle's modern atrophy. While the Supreme Court purports to adhere to a constitutional directive of nondelegation,[19] "this is a doctrine honored mostly in the breach. Statutory delegations of authority of wondrous breadth evade the nondelegation doctrine's supposed strictures."[20]

Although in its early applications the nondelegation doctrine was not employed to invalidate congressional action,[21] in three decisions in the 1930s the Supreme Court provided the doctrine with substantial force. In *Panama Refining Co. v. Ryan*[22] the Court utilized nondelegation as the basis for holding unconstitutional section 9(c) of the National Industrial Recovery Act of 1933.[23] Section 9(c), which authorized the president "to prohibit the transportation in interstate and foreign commerce of petroleum . . . in excess of the amount permitted to be produced or withdrawn from storage by any state law or valid regulation . . .," said the Court, "gives to the President unlimited authority to determine the policy" of when to interdict interstate commerce in petroleum produced in excess of state law.[24] In the words of Chief Justice Hughes, "Congress has declared no policy, has established no standard, has laid down no rule. . . . If section 9(c) were held valid, it would be idle to pretend that anything would be left of limitations upon the power of the Congress to delegate its lawmaking function."[25] Shortly thereafter, in *A.L.A. Schechter Poultry Corp. v. United States*,[26] the Court struck down section 3 of the same statute, which empowered the president to approve codes of "fair competition" for particular industries upon application by one or more trade or industrial associations or groups.[27]

The final member of the nondelegation trilogy was *Carter v. Carter Coal Co.*,[28] where the Court struck down the Bituminous Coal Conservation Act of 1935,[29] which required all coal producers to adhere to whatever maximum wage and hour limits were to be negotiated between miners and specified producers. In invalidating the delegation of power to private coal producers, the Court described the act as "legislative delegation in its most obnoxious form; for it is not even delegation to an official or an official body, presumptively disinterested, but to private persons whose interests may be and often are adverse to the interests of others in the same business."[30]

Subsequent decisions, however, illustrated the Court's dramatic retreat from the strict limits on congressional delegation represented by this trilogy of cases. For example, in *United States v. Rock Royal Co-Op.*,[31] the Court upheld the delegation to the secretary of agriculture made in the Agricultural Marketing Agreement Act of 1937,[32] which directed the secretary to issue orders fixing prices for specified commodities whenever he or she determines that the existing prices "are not reasonable in view of the price of feeds, the available supplies of feeds, and other economic conditions which affect market supply and demand for milk and its products in the marketing area."[33] The price-fixing order was to reflect the aforementioned factors, "insure a sufficient quantity of pure and wholesome milk, and be in the public interest."[34] In upholding the act, the Court reasoned that "[f]rom the earliest days the Congress has been compelled to leave to the administrative officers of the Government authority to determine facts which were to put legislation into effect and the details of regulations which would implement the more general enactments."[35]

In *National Broadcasting Co. v. United States*,[36] the Court upheld the delegation of power to the Federal Communications Commission to issue station licenses and regulations "as public convenience, interest, or necessity requires. . . ."[37] The Court argued that "[i]t is a mistaken assumption that this is a mere general reference to public welfare without any standard to guide determinations. The purpose of the Act, the requirements it imposes, and the context of the provision in question show the contrary."[38] Similar decisions, both those roughly contemporaneous with these cases[39] and more recent opinions,[40] have led to the widely shared view among scholars that the nondelegation doctrine today effectively imposes little, if any, effective limits on congressional power.[41]

To understand the problematic nature of legislative delegation, it is necessary to view the issue from the broader perspective of American separation-of-powers theory.[42] Unlimited legislative delegation to administrative agencies effectively undermines all three of the instrumental values that underly the political structure dictated by the Constitution: diversification, accountability, and checking.[43] Before proceeding to an analysis of these theoretical problems, however, it is helpful to explore the possibly significant differences in type of delegation, based on the nature of the recipient of the lawmaking power.

Judging Delegation by the Recipient: Drawing a Judicial-Administrative Distinction

Delegations may be made either to the executive branch or to the judicial branch, and the constitutionality of a delegation may well turn on which of the two branches has received the power. Although delegation to the executive branch gives rise to serious constitutional difficulties,[44] delegations of lawmaking power to the judiciary may be permissible, if certain procedural prerequisites are met in the judicial exercise of that lawmaking power.

When Congress authorizes the federal judiciary to establish substantive policy without any legislative guidance or direction, it is not authorizing the courts to "legislate," in the technical sense of the term, as long as the judiciary is authorized to exercise that power only in a manner incidental to the performance of its constitutionally dictated adjudicatory function. As explained in chapter 4, the primary distinction among the powers of the three branches is not generally the nature of the substantive decision being made but rather the procedural "baggage" tied to each branch's performance.[45] Congress may make substantive policy choices, as long as it does so in a generalized manner in accordance with the bicameralism and presentment requirements imposed by the Constitution.[46] On the other hand, assuming no contrary legislative directives, the judiciary has traditionally been able to fashion substantive policy choices through the evolution of the common law as an incident to the resolution of private disputes. The judiciary's power to fashion substantive common law flows ultimately from a court's obligation to resolve individualized disputes that come before it.[47] *Some* rule of decision must be ascertained in order that the court may choose between the parties to the dispute. Absent governing statute or constitutional provision, a court must fashion its own substantive rules of decision.

When applicable legislation exists, a court's job is solely to interpret and apply that legislation to the facts before it.[48] But when the legislature has not spoken to the specific issue raised by an individualized dispute, if only as a matter of necessity a court must be able to fashion substantive common law rules to fill the gaps left by the statutes. If no other governing body of substantive law is applicable, a court cannot resolve the dispute without fashioning its own substantive rules. Thus, as long as a court does so as part of the adjudication of a live case or controversy,[49] its fashioning of substantive policy choices in no way violates separation of powers.[50] By enacting the Rules of Decision Act,[51] however, Congress apparently concluded that the federal courts should not fashion their own substantive common law principles. Rather, largely in the interests of federalism,[52] Congress decided to require a federal court to apply state substantive law that is found to be applicable to the case before it.[53]

Thus, when Congress enacts a statute that vests authority in the federal courts to fashion substantive policy in the course of the adjudicatory process, Congress is effectively enacting a limited repeal of the bar on substantive common law creation imposed on the federal courts by the Rules of Decision Act. When viewed in this manner, statutory delegations of policymaking authority to the federal judiciary fit well within the structural framework established by our constitutional system. Under these circumstances, Congress has not delegated "legislative" power to the judiciary; it has merely authorized the federal courts to create law incident to performance of its adjudicatory function in specified contexts.

This does not mean, however, that *any* delegation of policymaking authority to the federal judiciary should be deemed constitutionally appropriate. If Congress vests such authority in the judiciary that is to be exercised apart from of the adjudication of live cases, then Congress has improperly delegated "legislative" power to the judicial branch. Both the constitutional text[54] and American political theory[55] prohibit the federal courts from issuing generalized, free-standing legal directives. But this defect is in no way limited to instances in which the judiciary is asked to create substantive law. The same could be said of a legislative directive to the federal courts to interpret or rule on the constitutionality of a statute, untied to the adjudication of specific cases, by means of an advisory opinion. In either case, the presence of a live dispute between affected adversaries is a constitutional prerequisite to judicial action.

Although Congress has not always confined delegations to the judiciary to the adjudication of live cases or controversies, when so confined such delegations are consistent with our governmental structure's system of separation of powers. Delegation of unguided policymaking authority to the executive branch (or, even worse, to so-called independent agencies), however, represents a fundamentally different situation. Pursuant to the pragmatic formalist model,[56] under no circumstances is the executive branch constitutionally authorized to exercise such creative policymaking authority. Hence it is appropriate to distinguish delegations on the basis of the branch receiving the delegated power.

Delegation of Legislative Power to the Executive Branch: Problems of Democratic and Republican Theory

If one accepts the definitional-doctrinal model dictated by the principle of pragmatic formalism,[57] there can be no question that "legislative" power may not be delegated to the executive branch. The only general authority vested by Article II of the Constitution in the executive branch is the obligation to "execute" the law.[58] Of course, the definitional problem of characterizing particular exercises of authority as "legislative" or "executive" would remain, but that does not alter the fact that, once characterized, such exercises can be definitionally distinguished.[59]

The textual directives, however, merely embody the fundamental values of political theory that underly our system of separation of powers. These are the principles of both democratic and republican theory that have been blended to form the cornerstones of our unique form of representative government. Briefly, broad legislative delegation to administrative agencies threatens to dilute the principle of electoral accountability, central to any notion of democratic theory,[60] by removing basic social policy choices from those who are most representative of and accountable to the electorate. Moreover, such delegation also undermines the republican-like limitations on governmental decisionmaking imposed by the Framers, in an attempt to reduce the dangers of factional tyranny.

The Checking Principle

Even if one were to proceed on the assumption that values of accountability and representationalism are not undermined by legislative delegation because of the executive branch's accountability, it would not necessarily follow that such delegation should be deemed constitutionally appropriate. The system of separation of powers was established in order to prevent undue accretion of political power in one branch.[61] Abandonment of the nondelegation doctrine effectively permits the executive branch to accumulate an almost unlimited amount of power, seemingly in violation of even the diluted balancing standard employed in current Supreme Court separation-of-powers doctrine.[62] While efficiency considerations are thought by some to justify abandonment of the nondelegation doctrine, if a balancing test is to serve as something more than a euphemism for total judicial abdication, surely it must impose at least *some* outer limits on delegation. Moreover, the fact that Congress voluntarily chooses to transfer its authority cannot circumvent separation-of-powers barriers, because those limitations were not included for the purpose of protecting the branches themselves, but rather to protect the public from tyranny.[63]

The Accountability Principle

Central to American political theory is the principle of popular sovereignty— the notion that the people are ultimately the governors.[64] Whatever one thinks about the issue as a matter of abstract political philosophy,[65] abandonment of the notion of representative government would dramatically alter our existing political structure. In vesting the legislative power in Congress, the Constitution assures that basic, free-standing decisions of social policy will be made by the branch of the federal government that is most responsive and accountable to the electorate.

Administrative agencies are, for the most part, unrepresentative bodies. Their members are neither chosen by the electorate in the first instance nor directly accountable to the electorate for their decisions. While their members are both selected and confirmed by the representative branches, the same could be said of Article III federal judges,[66] yet no one reasonably perceives such judges to be "representative" in any meaningful sense of the term. While the representative executive branch may have the authority to remove certain administrators on the basis of disagreement with their policies,[67] this is not true of the so-called independent agencies.[68] Moreover, one may question how accountable the executive's removal power actually renders administrative decisions. Such a conclusion would presuppose that the electorate (or at least a portion of the electorate) is likely to base its decision on the reelection of the president on the basis of his or her failure to remove an administrator—as a practical matter, a highly unlikely result. This indirect accountability comes, then, at best in an extremely diluted form. Thus, when Congress delegates the authority to make these social policy choices to administrators who are not directly accountable to the electorate, the fundamental prerequisite of democratic theory is seriously diluted as a result.[69]

Two lines of attack have been fashioned against this simple but nevertheless compelling argument from accountability. I have labelled one the "rejection" model, and the other the "avoidance" model. The avoidance model argues that whatever the impact of broad delegation on accountability, social and political concerns external to the accountability principle justify such delegation.[70] The rejection model, on the other hand, refuses to concede the validity of the accountability critique of delegation, and argues instead that the administrative policymaking to which delegation gives rise is as or more accountable to voter wishes than is legislative policymaking.

Responses to the Accountability Critique I:
The "Rejection" Model

Professor Jerry Mashaw has articulated the "rejection" response to the accountability critique.[71] His arguments fall basically into four categories: what I label "presidential accountability," "voter waiver," "responsive flexibility," and "dictatorial accountability." Careful examination reveals, however, that each of these arguments is seriously flawed.

Voter Waiver, Responsive Flexibility, and Presidential Accountability

Professor Mashaw challenges the entire premise of the asserted link between limits on legislative delegation and electoral accountability. His argument is threefold: (1) Voter knowledge of individual legislators' decisions on particular legislative matters is not likely to provide the basis for a voter's decision on retention of his legislative representative, (2) the head of the executive branch to which those legislative choices have been delegated is himself politically accountable to the voters, and (3) in any event, the voters' willingness to retain a legislator, despite her support of broad delegations of legislative power, constitutes a type of voter waiver.

Clearly the most dubious of these arguments is Mashaw's contention that voters do not need their legislators to make normative commitments through legislative votes in order to hold those legislators politically accountable. In support of his contention, Mashaw rhetorically asks,

[H]ow much better off are voters likely to be . . . in determining how well Congressman X is likely to represent them over a range of presently unspecified issues—by knowing that he or she voted yes or no on the specific language in certain specific bills in some preceding legislature? After all, the voter will also know that X could not have controlled all or even a substantial portion of the language of those bills.[72]

He asserts that "it is surely much more important that voters know the general ideological tendencies that inform those votes (prolabor, probusiness, prodisarmament, prodefense) than that X votes for or against the particular language of [a] particular bill."[73] It is unclear, however, why Mashaw believes that voter decisionmaking is not greatly assisted "by knowing that [the legislator] voted yes or no on the specific language in certain specific bills . . . ." If a voter's political predilections are probusiness or prodisarmament, surely his decisions in the voting booth will be aided considerably more by learning what his representative's votes are on bills to repeal governmental limitations on business activity or to reduce defense spending than on bills to authorize an administrative agency to make decisions on those issues.

Indeed, given the vacuous nature of much modern political rhetoric, absent such a required placing of the representative's "neck on the line" it is by no means clear that a voter will be able to learn his representative's ideological position. More importantly, even if (as Mashaw is so ready to assume) one were able to ascertain a representative's ideological position on various issues without knowing how a legislator voted on specific enactments, what difference does it make, if those ideological predilections will not influence the creation of law that affects the lives of citizens? Yet if we accept that in enacting legislation Congress need make absolutely no policy choice and instead simply delegate that decisionmaking power to an unelected administrative agency, the representative's ideological predispositions will have absolutely no impact on the eventual policy choices that are made. Once again using Mashaw's own hypotheticals, what practical effect does a representative's ideological position have on disarmament, if that representative votes in favor of (or against) a bill that does nothing more than delegate the disarmament decision to an unelected administrative agency? In such an event, the representative's ideology has absolutely no practical impact on actual governing decisions concerning disarmament. And if one accepts the constitutional validity of unlimited legislative delegation, there exists at least the theoretical possibility that *all* fundamental social policy choices will be made by unelected administrators, rather than by electorally accountable representatives. Under these circumstances, a voter's ability to ascertain her representative's ideological position will be of little relevance to either the democratic or governing processes.

It is true, of course, that given the substantial number of bills upon which a legislator is required to vote during her term, it will be impossible for a voter to reflect agreement or disagreement with each of those legislative votes through the making of choices in the voting booth. It is surely conceivable that a voter may agree with his representative's vote on bill *A* but not on bill *B*. In such an event, a voter's ability to hold his representative politically accountable for legislative decisions is obviously weakened. But the fact remains that, from the perspective of democratic theory and popular sovereignty, limited accountability is better than no accountability at all. Voters still have available a safety valve mechanism directly to reflect displeasure with a particular legislative vote—a mechanism that is, as a practical matter, unavailable to them in the case of administrative decisionmaking.

Professor Mashaw suggests, however, that to the extent that legislative delegation undermines accountability,[74] the voters have effectively received what they asked for. In his words:

> I find it difficult to understand why we do not presently have exactly the "clowns . . . we deserve." The dynamics of accountability apparently involve voters willing to vote upon the basis of their representative's record in the legislature. Assuming that our current representatives in the legislature vote for laws that contain vague delegations of authority, we are presumably holding them accountable for that at the polls. How is it that we are not being represented?[75]

In effect, Professor Mashaw appears to be advocating a type of "voter waiver": If the voters do not approve of either widespread legislative "buck passing" or legislative failure to alter the "buck passing" of previous legislatures, they may reflect that disapproval in the voting booth, by voting against representatives who had acted in such a manner. The voters are, then, being "represented" in a manner that satisfies their wishes.

This analysis is seriously flawed, from the perspectives of both constitutional theory and political reality. In an important sense, the "voter-waiver" analysis begs the constitutional question. If unlimited delegation is deemed to be a violation of the Constitution, no majority of the electorate may ratify that violation. If, for example, a president has openly and defiantly exceeded the constitutional limits on presidential authority, being reelected despite these transgressions cannot amount to an effective constitutional amendment that somehow ratifies the president's constitutional violation. The Constitution imposes a supermajoritarian requirement for the amendment process[76] for the very reason that it embodies enduring values, intended to be insulated from the changing attitudes of simple majorities. Professor Mashaw's analysis effectively authorizes the circumvention of the Constitution's inherently countermajoritarian protections.

Of course, Professor Mashaw's point delves more deeply than this analysis might suggest. He is not arguing merely that the electorate's decision ratifies a constitutional violation, but rather that the "representativeness" of the elected officials is all that the Constitution requires, and that by retaining elected officials who approve or accept broad delegation of legislative authority the voters are, in fact, "represented," because they have paradoxically chosen to be represented by those who do not represent them. The political realities, however, underscore why the supermajoritarian Constitution grants legislative power only to Congress in the first place, rather than leaving the decision on whether or not to transfer that power to the executive to a majority of the voters. It is unrealistic to expect a large portion of the electorate to judge their elected representatives not on their normative political positions but rather than on their *failure* to take political positions. Even if such an expectation of voter behavior were reasonable, legislative delegation generally does not come undisguised. Congress usually employs a linguistic sleight-of-hand by employing language that, to a casual observer, appears to take a stand but on more careful examination, is revealed as little more than a blank check to an administrative agency.[77] In such a situation, it is inaccurate to assume that the voters' failure to remove a representative on the grounds of her decision to accept wholesale delegation of legislative authority necessarily implies voter ratification of such delegation.

Professor Mashaw notes, however, that the executive branch to which legislative power has been delegated is headed by the president, who is himself both representative and accountable. "All we need do," Mashaw asserts, "is not forget there are also presidential elections and that . . . presidents are heads of administrations."[78] Indeed, he suggests that the president's broader-based constituency may actually make the president more representative than the individual members of Congress.[79] Further, he argues that absent broad legislative delegation to the executive branch, "presidential politics would be a mere beauty contest."[80] He articulates an argument grounded in the president's superior "responsive flexibility":

> [I]n the absence of a parliamentary system or a system of strict party loyalty, specific statutes [rather than broad legislative delegations] would mean that presidents and administrations could respond to voter preferences only if they were able to convince the legislature to make specific changes in the existing set of specific statutes. Arguments for specific statutory provisions constraining administrative discretion may reflect therefore a desire merely for conservative, not responsive, governance.[81]

In this passage, Professor Mashaw appears completely to ignore the avowedly "conservative" republican barriers to precipitant federal governmental action that were inserted into our constitutional structure.[82] If the Framers had desired the type of responsive flexibility that Professor Mashaw describes, the very last thing they would have done is create two distinct political branches, and then divide one of those branches even further, requiring something akin to approval of all segments before action may be taken.[83] Instead, the Framers would have allowed us simply to choose one elected official, who would then have free rein to undo everything that had been done previously. The values and benefits of these "checking" protections are discussed elsewhere in these pages,[84] but suffice it to say at this point that Professor Mashaw's criticisms derive from a set of political values very different from those on which our system is structured. Thus, the fact that "presidents and administrations could respond to voter preferences only if they were able to convince the legislature to make specific changes in the existing set of specific statutes," far from being the negative Mashaw assumes it to be, is actually an intended outgrowth of the political caution built into our governmental system.

Even from a pure accountability perspective, Professor Mashaw's "responsive flexibility" analysis suffers from numerous flaws. He seems implicitly to view Congress as some type of unelected House of Lords, sitting as an unrepresentative check on the elected president, ignoring the obvious fact that members of Congress, too, are elected—many of them at the very same time that the president is chosen. In light of this fact, it is difficult to understand why the president's inability to act without convincing a majority of Congress to concur somehow undermines the responsiveness of governmental decisionmaking to voter preferences.

Most importantly, the contention that policy decisions made by administrative agencies somehow satisfy the goals of representativeness and accountability because the president is elected ignores reality. As a practical matter, the president exercises relatively little day-to-day control over most agency decisionmaking.[85] This is especially true of the so-called independent agencies, whose members as a matter of law are immune from presidential removal, absent cause. While its reasoning remains a mystery to this very day, the Supreme Court long ago explicitly upheld the constitutionality of such agencies.[86] Thus, they are a political and legal reality. Even a strong and respected critic of the nondelegation doctrine has conceded that "[t]he recognition and reassertion of presidential control over agency policymaking is not complete because neither the Supreme Court nor the President has extended presidential control to policymaking by independent agencies."[87] Professor Pierce adds that "[o]nce that critical step is taken, the President and his political party can, and should, be held accountable at the ballot box for all agency policy decisions."[88] But surely his apparent optimism about the likelihood of such a step is dramatically overstated: there is no reason to expect an alteration in the structure of independent agencies in the foreseeable future. In any event, given general political perceptions and the bureaucratic layers of authority that separate the president from most administrative decisionmaking, it is unlikely that much of this decisionmaking will be attributed to the president by the voters.

"Dictatorial Accountability"

Defenders of broad delegation have on occasion asserted that such delegation to administrative agencies actually "might improve responsiveness."[89] In support, Professor Mashaw argues that "[l]umping alternatives together in a broad or vague statutory pronouncement and delegating choice to administrators is but another way of avoiding voting cycles through the establishment of dictators."[90] One might at first suspect that Mashaw's characterization of administrative agencies as "dictators" contradicts his earlier contention that use of such agencies is consistent with democratic values.[91] But Mashaw replies that "dictation may also be responsive":[92]

> Administrators at least operate within a set of legal rules (administrative law) that keep them within their jurisdiction, require them to operate with a modicum of explanation and participation of the affected interests, police them for consistency, and protect them from the importuning of Congressmen and others who would like to carry logrolling into the administrative process.[93]

Thus, to Mashaw, "delegation to experts becomes a form of consensus building that, far from taking decisions out of politics, seeks to give political choice a forum in which potential collective agreement can be discovered and its benefits realized."[94]

This argument misses the basic point of our governmental structure. Under a framework grounded in a commitment to societal self-determination, the concept of a benevolent dictator is, as John Stuart Mill suggested, an oxymoron.[95] While an administrative system that operates in accordance with law is of course preferable to one that does not, the basic fact remains that ultimate policy choices are being made by largely nonaccountable officials. No one can be assured that the nonaccountable administrative process will, in a particular instance, be able to attain the type of "consensus" envisioned by Professor Mashaw. More importantly, absent some means by which to allow the public meaningfully to express agreement or disagreement, even if only indirectly, the issue of political consensus is largely beside the point.

The argument has been made, however, that as unrepresentative as the administrative process may be, it is still more accountable than the means traditionally employed by our elected representatives to adopt legislation. Professor Richard Stewart, for example, contends that "delegation to administrative agencies [is] preferable to subdelegation within Congress, provided that agencies [are] required to observe procedural and other requirements designed to serve open, responsive, and reasoned decisionmaking."[96] Stewart believes that widespread delegation to congressional subcommittees probably "does not on balance lead to more desirable results than delegation to administrative agencies," because "[u]nlike administrative decisionmaking, subdelegated congressional decisionmaking often is not subject to public input through regularly established procedures. It is not required to be based on a public record, and is not subject to 'hard look' judicial review."[97]

Even if his unsubstantiated assertions about congressional behavior are assumed to be accurate, however, Professor Stewart's argument ignores the key fact that before any legislative policy choice made by a congressional subcommittee may be enacted into law, it must be approved through the processes of bicameralism and presentment, thereby assuring that those representative of and directly accountable to the electorate—members of Congress and the president—will have been forced to make a political commitment for or against that policy choice. That in doing so those representatives may be tacitly deferring to the policy choices of a congressional subcommittee (a factually unsubstantiated allegation in any event) does not alter this legal and political reality. It is this factor that inherently distinguishes legislative choices from those made by administrators for purposes of the accountability principle. This distinction applies, regardless of the procedures used by or judicial review given to administrative decisionmaking.

The "Judicial Review Purification" Theory

An additional argument that is sometimes utilized to defend the constitutional legitimacy of broad delegation is that the availability of judicial review of agency action provides an adequate safety net to assure that agencies do not act improperly. As Judge Harold Leventhal once argued:

> Congress has been willing to delegate its legislative powers broadly—and courts have upheld such delegation—because there is court review to assure that the agency exercises delegated power within statutory limits, and that it fleshes out objectives within those limits by an administration that is not irrational or discriminatory.[98]

The Supreme Court's majority in *INS v. Chadha*[99] expressly distinguished executive actions taken pursuant to permissible legislative delegations of authority from the unconstitutional one-house veto on the grounds that the former were subject to judicial review.[100]

Even if it were inaccurate to suggest, as has one commentator, that as an empirical matter such a view "overstates the extent to which judicial review controls administrative discretion in most cases,"[101] the argument would be unsuccessful, for two reasons. First, if a statute fails to provide an executive agency with sufficient guidance, it is difficult to see how a court will be in any position to confine the agency within the terms of the statute, when the very problem is that the terms of the statute fail to confine. Second, while it is true that even in such a case a reviewing court may seek to ensure that the agency's action is reasonable or wise, performance of such a function fails to cure the basic defect in unduly broad legislative delegation: the fundamentally undemocratic character of the resulting policy choices. The federal judiciary is even less representative and accountable than are administrative agencies. Thus, while vigorous judicial review might reduce the threat to the republican-like separation-of-powers concerns that in part underlie the nondelegation doctrine,[102] it totally fails to remedy the harm caused by delegation to the values of representationalism and accountability that lie at the heart of our system's commitment to some meaningful level of popular sovereignty.

Equality in Democratic Failure

The final argument raised against the accountability critique of delegation is that the legislative process is no better at attaining the goals of democratic theory than is the administrative process. Professor Pierce, for example, has pointed to "the inability of a collective body [such as Congress] to resolve many polycentric disputes in a manner consistent with democratic principles."[103] He relies on the works of Arrow and Sen[104] to support the assertion that "[e]ven if Congress had only one [polycentric] dispute on its agenda in a given session . . . Congress could not resolve that dispute without violating democratic principles."[105] Other scholars have also propounded this critique of the supposed democratic basis of the legislative process.[106] As Professor Cass Sunstein has asserted, "[i]n any representative democracy, there is simply too much slippage between legislative outcomes and constituent desires."[107]

Such fallacious "all-or-nothing" thinking fails to do justice to the values of the representative process. It is apparently assumed that because a representative legislative body cannot always ascertain or fulfill popular will in its decisionmaking, its processes' claim to democratic legitimacy is significantly undermined. Democratic theorist Robert Dahl has effectively responded to such criticisms of the democratic nature of the representational process: "[E]lections and political competition do not make for government by majorities in any very significant way, but they vastly increase the size, number, and varieties of minorities whose preferences can be taken into account by leaders making policy choices."[108] Thus, the election process is one method of helping to "make governmental leaders so responsive to non-leaders that the distinction between democracy and dictatorship still makes sense."[109] None of the arguments employed to support the "rejection" model, then alters the significant distinctions between the administrative and legislative processes in fulfilling the democratic goals inherent in American political theory.

Responses to the Accountability Critique II:
The "Avoidance" Model

Several theorists have opposed the nondelegation doctrine on grounds that, at least implicitly, either concede or ignore the validity of the accountability critique of legislative delegation. These arguments take two basic forms. The first is functional in nature, positing serious practical consequences from a return to the limits imposed by the nondelegation doctrine. The second argument is premised on the assumed impossibility of fashioning any workable standards for implementing the nondelegation doctrine. Careful consideration of these arguments, however, establishes that they are both overstated in their attacks on nondelegation, and in any event are insufficient to overcome the nondelegation doctrine's strong grounding in democratic theory.

The Functional Critique

"Congress creates rules based on highly imperfect knowledge and foresight," Professor Pierce has written.[110] "It then leaves those rules in effect long after they have become obsolete and destructive in their impact."[111] He asserts that arguments in favor of a return to nondelegation "are premised on an overestimate of the capabilities of the legislative branch."[112] He reasons that "[Congress] could not possibly make the hundreds, or perhaps thousands, of important policy decisions that agencies make annually."[113] He points to the numerous "transaction costs" that plague the legislative process: "large numbers of issues, large numbers of participants in a group decisionmaking process, inadequate information, and inadequate foresight. . . ."[114] Agencies, on the other hand, "encounter much lower transaction costs than Congress."[115] Pierce goes so far as to suggest that "Congress' creation of statutory rules to govern future conduct, when it lacks the ability to foresee the uncertain future, may be more irresponsible than delegating broad authority to make rules. . . ."[116]

Even if one were to find these arguments premised on considerations of practicality to be persuasive, that would not alter the dramatic differences between agencies and Congress from the perspective of democratic theory.[117] If efficiency in governmental decision making had been the sole or overriding concern of the Framers, surely our federal government would not have been structured in the manner in which it was.[118] If one places a high value on the public accountability of those making basic social policy choices, any gain in efficiency derived from the placing of decisionmaking authority in the hands of largely unaccountable administrative officials must be considered secondary. Moreover, the "inefficiency" of the federal legislative process may also be viewed as representing a value choice in favor of federalism, by enabling the states to fill the gaps left by Congress.[119] Reliance on the presumably more efficient federal agencies for federal policymaking, then, may be seen as a threat to the value of diversity in social policymaking, as well as to the values of representationalism and accountability.

To be sure, it is by no means certain that everyone drawing the balance would find that these threats to the values of democracy and federalism outweigh the efficiency values thought to be derived from reliance on the more flexible administrative process. One of the key problems with the arguments of those relying on the efficiency analysis, however, is that they fail to acknowledge the costs to the values embodied in American political theory engendered by heavy use of the largely unaccountable administrative process. This can be seen in Professor Pierce's assertion that Congress "leaves . . . rules in effect long after they have been obsolete and destructive in their impact."[120] Professor Pierce here apparently assumes that there can be no debate over the question of whether particular legislation has become "obsolete" or "destructive." Yet surely there can be no universal certainty as to whether a particular statute—for example, a civil rights or environmental law—could be characterized in these ways. By supporting the transfer of policy-making authority to largely unaccountable administrators, Professor Pierce fails to give sufficient attention to the "epistemological humility" about moral choices that underlies any democratic system and the resultant fundamental democratic premise that such policy choices are to be made by those representative of and accountable to the populace.[121] His position thus fits within what Professor Dahl has described as a "guardianship" model,[122] entrusting rulership not to a democratically elected representative body, but "to a minority of persons who are specially qualified to govern by reason of their superior knowledge and virtue."[123] Dahl posits two propositions upon which the guardianship model is premised:

> First, knowledge of the public good and the best means to achieve it is a "science" composed of objectively valid and validated truths, as the laws of physics or . . . mathematical proofs are usually thought to be "objective." Second, this knowledge can be acquired only by a minority of adults, quite likely a very small minority.[124]

The problem, of course, is that the world envisioned by the guardian model is not the world in which we live. To the contrary, recognition of our multicultural, pluralistic society suggests that the ideal of substantive universalism is illusory, and therefore that its pursuit is dangerous.

Equally important, however, is the fallacious "all-or-nothing" assumption which appears to underlie Professor Pierce's efficiency critique: either administrators must be given free and unlimited rein in policymaking, or the clumsy and unwieldy legislative process must attempt to foresee all conceivable issues and problems in the application of general directives to specific factual circumstances. But concern for the need for applicational flexibility does not necessarily lead to the conclusion that Congress may decline to make an initial substantive policy choice that provides administrators with guidance as to how individual situations should be handled. Recognition of this fact, however, leads to the second element of the "avoidance" model: the view that imposition of meaningful limitations on legislative delegations is either a practical impossibility, or would result in an "Internal Revenue Code" model of statutory detail. Neither concern, however, ultimately proves to be accurate.

The Supposed Impossibility of Fashioning Workable Standards

Scholars have in recent years suggested several methods for providing content to a meaningful nondelegation doctrine, with at best limited success. Professor Pierce points to four such standards: an analysis premised on "the relative importance of the policy issue Congress has delegated,"[125] a distinction between delegations are "motivated by 'inherent necessity' [that] are permissible [and] delegations motivated by 'lack of political will' [that] are forbidden,"[126] a standard that turns "on whether a statutory delegation permissibly creates a public good or impermissibly creates a private good,"[127] and a distinction between constitutionally valid "rules statutes" and invalid "goals statutes."[128]

Professor Pierce is correct in his assertion that "neither of the first two potential bases for distinction offers any prospect of application in a politically neutral manner." This is because "[p]olitically liberal jurists and politically conservative jurists inevitably would differ in their characterization of the relative importance of the thousands of policy issues Congress had delegated to agencies . . . [and] judges cannot distinguish between delegations motivated by a lack of political will and delegations motivated by an inherent necessity."[129] Moreover, there is no textual, theoretical, or historical basis on which to exclude delegations of so-called unimportant policy choices to unaccountable administrators from Article I's requirement that the legislative power be exercised by Congress. Such a theory, then, amounts to a wholly unprincipled basis of distinction.

Professor Pierce also correctly suggests that the "public-private good" distinction, associated with Professor Ernest Gellhorn,[130] "founders on the rocks of indeterminacy."[131] Gellhorn's concern is with statutes that allow agencies to redistribute wealth to politically favored special interests.[132] But Pierce quotes George Stigler for the proposition that "[m]onopoly aside, . . . there is no method in economics of predicting where externalities will arise or whether they will be worth talking about."[133] More problematic, however, is Gellhorn's implicit assumption that his suggested distinction between public and private goods is so embedded in our governmental theory that it rises to the level of a constitutional command. Nothing in the Constitution—with the possible exception of the Equal Protection Clause,[134] apparently not relevant to Gellhorn's analysis—even arguably dictates such a dichotomy. The principles of representationalism and accountability, central elements of American political theory which are, in fact, embodied in the Constitution,[135] are undermined just as much by a statute distributing public goods that delegates unlimited policymaking power to unelected administrators as by one distributing private goods. In short, the "public-private goods" distinction misses the point because it ignores the true constitutional difficulty plaguing legislative delegation, its inconsistency with representationalism and accountability.

Somewhat more complex is the fourth suggested dichotomy, that between "rules" statutes and "goals" statutes. Attempting to define Article I's directive that "the legislative power" be vested in Congress, Professor David Schoenbrod has argued that statutes which establish "rules" are constitutionally valid, while statutes which establish only "goals" are impermissible delegations of legislative power.[136] He asserts that "[r]ules statutes state rules demarcating permissible from impermissible conduct," while "[g]oals statutes state goals, which usually conflict, and delegate the job of reconciling such conflicts to others who are entrusted with promulgating the rules of conduct necessary to achieve those goals."[137] The latter are unconstitutional, Professor Schoenbrod asserts, because they delegate "legislative power," while the former category are constitutional, because they merely call for executive interpretation.[138]

Professor Schoenbrod argues that his suggested distinction "is fundamentally different from the 'intelligible principle' notion that has proved so unsatisfactory."[139] This is because "[a] goals statue can be relatively specific in that a goal may be quite precise . . . [and] a rule in a rules statute will always be general in the sense that it will require interpretation."[140] To the extent that these characterizations are accurate, however, it is questionable whether Professor Schoenbrod's suggested dichotomy actually fosters and protects the accountability and checking values inherent in the separation-of-powers system. For if a so-called rules statute actually is so vague that it is capable of multiple, equally plausible administrative interpretations, it is unclear why such statutes sufficiently constrain executive power.

Conversely, it is possible to hypothesize situations in which Congress could provide a detailed description of its normative goals, thereby enlightening the voting public and constraining executive power, yet be unable to provide specific rules of conduct because of the pragmatic need for immediate implementational adjustments. In light of the fact that the Framers apparently saw the need for the creation of the executive branch in light of the untenable practical situation caused by its absence under the Articles of Confederation,[141] it is not unreasonable to allow pragmatic considerations to influence the definition of the concepts of "executive" and "legislative" power.[142] This, in essence, is the premise of the "pragmatic formalist" model.[143] Under this standard, Congress should be allowed to adopt so-called goals statutes when (1) it provides a sufficiently detailed description of its goals to meet the political commitment principle, and (2) pragmatic considerations make it reasonable to conclude that it would be impossible to provide detailed, long-term implementational methodologies.

Thus, Professor Schoenbrod's dichotomy may simultaneously over- and underenforce the norms of American political theory that underlie the nondelegation doctrine. While in certain instances his dichotomy may dictate a correct constitutional result, it will be because such a result happens to coincide with the teachings of the political commitment principle, a more appropriate standard, which would return to the first principles of our system of separation of powers by asking simply whether congressional legislation evinces a sufficient political commitment to enable the voters to judge their representatives. It is to an analysis of the workings of this principle that the discussion now turns.

Fashioning the Political Commitment Principle

On one level, the political commitment principle is quite simple, in both purpose and implementation. In order to insure that social policy choices—at least in their most basic form—are made by those who are representative of and accountable to the electorate, every piece of legislation adopted by

Congress must make some recognizable normative commitment that will provides information to the voters about the views of their elected representatives. Under this standard, a reviewing court would ask itself whether the voters would be placed in a substantially better position to judge their representatives by learning whether they had voted for or against the challenged legislation. If the answer is no, then the law has failed to facilitate or preserve performance of the representative democratic function and therefore constitutes an unconstitutional delegation of legislative power.

Although such a doctrinal standard would undoubtedly fail to resolve all difficult or close cases, it should generally fare reasonably well in providing a workable method for distinguishing unconstitutional delegations from valid exercises of legislative power. However, if an additional doctrinal perspective is deemed necessary, a reviewing court could ask whether *any* conceivable action by the executive branch could reasonably be deemed to fall within the legislation's authorizing scope. If the answer is yes, the law exceeds the limits of the nondelegation doctrine. For example, a statute authorizing either the president or an executive agency to "take all necessary steps" to resolve the issue of affirmative action in employment in a "satisfactory manner" would constitute nothing more than a delegation of full legislative power to the executive branch. Adoption of the political commitment principle surely does not require Congress, in Chief Justice Rehnquist's words, to "fill in all the blanks."[144] However, the principle would guard against adoption of legislation in which "Congress simply abdicated its responsibility for the making of a fundamental . . . policy choice. . . ."[145]

It is important to contrast the political commitment principle with the "pragmatic formalist" model, previously used here as the guide for determining the constitutional contours of separation of powers among the branches.[146] While the political commitment principle requires at least some level of normative commitment by Congress, the degree of detail of that commitment may vary, depending on pragmatic considerations. It will often be practically infeasible for Congress to do more than provide a broad normative directive to those charged with statutory enforcement; individualized future circumstances will prevent more detail in Congress's normative commitment. However, Congress should be expected to provide as much detail in its normative commitment as pragmatic considerations will allow. While Congress will necessarily receive a degree of discretion under such an inescapably vague limitation, it should always be recalled that the political commitment principle imposes a floor, below which Congress may not fall under any circumstances. In enacting statutes, Congress must always make a normative commitment that could significantly improve voters' knowledge by learning whether their elected representatives voted for or against the law.

The intertwining of the political commitment principle and pragmatic formalism may be explored by examination of *Mistretta v. United States*,[147] where the Court upheld the federal sentencing guidelines against attack under the nondelegation doctrine. Pursuant to those guidelines, the Federal Sentencing Commission was to promulgate specific sentences for particular crimes.[148] Justice Blackmun, speaking for the Court, noted that nondelegation jurisprudence "has been driven by a practical understanding that in our increasingly complex society, replete with ever changing and more technical problems, Congress simply cannot do its job absent an ability to delegate power under broad general directives,"[149] and as a result the Court upheld Congress's delegation as "sufficiently specific and detailed to meet constitutional requirements."[150]

One may debate, however, whether the abstract determination of sentences for particular crimes is a subject that can be rationalized as "executive" power, under a pragmatic definitional analysis. As Justice Scalia pointed out in dissent:

> The whole theory of *lawful* congressional "delegation" is not that Congress is sometimes too busy or too divided and can therefore assign its responsibility of making law to someone else; but rather that a certain degree of discretion *inheres* in most executive or judicial action. . . .
>
> The focus of controversy in the long line of our so-called excessive delegation cases, has been whether the *degree* of generality contained in the authorization for exercises of executive or judicial powers in a particular field is so unacceptably high as to *amount to a delegation of legislative power.* . . . Strictly speaking, there is *no* acceptable delegation of legislative power.[151]

Justice Scalia then noted that while the act did in fact provide the commission with "intelligible standards" that did not alter the fact that what the commission was doing, as a definitional matter, amounted to "legislating." "It is irrelevant whether the standards are adequate," he concluded, "because they are not standards related to the exercise of executive or judicial powers; they are, plainly and simply, standards for further legislation."[152]

The generalized determination of sentences does not conceptually amount to an individualized exercise of *applicational* discretion under the circumstances of a specific situation. Hence, under Justice Scalia's analysis, the fact that Congress may have made a political commitment in the delegating statute cannot justify the delegation of what is properly defined as *legislative* power to the executive branch. Under Justice Scalia's analysis, then, although meeting the political commitment principle apparently serves as a necessary condition for the validation of delegation, it will not always prove to be a sufficient one: unless the power that has been delegated is capable of classification as "executive" in nature, the fact that Congress has made a political commitment in the delegating statute provides an insufficient basis for a finding of constitutionality.

While Justice Scalia's analysis possesses a superficial appeal, its acceptance would seem logically to lead to a dramatic result: total abandonment of all administrative rulemaking power. For by definition, rulemaking is generalized in its nature; it does not constitute the "application" of a generalized legislative directive to a specific set of facts. Thus, statutes authorizing rulemaking could be subjected to the same attack that Justice Scalia leveled at the sentencing guidelines in *Mistretta:* they are simply "standards for further legislation."[153]

Certainly, the mere fact that a particular constitutional interpretation will have a dramatic practical impact is not, standing alone, a sufficient basis on which to reject it. However, it should be recalled that the main concern of American political theory underlying the nondelegation doctrine is that the legislature make a normative commitment sufficient to enable the public to judge its legislators in the voting booth. In determining whether that prerequisite has been met, the pragmatic formalist model takes into account the pragmatic rationales underlying the initial division of power between the legislative and executive branches.[154] As long as the executive agency is truly engaged in interpretation and application of normative principles fashioned by Congress, the provision of implementational details of the legislative directive—even in the generalized form of rulemaking—should be deemed constitutionally acceptable.

Applying the Political Commitment Principle

A better understanding of the political commitment principle can be attained by examining its application to several existing congressional statutes. The Securities Exchange Act of 1934 provides that

> [i]t shall be unlawful . . . [t]o use or employ, in connection with the purchase or sale of any security . . ., any manipulative or deceptive device or contrivance in contravention of such rules and regulations as the [Securities and Exchange] Commission may prescribe as necessary or appropriate in the public interest or for the protection of investors.[155]

There can be little doubt that this statute fails to meet the standards of the "political commitment" principle. By its terms, the statute fails to provide the slightest hint—to either the electorate or the enforcement agency—of Congress's guiding normative principles. As proof, one need only ask whether there is *any* reasonably conceivable agency implementation of the act's legislative directive that a reviewing court could invalidate as not falling within that directive. The answer is, obviously, no.

Thus, in much the same manner as the Federal Communications Act,[156] the statute does nothing more than delegate *both* policymaking *and* implementational authority to the largely unrepresentative agency. These two statutes, then, make clear that whatever close calls might arise in application of the "political commitment" principle, there presently exist a number of enactments which unambiguously fail any meaningful nondelegation standard.

An example of a closer case is the Federal Trade Commission Act,[157] which empowers the Federal Trade Commission to issue regulations to prevent "unfair or deceptive acts or practices in or affecting commerce." On one level, this statute comes closer to meeting the "political commitment" standard than do either the Securities Exchange Act or the Federal Communications Act. Prohibiting the use of "deceptive acts" provides substantial notice of Congress's guiding normative principles, even though it leaves room for implementational discretion. Arguably more questionable is the prohibition of "unfair methods of competition," a phrase which is potentially subject to a broad range of interpretation. On the one hand, it is conceivable that the preexisting common law interpretations of that concept in the context of tort law may provide a narrowing construction. On the other hand, if the focus of the nondelegation doctrine is placed on the interest of the electorate in learning about its representatives, it is questionable whether the existence of a common law history should suffice. In any event, the term clearly provides more guidance than do statutes which undoubtedly fail the political commitment test.

Whether the term "unfair" in the Federal Trade Commission Act meets the requirements of pragmatic formalism, despite its questionable status under the political commitment principle, will ultimately depend on whether a legislature could feasibly be expected to provide more detail in its generalized directives, or whether the reality is that there exists too great a need for case-by-case implementational discretion. Viewed from this perspective, one may wonder whether Congress could not reasonably be expected at least to enumerate certain specific prohibited practices. In order to satisfy the need for implementational flexibility, the statute could also contain a residuary clause, enabling the implementing agency to prohibit other "unfair" trade practices. Under a pragmatic formalist perspective, then, the Federal Trade Commission Act should probably be deemed unconstitutional.

The Political Commitment Principle and Political Reality

Perhaps the strongest attack on the political commitment principle is the argument that it is both naive and unrealistic to assume that the electorate pays significant attention to how its representatives have voted on specific pieces of legislation. But while this is likely to be true for many of the more technical and esoteric statutes, it is quite probably untrue for proposed legislation that generates wide and controversial public interest. For example, it is reasonable to believe that many voters would choose whether or not to retain their representatives on the basis of how they voted on a proposed "freedom-of-choice" abortion act. Legislation delegating to an executive agency the power to decide that question, then, could greatly disrupt the performance of the democratic process.

Once it is conceded that how legislators vote on certain legislation can have a significant impact on voter behavior, there exists no principled means by which a court may distinguish such proposed enactments from the rest. A court should not be allowed to fashion principles of constitutional law on the basis of its own assessment of how effectively the democratic process is operating. Such judgments are too speculative, subjective, and vulnerable to shifting influences and conditions to provide sound bases for judicial judgment.

More importantly, it is appropriate and advisable to view the democratic process from the perspective of its normative ideal, rather than its supposed realities. Otherwise, empirically inaccurate assessments of the democratic process are in danger of becoming self-fulfilling prophecies: because we structure judicial review on the basis of assumed reality of political behavior, we effectively encourage the continuation of that behavior. It is only by fashioning constitutional principles with a view toward attaining the normative democratic ideal that judicial review may further the values that inhere in American political theory.

Doctrinal Implications of the
Political Commitment Principle:
The Legislative Veto

Inextricably intertwined with the nondelegation doctrine is the question of the constitutionality of the legislative veto. In *Immigration & Naturalization Service v. Chadha,*[158] the Supreme Court held that legislation authorizing one house of Congress to veto administrative action was unconstitutional because it violated the constitutional requirements of bicameralism and presentment found in Article I of the Constitution.[159] The Court reasoned that Congress was effectively legislating through the definitive action of one house, while the Constitution required the assent of both houses and the signature of the president.[160] In the abstract, such a conclusion fits well within the framework of pragmatic formalism. Under that model, the formalistic requirements of separation of powers and checks and balances are to be followed, without requiring a showing that those requirements are necessary or advisable under the particular circumstances.[161]

Problems arise, however, when *Chadha* is viewed in light of the current status of the nondelegation doctrine. As previously noted,[162] that doctrine is currently in a state of atrophy. It would not be a significant exaggeration to assert that for all practical purposes, agencies may today "legislate" without substantial fear of judicial invalidation. When *Chadha* is paired with the current version of the nondelegation doctrine, one is left with the dubious conclusion that as long as "legislation" is enacted with the assent of *one* house, it is unconstitutional for failure to meet the bicameralism and presentment requirements, but when what amounts to "legislation" is promulgated by *neither* house but rather by an unelected administrative body, it is valid. On a theoretical level, then, the *Chadha* decision should be found to have significant implications for the nondelegation doctrine. For if the requirements of bicameralism and presentment are violated when legislation is enacted by *one* house of Congress, surely they are violated when legislation is enacted by neither house.

In apparent anticipation of this reasoning, the Court in *Chadha* argued that the dangers caused by congressional evasion of the bicameralism and presentment requirements are not present when lawmaking power is delegated to the executive or to an independent agency.[163] The reason for this suggested dichotomy is generally thought to be that the availability of judicial review of administrative action cures the dangers—a cure that is unavailable for congressional excesses. As noted previously,[164] however, any cure of unduly broad delegation thought to be provided by judicial review of administrative action is wholly illusory. For if the delegating statute provides no meaningful guidance to the implementing agency, there is little that judicial review can do to confine agency discretion. Moreover, there is no way that judicial review can cure the lack of political commitment on the face of the statute.

Chadha also gives rise to serious practical problems, in light of the Court's virtual abandonment of the nondelegation doctrine. Given the total delegation by Congress of policymaking authority to largely unrepresentative executive agencies, the one-house veto remains virtually the only practical method by which Congress may retain at least some level of control. To be sure, such reasoning could be criticized for implying that two wrongs can make a right. Acceptance of the legislative veto solely on the grounds that it dilutes the damage already done by abandonment of the nondelegation doctrine could be thought to compound constitutional breach upon constitutional breach. The reality, however, is that given the Court's validation of total legislative delegations to executive agencies, its invalidation of the one-house veto in *Chadha* seriously compromises a potential congressional safety valve for this abandonment of the nondelegation doctrine. The fact remains that the Court's approach undermines both the accountability and checking values that are central to the American governmental system. Article I of the Constitution wisely vests the legislative power in the branch that is most directly and locally accountable to the electorate. Judicial validation of congressional delegation of this power to agencies whose representativeness is at best remote and indirect significantly undermines and disrupts the electorate's ability to judge the work of its chosen representatives. Moreover, allowing one branch of government to combine both basic policymaking authority and implementational discretion dangerously concentrates political power, in contradiction of our system's concern with the threat of tyranny that inevitably flow from such concentrations.

Conclusion

The currently moribund state of the nondelegation doctrine allows significant departures from both the republican and democratic underpinnings of American political theory. By authorizing one branch of government—the executive branch—to combine the powers of legislation and execution, abandonment of nondelegation undermines the barriers to the dangerous accretion of political power in one governmental unit. By enabling Congress to avoid its obligation to make legislative policy choices, the doctrine's abandonment undermines the principles of representative democracy by making simultaneously more difficult and less meaningful the electorate's selection of its representatives.

To ameliorate the political and constitutional harms of the current structure, one need not totally abandon the post–New Deal administrative state as it currently exists. Under adoption of the political commitment principle advocated here as the guiding principle for a newly invigorated nondelegation doctrine, administrative agencies would continue to exercise substantial political authority in the implementation of congressional statutory directives. Neither modern social nor political realities could tolerate a system in which Congress is forced to promulgate every conceivable implementing regulation. What administrative and executive bodies could not be permitted to do under the structure urged here, however, would be effectively to make basic policy choices reserved, in a representative democratic system of government, for those directly accountable to the people.

Reinvigoration of the nondelegation doctrine by use of the political commitment principle would give rise to neither the hopeless problems of interpretation nor the required proliferation of detailed legislative codes feared by the doctrine's opponents. To be sure, questions will arise about particular statutes over which reasonable people may differ. But that fact does not distinguish this inquiry from the great majority of modern constitutional questions. More importantly, the costs of abandoning the nondelegation doctrine to the central values of our political structure far outweigh the added interpretive burdens that might result from the doctrine's reinvigoration.

6

Conclusion: Liberalism, Constitutional Theory, and Political Structure

One reading the preceding chapters might conclude, not unreasonably, that their author adopts a general approach to constitutional interpretation consistent with the views of scholars of the political right. Those chapters, have, after all, argued that the Supreme Court should enforce constitutional limitations on federal power in order to preserve the values of federalism; abandon the limitations imposed by the dormant Commerce Clause on state power to regulate interstate commerce; enforce the constitutional separation of powers in at least a partially formalistic manner; and reinvigorate the limits of the nondelegation doctrine. For the most part, these are positions that are traditionally associated with politically conservative scholars and jurists.[1]

Yet the most important message intended to be conveyed in these pages is that at some point in the process of constitutional interpretation, immediate political objectives must give way to the broader goals of American constitutional and political theory. It is this broader-based commitment that, in the long run, will better protect the values associated with liberal precepts. For it is this commitment that will ultimately assure the avoidance of tyranny and the preservation of liberty. In a certain sense, then, I have attempted to apply the lessons of Professor Herbert Wechsler's concept of "neutral principles," which requires that the Court's constitutional decisions be premised on normative principles that transcend the immediate consequences of the case at bar.[2]

One who appreciates the values of popular sovereignty and individual liberty, yet who is also aware of the continually vulnerable status of those precepts throughout history, must be willing to accept the loss of individual political battles in order to win the political-constitutional war. For example, the fact that one finds politically advisable the use of an independent prosecutor should not lead to the upholding of such a scheme, if it is found to contravene the clear constitutional directives of Articles I, II, and III,[3] which in turn are designed to protect the values of branch separation so vital to the preservation of liberty and the avoidance of tyranny.[4] The long-term values embodied in the constitutional provisions establishing political structure are both too important and too vulnerable to justify judicial failure to enforce them.

Those scholars who urge vigorous judicial protection of the individual liberty guaranteed in the Constitution yet who simultaneously urge judicial abdication in enforcement of the constitutional directives concerning political structure apparently fail to recognize that their suggested dichotomy would ultimately threaten attainment of their own constitutional goals. First, authorizing the judiciary to pick and choose among the Constitution's provisions for purposes of enforcement on the basis of its own political value system creates the risk that the courts will at some point choose to ignore the very individual liberty provisions that these scholars believe deserve vigorous protection. Indeed, at least one respected constitutional scholar has effectively turned the tables by urging virtual judicial abdication in the enforcement of free speech rights while simultaneously advocating vigorous enforcement of the Constitution's federalism protections, seemingly for no reason other than his personal ranking of their respective normative values.[5] If the judiciary is given authority to choose which provisions to enforce, abandonment of the individual liberty provisions in favor of the structural guarantees is just as conceivable a judicial option as the reverse. Neither alternative, however, should be available to the judiciary.

Ironically, by choosing not to enforce a constitutional limitation on the majoritarian branches because of disagreement with its social or political purpose or impact, the courts are engaging in undue judicial activism. For in so doing the courts are judging the wisdom and advisability of the provisions of the Constitution, a power they were never given and one that would surely threaten the people's ability to enshrine values in a supermajoritarian Constitution. Even more important, the judiciary's enforcement of the Constitution's individual liberty provisions while abdicating enforcement of the guarantees of political structure would ultimately prove to be counterproductive. For as the preceding chapters have demonstrated, allowing the centralization of political power substantially increases the dangers to the very individual liberty that we seek to guard.[6]

Adherence to the political structure contemplated in the Constitution may well give rise to a certain degree of inefficiency and delay in accomplishing substantive political goals. But to a certain extent, that was the very design of the system in the first place.[7] In a governmental system lacking the protections of separation of powers and federalism, a popularly elected leader could summarily accomplish political or social results dramatically inconsistent with long-established and currently popular policies, with the only conceivable check coming from a future election. And we cannot know, a priori, whether the abandoned policies will be those with which we agree or disagree. While it may seem absurd to contemplate such radical consequences occurring in our nation, that is quite probably because of our accepted traditions of the separation and division of political power, derived from the political structure established by the Constitution.

It should be noted that reinvigorated judicial enforcement of the structural dictates established by the Constitution would not require a return to the jurisprudence of the pre–New Deal period. The Supreme Court need not construe the Constitution's structural provisions so grudgingly as to tie the hands of the federal government to deal with changing social needs and conditions. The Constitution's text and structure leave sufficient room for the courts to take into account modern social and economic realities without requiring abandonment of its directives.[8]

Those who drafted the Constitution wisely recognized the moral and political benefits to be derived from the use of a constitutional democratic system, as well as the existence of constant threats to the viability of such a system. We ignore the lessons they learned—and sought to convey to us through the governing document they created—at our peril.

NOTES

Chapter 1

1. See, e.g. Jesse H. Choper, *Judicial Review and the National Political Process: A Functional Reconsideration of the Role of the Supreme Court* (1980); Michael J. Perry, *The Constitution, the Courts and Human Rights: An Inquiry into the Legitimacy of Constitutional Policymaking by the Judiciary* 37–60 (1982) (discussing noninterpretive review with respect to separation of powers issues); see discussion infra pp. 16–20.

2. Recently, in New York v. United States, 112 S. Ct. 2408 (1992), the Court struck down portions of federal legislation on the grounds that it interfered with states' rights under the Tenth Amendment. Id. at 2427–49. See also Gregory v. Ashcroft, 111 S. Ct. 2395 (1991). The extent to which this decision signals a renewed agressiveness on the part of the Court to protect constitutional federalism remains unclear. See discussion in chapter 2, infra pp. 44–48.

3. See, e.g., Garcia v. San Antonio Metro. Transit Auth., 469 U.S. 528 (1985). See generally chapter 2.

4. See, e.g., Bowsher v. Synar, 478 U.S. 714 (1986), discussed in chapter 4, infra pp. 123–24. Most recently, the Court appears to have returned to this formalistic analysis. See Metropolitan Washington Airports Auth. v. Citizens for the Abatement of Aircraft Noise, Inc., 111 S. Ct. 2298 (1991) (discussed infra p. 215). This is so, even though the clear trend prior to this decision was toward a considerably more functional approach. See Arthur C. Leahy, Note, "*Mistretta v. United States:* Mistreating the Separation of Powers Doctrine?," 27 *San Diego L. Rev.* 209, 221–22 (1990).

5. See, e.g., Morrison v. Olson, 487 U.S. 654 (1988), discussed in chapter 4.

6. In the words of one perceptive commentator, "the Supreme Court's treatment of the constitutional separation of powers is an incoherent muddle." Rebecca L. Brown, "Separated Powers and Ordered Liberty," 139 *U. Pa. L. Rev.* 1513, 1517 (1991); see also Erwin Chemerinsky, "A Paradox Without a Principle: A Comment on the Burger Court's Jurisprudence in Separation of Powers Cases," 60 *S. Cal. L. Rev.* 1083, 1084–86 (1987) (discussing the Burger Court's differing and inconsistent approach with respect to executive, as opposed to legislative, challenges for separation of powers violations); E. Donald Elliott, "Why Our Separation of Powers Jurisprudence Is So Abysmal," 57 *Geo. Wash. L. Rev.* 506, 531–32 (1989) (discussing literalism and its negative impact on separation-of-powers jurisprudence).

7. See sources cited supra note 1; discussion infra pp. 16–20.

8. See generally Catherine D. Bowen, *Miracle at Philadelphia: The Story of the Constitutional Convention, May to September 1787* (1966).

9. See, e.g., John Hart Ely, *Democracy and Distrust: A Theory of Judicial Review* 92 (1980) (noting that the Constitution was "overwhelmingly dedicated to concerns of process and structure"); see also Brown, supra note 6, at 1531; cf. Geoffrey P. Miller, "Rights and Structure in Constitutional Theory", *Soc. Phil. & Pol'y*, Spring 1991, at 196:

> [T]he Framers were overwhelmingly concerned with matters of government structure: separation of powers . . . and federalism. Separation of powers and federalism form the fundamental matrix or Euclidian plane of our constitutional law. These questions of individual rights dominate contemporary constitutional thought.

The primary direct protections of individual liberty contained in the body of The primary direct protections of individual liberty contained in the body of the Constitution appear in Article I, Section 9. They include the protection of the writ of habeas corpus and the prohibition of bills of attainder. See U.S. Const. art. I, § 9, cls. 2–3.

10. Modern commentators have suggested—arguably anachronistically—that the Framers' theoretical sophistication was severely limited because of their failure to comprehend the dramatic impact of interest group pluralism and social choice theory on the functioning of popular sovereignty. See, e.g., Stephen L. Carter, "Constitutional Adjudication and the Indeterminate Text: A Preliminary Defense of an Imperfect Muddle", 94 *Yale L.J.* 821, 863 (1985). Yet *The Federalist* No. 10, authored by Madison, is famous for its recognition of the threat posed by factions to the democratic process. See *The Federalist* No. 10 (James Madison). In any event, whatever the limiting impact of modern social choice theory on the values of democracy (see William H. Riker, *Liberalism Against Populism: A Confrontation Between the Theory of Democracy and the Theory of Social Choice* (1982); Cass R. Sunstein, "Beyond the Republican Revival", 97 *Yale L.J.* 1539, 1545–56 (1988)), the fact remains that a system ultimately premised on the concept of popular sovereignty is still qualitatively different from a totalitarian state.

11. For a detailed discussion of the link between separation of powers and the preservation of liberty, see Brown, supra note 6, at 1531–40.

12. See, e.g., Gordon Wood, *The Creation of the American Republic, 1776–1787* 330 (1969), suggesting that prior to the Revolution, "[t]he people were the undisputed, ubiquitous source that was appealed to by both the advocates and the opponents of independence."

13. See Alexis de Tocqueville, *Democracy in America* 55 (Richard D. Heffner ed., 1956), suggesting that "[w]henever the political laws of the United States are to be discussed, it is with the doctrine of the sovereignty of the people with which we must begin."

It it true, of course, that in adopting an underlying principle of popular sovereignty, our society at the outset excluded numerous groups of people on the basis of race or gender. However, it is appropriate, for purposes of current theoretical discussion, to impose a modern, admittedly anachronistic gloss on this original commitment to popular sovereignty.

14. See U.S. Const. arts. I, II. Any discussion of our society's historical commitment to popular sovereignty must acknowledge the significant diluting effect intentionally imposed by the Framers' insertion of various republican-like limitations on popular rule. Indeed, many of the structural portions of the Constitution were de-

signed to dilute precipitous changes in and abuses of popular will. See discussion infra p. 116. But at no point did these limitations ever authorize outright rejection of society's ultimate reliance on legitimacy through popular will. Moreover, by subsequent modification society reduced the diluting effect of popular sovereignty, as by authorization of the direct election of senators. U.S. Const. amend. XVII.

15. See U.S. Const. art. V, requiring approval of two-thirds of both houses of Congress and three-fourths of the state legislatures for approval of an amendment, or through the holding of a constitutional convention.

16. I have made such an attempt in my previous writing. See Martin H. Redish & Gary Lippman, "Freedom of Expression and the Civic Republican Revival in Constitutional Theory: The Ominous Implications," 79 *Cal. L. Rev.* 267, 276–81 (1991).

17. See, e.g., Robert H. Bork, *The Tempting of America: The Political Seduction of the Law* 143–86 (1990).

18. See discussion in chapters 2 and 4.

19. See, e.g., Marbury v. Madison, 5 U.S. (1 Cranch) 137 (1803) where the Court invalidated a congressional grant of original jurisdiction to the Supreme Court because the subject matter of the grant did not fall within the categories of cases to which the Court's original jurisdiction was extended in the text of Article III, Section 2, Clause 2 of the Constitution.

20. See generally chapters 2 and 3.

21. More recently, attacks on the validity of textualism have extended to the area of statutory construction. See, e.g., William N. Eskridge, Jr., "The New Textualism," 37 *UCLA L. Rev.* 621 (1990). In this area, however, there has been something of a protextualist resurgence. See, e.g., Frank H. Easterbrook, "Statute's Domain," 50 *U. Chi. L. Rev.* 533 (1983).

22. E.g., Peter Bachrach, "Interest, Participation and Democratic Theory, in Participation in Politics" 16 *Nomos* 39 1975) ("Democratic participation . . . is a process in which persons formulate, discuss and decide public issues that are important to them and directly affect their lives.").

23. See John Agresto, *The Supreme Court and Constitutional Democracy* 52–55 (1984).

24. Under Article III of the Constitution, federal judges are provided life terms during good behavior, and their salaries cannot be reduced. See, e.g., *The Federalist* No. 78, at 492 (Alexander Hamilton) (Benjamin F. Wright, ed. 1974) ("The interpretation of law is the proper and peculiar province of the courts. A constitution is, in fact, and must be regarded by judges, as fundamental law. It therefore belongs to them to ascertain its meaning. . . ."). I have explored the connection between judicial review and the judiciary's insulation from political pressure in previous writing. See Martin H. Redish, *The Federal Courts in the Political Order: Judicial Jurisdiction and American Political Theory* 75–85, 491 (1991). For that reason, the issue will not be considered in detail here.

25. See Marbury v. Madison, 5 U.S. (1 Cranch) 137, 176–80 (1803).

26. *The Federalist* No. 78, at 493 (Alexander Hamilton) (Benjamin F. Wright, ed. 1974).

27. U.S. Const. art. III, § 2.

28. To a great extent, this logic formed the basis for Chief Justice Marshall's adoption of the principle of judicial review in Marbury v. Madison, 5 U.S. (1 Cranch) 137 (1803). See generally Redish, supra note 24, at 75–80.

It might be responded that the British democratic system functions effectively absent an overriding power of judicial review, so that the necessity of the concept in our system is unestablished.00But our nation's founders consciously rejected the British system by choosing to adopt a formal, written, countermajoritarian constitution. The function of formally controlling the majoritarian branches by means of a written constitution would thus be undermined absent judicial review.

29. The analysis here does not consider here the legitimacy, as a matter of constitutional theory, of the Supreme Court's use of what Professor Bickel labelled the "passive virtues" as a means of avoiding politically or socially difficult issues of constitutional interpretation. See Alexander Bickel, "The Supreme Court, 1960 Term—Foreword: The Passive Virtues", 75 *Harv. L. Rev.* 40 (1961). The phrase refers to the resort to procedural doctrines of standing, ripeness, mootness, and political question as forms of camouflage to insulate the Court from difficult or sensitive substantive decision making. Professor Bickel's theory, however, has been perceptively attacked. See Gerald Gunther, "The Subtle Vices of the 'Passive Virtues'—A Comment on Principle and Expediency in Judicial Review," 64 *Colum. L. Rev.* 1 (1964). See generally Redish, supra note 24, at 97–100.

30. Robert W. Bennett, "Objectivity in Constitutional Law," 132 *U. Pa. L. Rev.* 445, 458 (1984) (footnote omitted).

31. Frederick Schauer, "An Essay on Constitutional Language," 29 *UCLA L. Rev.* 797, 828 (1982).

32. See generally H. Jefferson Powell, "The Original Understanding of Orignal Intent," 98 *Harv. L. Rev.* 885 (1985).

33. McCulloch v. Maryland, 17 U.S. (4 Wheat.) 316, 407 (1819) (Marshall, C.J.):

> A constitution, to contain an accurate detail of all the subdivisions of which its great powers will admit, and of all the means by which they may be carried into execution, would partake of the prolixity of a legal code, and could scarcely be embraced by the human mind. It would probably never be understood by the public. Its nature, therefore, requires, that only its great outlines should be marked, its important objects designated, and the minor ingredients which compose those objects be deduced from the nature of the objects themselves. That this idea was entertained by the framers of the American constitution, is not only to be inferred from the nature of the instrument, but from the language.

34. See the discussion in chapters 4 and 5, infra pp. 113–25; 155–57.

35. See, e.g., Paul Brest, "The Misconceived Quest for the Original Understanding," 60 *B.U.L. Rev.* 204 (1980); Thomas C. Grey, "Do We Have an Unwritten Constitution?," 27 *Stan. L. Rev.* 703 (1975).

36. See, e.g., Sanford Levinson, "Law As Literature," 60 Tex. L. Rev. 373 (1982).

37. See, e.g., Stanley Fish, *Is There a Text in This Class?* (1980). In Professor Fish's words, "[t]he objectivity of the text is an illusion and, moreover, a dangerous illusion, because it is so physically convincing." Id. at 327.

38. For a critical discussion of this theory, see Martin H. Redish & Karen L. Drizin, "Constitutional Federalism and Judicial Review: The Role of Textual Analysis," 62 *N.Y.U. L. Rev.* 1, 23–28 (1987).

39. See discussion supra pp. 7–9.

40. For an attack on the use of deconstructionism in legal interpretation, see Gerald Graff, "'Keep off the Grass,' 'Drop Dead,' and Other Indeterminacies: A Response to Sanford Levinson," 60 *Tex. L. Rev.* 405 (1982). Professor Graff argues that those advocating something approaching legal deconstructionism "begin[ ] with an unrealistic expectation about interpretation and then adopt[ ] an unnecessary skepticism when the expectation isn't met," and that such scholars have "merely

inverted the gesture of the interpretive absolutist, who insists that there is One True Meaning and that he alone possesses it." He concludes that "[t]he alternatives [suggested by the deconstructionists] are simply unreal." Id. at 410–11.

41. Brest, supra note 35.

42. Id. at 229. Because he endorses nonoriginalist adjudication, Brest views textualism as helpful but not binding on constitutional interpretation.

43. Id. at 225 (footnote omitted).

44. Id. (footnote omitted).

45. Id. at 225–26.

46. I should once again emphasize that I do not mean to suggest that interpretations of the Constitution may not change over time. Given the broad constitutional language and acceptance of the Constitution as a "living" document, such changes are not precluded. What is precluded, however, is abandonment of even the broadest rational construction of the text.

47. Brest, supra note 35, at 225.

48. See discussion in chapter 2, infra pp. 38–39.

49. This is a course of action that commentators have on occasion urged the Court to take. See, e.g., Suzanna Sherry, "The Founders' Unwritten Constitution," 54 *U. Chi. L. Rev.* 1127 (1987).

50. See, Choper, supra note 1, at 136–37.

51. The Supreme Court's appellate jurisdiction, unlike its original jurisdiction, is given "with such Exceptions and under such Regulations as the Congress shall make." U.S. Const. art. III, § 2, cl. 2.

52. See Martin H. Redish, "Congressional Power to Regulate Supreme Court Appellate Jurisdiction Under the Exceptions Clause: An Internal and External Examination," 27 *Vill. L. Rev.* 900, 925–27 (1982).

53. See id. at 902 nn.9–11 (describing the proposed legislation dealing with school prayer, abortion, and busing).

54. See, e.g., Paul M. Bator, "Congressional Power Over the Jurisdiction of the Federal Courts," 27 *Vill. L. Rev.* 1030, 1039 (1982) (emphasis in original):

> We should . . . not be embarrassed to take the position that Congress may have the authority to carve out subject matters and withdraw them from the Supreme Court's appellate jurisdiction, but should not do so, not only because they represent bad policy but because they violate the structure and spirit of the instrument.

55. See Choper, supra note 1, at 146.

56. See J. Carlson, *George C. Wallace and the Politics of Powerlessness* 127–30 (1981) (discussing role of "law and order" issues in American presidential campaigns); Richard Scammon & Ben Wattenberg, *The Real Majority* 17, 21, 37–39, 40–41, 180, 207–08 (1970) (same); Jules Witcover, *Marathon: The Pursuit of the Presidency, 1972–76,* at 100, 206–07, 549, 551, 564–65, 609, 647 (1977) (discussing role of abortion and church-state issues in presidential campaigns).

57. Brest, supra note 35, at 225–26.

58. Id. at 226.

59. At one point, Brest acknowledges that the conditions required for actual consent "perhaps can never be met in a large industrial society." Id.

60. See Bruce A. Ackerman, *We the People* 47–50 (1991); Bruce A. Ackerman, "Constitutional Politics/Constitutional Law," 99 *Yale L.J.* 453 (1989); Bruce A. Ackerman, "The Storrs Lecturers: Discovering the Constitution," 93 *Yale L.J.* 1013 (1984).

See also Cass R. Sunstein, "Constitutionalism After the New Deal,"101 *Harv. L. Rev.* 421, 448 (1987) (The New Deal "altered the constitutional system in ways so fundamental as to suggest that something akin to a constitutional amendment has taken place.").

61. U.S. Const. art. V. See Ackerman, "Constitutional Politics," supra note 60, at 491.

62. See Ackerman, "Constitutional Politics," supra note 60, at 456–61.

63. See, e.g., Dennis v. United States, 341 U.S. 494 (1951).

64. See generally Powell, supra note 32.

65. It is my position that much of the New Deal can survive a proper textual analysis of the Constitution. See chapter 6.

66. Five amendments have been either declared ratified or adopted in the post–New Deal period. On the other hand, numerous unsuccessful attempts to amend the Constitution—on such varied subjects as equal rights for women, abortion rights, school prayer, and busing to achieve integration—have also been made.

67. Ackerman, "Constitutional Politics," supra note 60, at 496. See also Coleman v. Miller, 307 U.S. 433, 449–50 (1939).

68. U.S. Const. amend. IX: "The enumeration in the Constitution, of certain rights, shall not be construed to deny or disparage others retained by the people."

69. U.S. Const. amend. XIV, § 1, cl. 2: "No State shall make or enforce any law which shall abridge the privileges or immunities of citizens of the United States . . . ."

70. I should emphasize, however, that I do not intend here necessarily to endorse the concept of unenumerated rights. The point is simply that the relevance of textualism to enforcement of the Constitution's structural provisions could be thought to present a question different from that concerning unenumerated individual rights.

71. See chapter 2.

72. See chapter 4.

73. See generally Choper, supra note 1.

74. See id. at 260–75. Choper argued that "the ultimate constitutional issues of whether executive action (or inaction) violates the prerogatives of Congress or whether legislative action transgresses the realm of the President should be held nonjusticiable, their final resolution to be remitted to the interplay of the national political process." Id. at 263.

75. See id. at 275 ("[T]he participation of the Supreme Court is unnecessary to police constitutional violations by one political department against the other.").

76. See, e.g., Erwin Chemerinsky, "Controlling Inherent Presidential Power: Providing a Framework for Judicial Review," 56 *S. Cal. L. Rev.* 863, 888 (1983); Thomas O. Sargentich, "The Contemporary Debate About Legislative-Executive Separation of Powers," 72 *Cornell L. Rev.* 430, 441–44 (1987).

77. U.S. Const. art. III, § 2, cl. 1.

78. See U.S. Const. art. III, § 1 (guaranteeing federal judges protection of their salary and tenure).

79. Of these, the most important were the guarantee of habeas corpus, U.S. Const. art. I, § 9, cl. 2; the prohibition of bills of attainder and ex post facto laws by the federal government, id. art. I, § 9, cl. 3; and by state government, id. art. I, § 10, cl. 1; and the prohibition on states' impairing the obligation of contract, id. art. I, § 10, cl. 1.

80. See generally *The Federalist* No. 39 (Benjamin F. Wright, ed. 1974).

81. See Choper, supra note 1, at 263.

82. Sargentich, supra note 76, at 442.
83. See id.
84. See Chemerinsky, supra note 76, at 888.
85. See id. These informal barriers may include:

[Congress may not want] to be viewed as disruptive; or Congresspersons may not want to embarrass the President, or Congress may want to score political points by attacking the executive's action rather than accepting political responsibility for some action itself; or Congresspersons may be busy running for reelection or tending to constituents' individual problems . . . ."

Paul Gewirtz, "The Courts, Congress, and Executive Policy-Making: Notes on Three Doctrines," *Law & Contemp. Probs.*, Summer 1976, at 46, 79.

86. See Choper, supra note 1, at 275; Sargentich, supra note 78, at 443.
87. See the discussion in chapter 4, infra pp. 99–100.
88. See Choper, supra note 1, at 169 (contending that the Court need not involve itself in federalism issues "because its activity there is unnecessary to effective preservation of the constitutional scheme").
89. Id. at 175.
90. Id. at 175–84. See Herbert Wechsler, "The Political Safeguards of Federalism: The Role of the States in the Composition and Selection of the National Government," 54 *Colum. L. Rev.* 543 (1954).
91. See Kenneth Stampp, *The Era of Reconstruction, 1865–77*, at 143–45 (1968).
92. See discussion in chapter 2, infra pp. 38–39.
93. Choper, supra note 1, at 242, 246–47.
94. Id. at 243.
95. See discussion in chapter 2, infra p. 44.
96. Choper, supra note 1, at 235–40.
97. See Redish, supra note 24, at 75–85.
98. Id. at 169. see Choper, supra note 1, at 169.
99. U.S. Const. art. V.
100. E.g., Roe v. Wade, 410 U.S. 113 (1973).
101. E.g., Engel v. Vitale, 370 U.S. 421 (1962).
102. E.g., North Carolina State Bd. of Educ. v. Swann, 402 U.S. 43 (1971).
103. E.g., Miranda v. Arizona, 348 U.S. 436 (1966).
104. See Brown, supra note 6, at 1513–17. See discussion in chapter 4, infra pp. 105–08.
105. Article III provides protections of judicial salary and tenure, see U.S. Const. art. III, § 1, designed to insulate federal judges from acute political pressures. See Martin H. Redish & Lawrence C. Marshall, "Adjudicatory Independence and the Values of Procedural Due Process," 95 *Yale L.J.* 455, 496–97 (1986).
106. See Redish, supra note 24 at 75–85.
107. See discussion infra at pp. 59–60; 111–13.
108. This is true of the so-called dormant Commerce Clause doctrine. See generally chapter 3.

Chapter 2

1. See, e.g., Hammer v. Dagenhart, 247 U.S. 251 (1918) (striking down congressional attempt to regulate child labor).

2. See, e.g., Wickard v. Filburn, 317 U.S. 111 (1942) (upholding application of federal quotas to production of wheat for domestic consumption); United States v. Darby, 312 U.S. 100 (1941) (upholding a federal labor law, finding Congress's intent to regulate local production irrelevant).

3. 426 U.S. 833 (1976) (Tenth Amendment prohibits application of federal minimum wage and overtime pay laws to state governments).

4. 469 U.S. 528 (1985) (state interests more protected by representational protections inherent in federal system than by substantive limits on federal power).

"Flip-flopped" may be somewhat misleading because it suggests that nothing happened during the nine years between *National League of Cities* and *Garcia*. In fact, during that period the Court struggled to apply the *National League of Cities* test. See, e.g., Equal Employment Opportunities Comm'n v. Wyoming, 460 U.S. 226 (1983) (upholding extension of age discrimination legislation to state and local government employers as valid exercise of commerce power not precluded by Tenth Amendment); United Transp. Union v. Long Island R.R. Co., 455 U.S. 678 (1982) (upholding application of federal law to state-owned railroad, stressing that operation of railroads is not traditional function of state and local governments).

5. *Garcia*, 469 U.S. at 550–51 and 551 n.11 (citing Jesse Choper, *Judicial Review and the National Political Process* 175–84 (1980); Herbert Wechsler, "The Political Safeguards of Federalism: The Role of the States in the Composition and Selection of the National Government," 54 *Colum. L. Rev.* 543 (1954)).

6. 112 S. Ct. 2408 (1992).

7. See, e.g., D. Bruce La Pierre, "The Political Safeguards of Federalism Redux: Intergovernmental Immunity and the States as Agents of the Nation," 60 *Wash. U. L.Q.* 779 (1982).

8. See discussion infra pp. 43–48.

9. See the discussion in chapter 1, supra pp. 16–20; see also infra pp. 48–49.

10. See U.S. Const. art. I, § 8.

[1] The Congress shall have Power To lay and collect Taxes, Duties, Imposts and Excises, to pay the Debts and provide for the common Defence and general Welfare of the United States; but all Duties, Imposts and Excises shall be uniform throughout the United States; [2] To borrow money on the credit of the United States; [3] To regulate Commerce with foreign Nations, and among the several States, and with the Indian Tribes; [4] To establish an uniform Rule of Naturalization, and uniform Laws on the subject of Bankruptcies throughout the United States; [5] To coin Money, regulate the Value thereof, and of foreign Coin, and fix the Standard of Weights and Measures; [6] To provide the Punishment of counterfeiting the Securities and current Coin of the United States; [7] To establish Post Offices and post Roads; [8] To promote the Progress of Science and useful Arts, by securing for limited Times to Authors and Inventors the exclusive Right to their respective Writings and Discoveries; [9] To constitute Tribunals inferior to the supreme Court; [10] To define and punish Piracies and Felonies committed on the high Seas, and Offenses against the Law of Nations; [11] To declare War, grant Letters of Marque and Reprisal, and make Rules concerning Captures on Land and Water; [12] To raise and support Armies, but no Appropriation of Money to that Use shall be for a longer Term than two Years; [13] To provide and maintain a Navy; [14] To make Rules for the Government and Regulation of the land and naval Forces; [15] To provide for calling forth the Militia to execute the Laws of the Union, suppress insurrections and repel Invasions; [16] To provide for organizing, arming,

and disciplining, the Militia, and for governing such Part of them as may be employed in the Service of the United States, reserving to the States respectively, the Appointment of the Officers, and the Authority of training the Militia according to the discipline prescribed by Congress; [17] To exercise exclusive Legislation in all Cases whatsoever, over such District (not exceeding ten Miles square) as may, by Cession of particular States, and the Acceptance of Congress, become the Seat of the Government of the United States, and to exercise like Authority over all Places purchased by the Consent of the Legislature of the State in which the Same shall be, for the Erection of Forts, Magazines, Arsenals, dock-Yards, and other needful Buildings;-And [18] To make all Laws which shall be necessary and proper for carrying into Execution the foregoing Powers, and all other Powers vested by this Constitution in the Government of the United States, or in any Department or Officer thereof.

11. See the discussion in chapter 1, supra pp. 7–16.

12. See, e.g., Wickard v. Filburn, 317 U.S. 111 (1942); United States v. Darby, 312 U.S. 100 (1941); discussion infra pp. 49–59.

13. See discussion infra pp. 49–59.

14. Clark Carey, *The Rise of a New Federalism* 4 (1938).

15. Daniel Elazar, *The American Partnership* 22 (1962).

16. Edward S. Corwin, "The Passing of Dual Federalism", 36 *Va. L. Rev.* 4 (1950).

17. Alpheus Mason, "Federalism: The Role of the Court", in *Federalism: Infinite Variety in Theory and Practice* 24–25 (Valerie A. Earle ed. 1968).

18. Corwin, supra note 16 at 19 (emphasis omitted).

19. Carey, supra note 14, at 10.

20. Morton Grodzins, "Centralization and Decentralization in the American Federal System," in *A Nation of States* (Robert A. Goldwin ed., 1963). Professor Grodzins, it should be noted, was one of the modern theoretical pioneers of the concept of cooperative federalism. See Richard Leach, *American Federalism* 14 (1970).

21. Leach, supra note 20, at 15.

22. As will be seen below, my view is that, at least in their rigid form, neither theory represents an accurate characterization, either as a descriptive or normative matter, of American federalism. See discussion infra pp. 27–30.

23. See discussion supra p. 26.

24. Historian Harry Scheiber, for example, associates cooperative federalism with "[i]ncreases in both the extent and intensity of federal regulation." Harry Scheiber, "Federalism and Legal Process: Historical and Contemporary Analysis of the American System", 14 *Law & Soc'y Rev.* 663, 680 (1980). Professor Corwin similarly believed that the passing of dual federalism necessarily portended an effective abandonment of state automony in favor of heavily dominant national power:

> In the process of remolding the Federal System . . . the instrument has been overwhelmed and submerged in the objection sought, so that today the question faces us whether the constituent States of the System Can be saved for any useful purpose, and thereby saved as the vital cells that they have been heretofore of democratic sentiment, impulse, and action.

Corwin, supra note 16, at 23.

25. See Elazar, supra note 15, at 324, where he states:

[W]herever strict adherence to the separatist theory of federalism was maintained in a major area of governmental concern, there followed a centralization of power in the hands of the federal government because no smaller
unit of government could properly deal with the problems that arose. In
most cases, however, the desire for local control over the effects of government locally, coupled with a realization of the need for some type of participation on the part of the federal government (usually fiscal or standard-
setting), led to the emergence of a federalism based on the sharing principle.

Professor Grodzins argued that a formal division of state and federal functions "would
probably result in putting virtually all functions in the hands of the national government." Grodzins, supra note 20, at 15.

26. See, e.g., Grodzins, supra note 20, at 19 ("[T]he national government steps in
as an emulator when the states produce useful innovations, making national programs
of state successes.").

27. Cf. Daniel Elazar, "Federalism and Intergovernmental Relations", in *Cooperation and Conflict* 11 (1969) ("[M]uch of the sharing among [federal and state]
governments is . . . through conferences, the provision of advisory and training
services, the exchange of general services, the lending of equipment and personnel,
and the performance of services by one government in place of another.").

28. Richard Stewart, "Pyramids of Sacrifice? Problems of Federalism in Mandating State Implementation of National Environmental Policy," 86 *Yale L.J.* 1196, 1201
(1977). Professor Stewart notes:

Often federal air and water pollution control statutes give the states initial
responsibility (subject to federal review and "backup" enforcement) for
achieving federal objectives. In other instances, the EPA is authorized to
delegate certain of its own implementation and enforcement respon-
sibilities, an option which overburdened federal officials have readily utilized. Even where no formal delegation has occurred, the EPA in practice
relies heavily upon the cooperation of state officials.

Id. (footnotes omitted).

29. See Elazar, supra note 15, at 330 ("Under a co-operative arrangement, neither side of the partnership could work its will unopposed to cripple or destroy the
other or the interests represented by the other.") Professor Elazar suggests that
cooperative federalism "was as much a vehicle by which the enlightened champion of
states' rights might strengthen the states by giving them more to do and more power
with which to do it, as it was a vehicle by which the nationalist might secure programs
that covered the entire Union." Id. at 328.

30. The term is employed by Professor Wildavsky. Aaron Wildavsky, "Birthday
Cake Federalism," in *American Federalism: A New Partnership for the Republic* 185
(Robert B. Hawkins ed., 1982).

31. See, e.g., Wickard v. Filburn, 317 U.S. 111, 128–29 (1942) (federal regulation
of wheat intended for consumption on the farm is within the power conferred by the
Commerce Clause); United States v. Darby, 312 U.S. 100 (1941) (Commerce Clause
justifies Congress's prohibition of interstate shipment of goods produced under sub-
standard labor conditions). See discussion infra pp. 52–53.

32. See, e.g., Heart of Atlanta Motel, Inc., v. United States, 379 U.S. 241, 258
(1964) (Title II of Civil Rights Act of 1964 is a valid exercise of Congress's commerce
power as applied to hotels and restaurants serving interstate travelers). See discussion
infra pp. 52–53.

33. See chapter 3.

34. Compare Goldstein v. California, 412 U.S. 546, 560–61 (1973) (state copyright statute not void because of unlimited duration, even though power of Congress to grant copyrights is subject to durational limitation) with Sears, Roebuck & Co., v. Stiffel Co. 376 U.S. 225, 231 (1964) (state cannot give unfair competition protection of a kind that clashes with the objectives of federal patent laws).

35. See discussion infra pp. 33–38.

36. I employ the term "interactive" federalism with some trepidation, in light of one commentator's observation that "[a]mong groups of scholars, federal theorists have been particularly prone to use ostensible crude, nonmathematical, frequently metaphorical conceptualizations to label changes in governmental roles." William Stewart, "Metaphors, Models, and the Development of Federal Theory," *Publius*, Spring 1982, at 5. Nevertheless, I believe the "interactive" label, used as a contrast to the dual model, communicates a basic tone that pervades modern federalism.

I should also note that according to Professor Scheiber, there are presently forty-four descriptions or labels of federalism in use by modern scholars. Scheiber, supra note 24, at 669 n.2. They do not, however, include the term "interactive."

37. See generally Elazar, supra note 15; Leach, supra note 20.

38. Cf. Carl Friedrich, *Trends of Federalism in Theory and Practice* 7 (1968):

[I]t is possible to define federalism and federal relations in dynamic terms. . . . [F]ederalism should not be seen only as a static pattern or design, characterized by a particular and precisely fixed division of powers between government levels. Federalism is also and perhaps primarily the process of federalizing a political community, that is to say, the process by which a number of separate political communities enter into arrangements for working out solutions, adopting joint policies, and making joint decisions on joint problems. . . .

39. It is true that in Gibbons v. Ogden, 22 U.S. (9 Wheat.) 1 (1824), Chief Justice Marshall hinted that the grant to Congress of power to regulate interstate commerce excluded state authority to do so. He recognized, however, the equivalent of inherent state "police power" to preserve state health and safety. Since "a state law may regulate health and safety and yet also regulate or affect commerce among the states," John Nowak & Ronald Rotunda, *Constitutional Law* 227 (4th ed. 1991), in effect Marshall was recognizing an overlapping state and federal power to regulate interstate commerce, power that continues to be recognized—within constitutionally derived limits—to this day. See chapter 3.

40. Cf. William Anderson, *The Nation and the States, Rivals or Partners?* 19–20 (1955):

Some [public functions] are performed almost entirely by the units in a single level [of government]. Examples at the local level are the furnishing of fire protection and water supplies in cities and villages and the operation of primary and secondary education . . . in the various types of local school districts. Centered almost entirely at the state level we find the regulation of insurance companies and the licensing of professions. The national government . . . has the sole responsibility for national defense.

Far more numerous, however, are the functions in which there is a joint interest and a sharing or division of responsibility between two or three levels of government.

41. See discussion infra pp. 38–59.

42. See Corwin, supra note 16, at 19 (modern cooperative federalism has

emerged from the original competitive federalism); Scheiber, supra note 24, at 681 ("Many areas of policy for which state and local government were responsible before 1933 have now become strongly centralized.").

43. See supra note 38.

44. It is, of course, conceivable that modern departures from historical conceptions of federalism could violate one or more constitutional provisions. But it does not appear that the concept of "interactive" federalism was in any sense constitutionally prohibited. See discussion infra pp. 38–59.

45. Friedrich, supra note 38, at 14.

46. According to Professor Leach:

> [W]hile there is no doubt that the framers visualized two levels of government, each exercising power over the nation's affairs at the same time, they failed to make clear what should be the precise relationship between them or how either level might relate to local and private sources of power.

Leach, supra note 20, at 8. Moreover, he notes:

> Though . . . the stage was set for a lengthy and revealing debate on federalism, in fact such a debate did not materialize. Instead, the energies of the Convention were devoted to solving the problem of reconstituting Congress . . . and it never came back again to the question of the nature of the federalism. In the end, the Constitution emerged with no real clues as to what was in the framers' minds as they voted on the several resolutions before them or how they expected the federal system they had brought into being to work in practice.

Id. at 7. According to another scholar:

> No great debate . . . occurred in the Convention on the nature of federalism. How could it? The bundle of critical decisions that established federalism were made in an ad hoc fashion and their overall significance probably was not appreciated until must later, though Madison's expositions in *The Federalist,* and to a lesser extent Hamilton's reveal considerable awareness of what had been wrought in Philadelphia.

David Walker, *Toward a Functioning Federalist* 40 (1981). Professor Walker adds: "Little overt attention was given to intergovernmental relations as such either in the Convention debates or *The Federalist.*" Id. at 41. See also Gordon Wood, *The Creation of the American Republic, 1776–1787,* at 525 (1969) ("as crucial as the idea of federalism was to the Federalists in explaining the operation of their new system, it seems clear that few of them actually conceived of it in full before the Constitution was written and debated). Wood observes that "[a]s late as the spring of 1787 Madison . . . showed little comprehension of a political system in which the national and state governments would coexist as equal partners." Id.

47. K. C. Wheare, *Federal Government* 1 (4th ed. 1963) (footnote omitted).

48. See discussion infra pp. 48–59.

49. Cf. Elazar, supra note 15, at 308: "Just as the founding fathers did not perceive the future role of political parties in the United States, they also appear not to have planned for the development of co-operative federalism as we know it." While Professor Elazar notes that "[t]he document does make explicit provision for some intergovernmental co-operation in several important fields as varied as national defense, conduct of elections, and standards of measurement," he adds that "[m]ost sections . . . do not clearly indicate whether the powers of the two levels of government are to be exclusive or concurrent, leaving the matter open to interpretation." Id.

50. See discussion infra at pp. 49–59.

51. U.S. Const. art. I, § 10:

> No State shall enter into any treaty, alliance, or confederation; grant Letters of Marque and Appraisal; coin money; emit Bills of Credit; make anything but gold and silver coin a tender in payment of debts; pass any bill of attainder, ex post facto law, or law impairing the obligation of contracts, or grant any title of nobility.
>
> No State shall, without the Consent of the Congress, lay any Imposts or Duties on Imports or Exports, except what may be absolutely necessary for executing its inspection Laws: and the net Produce of all Duties and Imposts, laid by any State on Imports or Exports, shall be for the Use of the Treasury of the United States; and all such Laws shall be subject to the Revision and Control of the Congress.
>
> No State shall, without the Consent of Congress, lay any Duty of Tonnage, keep Troops, or Ships of War in Time of Peace, enter into any Agreement or Compact with another State, or with a foreign Power, or engage in War, unless actually invaded, or in such imminent Danger as will not admit of delay.

52. See discussion infra p. 49.

53. See supra note 51.

54. See Martin H. Redish, "Congressional Power to Limit Supreme Court Appellate Jurisdiction Under the Exceptions Clause: An Internal and External Examination," 27 *Vill. L. Rev.* 900 (1982).

55. Harry Scheiber, "American Federalism and the Diffusion of Power: Historical and Contemporary Perspectives," 9 *U. Tol. L. Rev.* 619, 626 (1978) (quoting *The Federalist* No. 46 at 311 (James Madison) (Jacob E. Cooke ed., 1961)).

56. *The Federalist* No. 46, at 331 (James Madison) (Jacob E. Cooke ed., 1961).

57. Madison noted that "[t]he prepossessions, which the members themselves will carry into the federal government will generally be favorable to the States." Id.

58. Scheiber, supra note 55, at 626 (quoting *The Federalist* No. 46, at 330 (James Madison) (Jacob E. Cooke ed., 1961)).

59. For example:

> The Federal and State governments are in fact but different agents and trustees of the people, constituted with different powers and designed for different purposes. The adversaries of the Constitution seem to have lost sight of the people altogether in their reasoning on this subject; and to have viewed these different establishments not only as mutual rivals and enemies, but as uncontrolled by any common superior in their efforts to usurp the authorities of each other.

The Federalist No. 46, supra note 55, at 330.

In fact, according to Gordon Wood, in 1787 Madison's view "was not the federalism of 1788, but . . . rather 'a due supremacy of the national authority' with 'the local authorities' left to exist only in 'so far as they can be subordinately useful.'" Wood, supra note 46, at 525. Wood notes:

> But Madison and James Wilson fought hard in the Convention to prevent both equal representation of the states in the Senate and elimination of the congressional veto of all state laws that Congress deemed unjust and unconstitutional. Both proportional representation and the congressional veto, they believed, would deny any recognition of state sovereignty in the Constitution, and thus prevent a reversion to the evils of the Confederacy.

Id. at 525–26.

60. *The Federalist* No. 46, supra note 56, at 330.

61. See Wood, supra note 46, at 529 (statement of Edmund Pendleton).

62. Id. at 529.

63. Id. at 530–32 (people are the "fountain of all power").

64. One illustrative example cited by Wood occurred at the Virginia ratification convention. Anti-Federalist Patrick Henry

> would not leave the issue of federal taxing power alone and continually denied the possibility of concurrent justification between the states and the national government. Without effect Madison argued that the tax collections between the general government and the states would be similar to those between the states and the various counties and petty corporations within their boundaries. "The comparison," retorted Henry, "will not stand examination." The taxes collected within the state, whether from the state, county, or parish level, all "radiate from the same center. They are not coequal or coextensive. There is no clashing of power between them. Each is limited to its own particular objects, and all subordinate to one supreme, controlling power—the legislature." All right, answered Madison. If there had to be one supreme, controlling power over the tax collections of the general and state governments, then one could be found. "To make use of the gentleman's own terms, the concurrent collections under the authorities of the general government and state governments all radiate from the people at large. The people is their common superior."

Id. at 531–32 (footnote omitted).

65. Professor Scheiber states that "most contemporary scholarship on federalism seems to have moved to the ground held all along by historians and legal scholars: acceptance of the historical reality of dual federalism. Even some prominent political scientists aligned with the Grodzins-Elazar school on ideological questions seem ready to dissent on issues historical." Scheiber, supra note 55, at 677.

66. See, e.g., Elazar, supra note 15, at 304:

> Despite a theory which held that the federal system functioned best when each plane was functionally as well as structurally separate, the necessity of shared interests and publics led to substantial intergovernmental cooperation in those fields where governments were active throughout the nineteenth century. The federal governments, the states, and the localities cooperated in developing educational systems; in constructing roads, canals and railroads; in creating rudimentary public welfare institutions; in providing for the common defense; in maintaining a national financial system; and in numerous other ways after 1790.

Id. See also Daniel Elazar, *American Federalism: A View from the States* 51 (3d ed. 1984) (since 1796, virtually all possible restrictions on joint state-federal action have been eliminated). According to another commentator:

> "[D]ual federalism" was a marvelous invention which offered reassurance to contending partisans that they could have the best of both worlds. . . .
> But the price of the invention was a conception of intergovernmental relations which diverges from the data. Theory dominated interpretation of the data and federal tasks were sharply distinguished from state tasks, despite abundant evidence that in the 19th century, functions were shared. The gap between theory and practice contributed to the conceptual confusion surrounding the American theory of federalism.

David J. Rothman, "The Ambiguity of American Federal Theory," *Publius*, Summer 1983, at 303, 313 (footnote omitted).

67. The Supreme Court has noted:

[T]he States have been able to direct a substantial proportion of federal revenues into their own treasuries in the form of general and program-specific grants in aid. The federal role in assisting state and local governments is a longstanding one; Congress provided federal land grants to finance state governments from the beginning of the Republic, and direct cash grants were awarded as early as 1887 under the Hatch Act.

Garcia v. San Antonio Metro. Transit Auth., 469 U.S. 528, 552 (1985) (footnote omitted). It should be noted, however, that this fact does not necessarily imply that the Court need play no role in enforcing the constitutional protection of federalism. See discussion infra pp. 48–59.

68. See discussion supra p. 31.

69. One commentator has observed that "[d]espite the Marshall Court's resounding affirmation of the breadth of the powers conferred on the national government, the use made of these powers through the first century of our history under the Constitution was restrained." Henry J. Friendly, "Federalism: A Foreword," 86 *Yale L.J.* 1019, 1020 (1977) (footnote omitted).

70. See discussion infra pp. 51–59.

71. As Professor Elazar has noted, "In the years since the establishment of the Republic, intergovernmental collaboration has expanded along with the growth in the velocity of government to include virtually every governmental function." Elazar, *American Federalism,* supra note 66, at 51.

No one appears to dispute the substantial expansion of state-federal involvement in the twentieth century. See, e.g., Walker, supra note 46, at 65. The Supreme Court noted in *Garcia,* "In the past quarter-century alone, federal grants to States and localities have grown from $7 billion to $96 billion. . . . The States have obtained federal funding for such services as police and fire protection, education, public health and hospitals, parks and recreation, and sanitation." Garcia v. San Antonio Metro. Transit Auth., 469 U.S. at 552–53 (1985) (footnotes omitted). For a detailed description and analysis of existing forms of intergovernmental sharing, see Elazar *American Federalism,* supra note 66, at 74–80.

72. See, e.g., Robert C. Welsh, "Reconsidering the Constitutional Relationship Between State and Federal Courts: A Critique of *Michigan v. Long,*" 59 *N. Dame L. Rev.* 1118 (1984).

73. 401 U.S. 37 (1971). In his opinion for the Court, Justice Black emphasized the need to recognize that "the entire country is made up of a Union of separate state governments," and that "the National Government will fare best if the States and their institutions are left free to perform their separate functions in their separate ways." Id. at 44.

74. See Scheiber, supra note 24, at 684–85 (Court has invoked federalism to reduce federal court oversight of state court procedure).

75. The *Younger* doctrine is designed in large part to avoid the "unseemly failure to give effects to the principle that state courts have the solemn responsibility, equally with the federal courts 'to guard, enforce, and protect every right granted or secured by the [C]onstitution of the United States.'" Steffel v. Thompson, 415 U.S. 452, 460–61 (1974). See generally Martin H. Redish, "*Younger v. Harris:* Deference in Search of a Rationale," 63 *Cornell L. Rev.* 463 (1978) (discussion of alternative bases, as suggested by the Court, for limiting the injunctive power of federal courts).

76. Scheiber, supra note 55, at 624.

77. See Redish, supra note 75, at 468–72 (discussion of the need for federal courts to avoid interference with substantive state legislative goals).

78. See *Younger*, 401 U.S. at 49 (defendant has adequate opportunity to raise his constitutional claims in the state court proceedings).

79. Paul M. Bator et al., *Hart & Wechsler's The Federal Courts and the Federal System* 384 (3d ed. 1988). [hereinafter cited as Hart & Wechsler]. See Martin H. Redish & Curtis Woods, "Congressional Power to Control the Jurisdiction of Lower Federal Courts: A Critical Review and a New Synthesis," 124 *U. Pa. L. Rev.* 45, 52–56 (1975) (discussion of Madisonian Compromise as based on the assumption that state courts could provide adequate federal remedies).

80. The Constitution provides: "The judicial power of the United States shall be vested in one supreme Court, and in such inferior courts as the Congress may from time to time ordain and establish." U.S. Const. art. III, § 1. It should be noted that certain modern scholars reject the understanding that the Framers intended to leave to congressional discretion the decision whether to create lower federal courts. See, e.g., Lawrence G. Sager, "The Supreme Court 1980 Term—Foreword: Constitutional Limitations on Congress' Authority to Regulate the Jurisdiction of the Federal Courts," 95 *Harv. L. Rev.* 17 (1981) (discussing reasoned claims that lower federal courts are a constitutional necessity). This is a position which, at least as a historical matter, I reject. See Martin H. Redish, "Constitutional Limitations on Congressional Power to Control Federal Jurisdiction: A Reaction to Professor Sager," 77 *Nw. U. L. Rev.* 143 (1982). Note, however, that as a general matter even those scholars who believe that Congress was obligated by Article III to create lower federal courts do not deny Congress's power simultaneously to rely upon state courts for adjudication and enforcement of federal law.

81. The Supremacy Clause provides:

> This Constitution, and the Laws of the United States which shall be made . . . under the Authority of the United States, shall be the supreme Law of the Land; and the judges in every State shall be bound thereby, any Thing in the Constitution or Laws of any State to the contrary notwithstanding.

U.S. Const. art. VI, cl. 2.

82. See Martin v. Hunter's Lessee, 14 U.S., (1 Wheat.) 304, 331 (1816) (Constitution extends state court jurisdiction to issues of federal law).

83. Henry M. Hart, Jr., "The Power of Congress to Limit the Jurisdiction of Federal Courts: An Exercise in Dialectic," 66 *Harv. L. Rev.* 1362, 1401 (1953).

84. 93 U.S. 130 (1876).

85. See Martin H. Redish, *Federal Jurisdiction: Tensions in the Allocation of Judicial Power* 149–56 (2d ed. 1990).

86. See Charles Dowd Box Co. v. Courtney, 368 U.S. 502, 507 (1962) (ruling that "nothing in the concept of our federal system prevents state courts from enforcing rights created by federal law").

87. 330 U.S. 386 (1946).

88. See Redish, supra note 85, at 169–78 (general discussion of the valid excuse doctrine and criticism of a portion of it).

89. Welsh contended that "there is little evidence to support [the assertion] that the Constitution vested state courts to hear suits arising directly under federal law." Welsh, supra note 72, at 1137 (footnote omitted).

90. 463 U.S. 1032 (1983).

91. See Welsh, supra note 72 at 1124.

92. See id. at 1133–38 (discussion of debate at the Constitutional Convention).

93. See id. at 1138–41 (discussing Ableman v. Booth, 62 U.S. (21 How.) 506 (1858)).

94. See id. at 1143.

95. Id. at 1134

96. See id. at 1134–35.

97. According to Judge Gibbons:

> [I]n the beginning, our republic survived with a national judiciary which, by today's standards, amounted to very little. The Judiciary Act of 1789 provided for few places for holding court and fewer federal judges authorized to exercise original jurisdiction. Even the Supreme Court's appellate jurisdiction over state courts was limited to what was considered the bare minimum essential for the preservation of the supremacy of national law.

John J. Gibbons, "Federal Law and the State Courts 1790–1860," 36 *Rutgers L. Rev.* 394, 394 (1984). He also notes that "[t]he minimal resort to federal courts of original jurisdiction undoubtedly reflected hostility among opponents of the Constitution to the very existence of federal courts." Id. at 399–400.

98. Judiciary Act of 1875, 18 Stat. 470.

99. Welsh relies in part upon the debates in the first Congress over the creation of lower federal courts. He notes that during the course of the debates,"[t]he familiar arguments appeared again. The anti-Federalists contended that an independent federal judiciary threatened state autonomy. The Federalists countered that state courts could not be trusted to vindicate national interests." Welsh, supra note 72, at 1136. Professor Welsh apparently does not see how this evidence seriously undermines his position. If, as he argues, in adopting Article III the Framers did not assume that state courts could perform all the functions of lower federal courts, why should the first Congress have debated the issue so strenuously? Why did they not understand that, under the recently adopted Constitution, the state courts could not exercise such power? In fact, the existence of these early congressional debates confirms the traditionally held view of Article III—that the Framers chose to leave the allocation of judicial power between state and federal courts to congressional discretion.

100. Id. at 1137.

101. Id. at 1137–38 (footnote omitted).

102. Id. at 1135.

103. Welsh argues:

> The provision for concurrent jurisdiction . . . does not support the . . . thesis of state and federal court equivalence. The First Congress never claimed the power to alter or enlarge the jurisdiction of state tribunals. Instead, these jurisdictional provisions only indicated that federal law did not preclude state courts from hearing federal claims if state law granted jurisdiction over such claims. . . . Thus, the First Congress realized that determining the actual scope of state court jurisdiction was ultimately a matter of state rather than federal law.

Id at 1137. Today, however, it is clear that state courts do not have such discretion in declining to enforce federal law. Instead, to decline to adjudicate a federal claim a state court must meet the requirements of a narrow "valid excuse" doctrine developed by the Supreme Court. See Testa v. Katt, 330 U.S. 386, 392 (1947) (failure to adjudicate case involving federal "penal" statute as contrary to state policy is not a "valid excuse"); Mondou v. New York, N.H. & H.R.R., 223 U.S. 1, 58 (1912); Redish, supra note 85, at 169–78 (discussion of state court requirements to hear federal claims). Moreover, it is unlikely that the first Congress would have agreed with Welsh's historical description, in light of the fact that Congress had vested so little of the federal judicial power in the lower federal courts. If state courts could have chosen, at will, to decline to adjudicate federal claims, it is likely that in many cases no trial forum would have been available to vindicate federal law.

In any event, it is difficult to see any significance in this fact, even if Welsh's assertions are correct. That the state courts might not be obligated to adjudicate federal claims would seem to be irrelevant to the question of whether they exercise the federal power when they do adjudicate such claims.

104. 62 U.S. (21 How.) 506 (1858).

105. 80 U.S. (13 Wall.) 397 (19871). In *Tarble,* the Court extended the holding of *Ableman* to a writ of habeas corpus issued to a federal military officer concerning the detention of an allegedly underage enlistee. See Redish & Woods, supra note 79, at 84–88 (discussion of *Tarble*).

106. *Ableman,* 62 U.S. at 515–16.

107. See, e.g., Hart & Wechsler, supra note 79, at 488–92 (discussion of and questions concerning holding in *Tarble*).

108. Gibbons, supra note 97, at 447.

109. See discussion supra p. 27.

110. See Redish, supra note 85, at 157–61 (discussion of presumptions of congressional intent in *Tarble*); Redish & Woods, supra note 79, at 93–108 (discussion of current validity of *Tarble* and its relation to congressional authority over lower federal court jurisdiction).

111. See, e.g., Redish, supra note 85 at 1–4 (changes in philosophy of federalism preclude interchanging federal and state courts as enforcers of federal rights); Id., at 483–84 (institutional factors may affect ability of state courts to protect federal rights with the same vigor as federal courts).

112. 330 U.S. 386 (1947).

113. See discussion supra p. 29.

114. Judge Gibbons notes, for example:

> [T]he significance of *Abelman* [sic]*v. Booth* lies in the Court's appreciation of the extent to which the state courts could, by ordering habeas corpus release of alleged fugitive slaves, effectively frustrate the enormous federal apparatus dedicated to their apprehension, which had been adopted as national policy in the Fugitive Slave Act of 1850.

Gibbons, supra note 97, at 447 (footnote omitted).

115. See discussion infra pp. 37–38.

116. See, e.g., Younger v. Harris, 401 U.S. 37 (1971).

117. See Burt Neuborne, "The Myth of Parity," 90 *Harv. L. Rev.* 1105 (1977) (criticism of assumption that state and federal courts are equally competent to protect federal rights); Martin H. Redish and Lawrence C. Marshall, "Adjudicatory Independence and the Values of Procedural Due Process," 95 *Yale L. J.* 455, 496 (1986) (discussing possible state governmental influences over state judges).

118. See Mitchum v. Foster, 407 U.S. 225, 238–42 (1972).

119. See generally Martin H. Redish, "Abstention, Separation of Powers and the Limits of the Judicial Function," 94 *Yale L.J.* 71 (1984).

120. Welsh, supra note 72, at 1124.

121. See 28 U.S.C. § 1332.

122. Until the decision in Erie R.R. v. Tompkins, 304 U.S. 64 (1938), the doc-

trine of Swift v. Tyson, 41 U.S. (16 Pet.) 1 (1942), required the federal courts in many diversity cases to develop their own common law. Even under *Swift,* however, federal courts sitting in diversity were bound by state statutes, and, in some cases, even by state common law.

123. Judge Skelly Wright, for example, referred to the "healthful interplay between federal and state judicial establishments" as an accomplishment of the diversity jurisdiction. "In truth," he adds, "each of the systems often has vital lessons to confer on the other." J. Skelly Wright, "The Federal Courts and the Nature and Quality of State Law," 13 *Wayne L. Rev.* 317, 327 (1967).

124. See, e.g., Comment, "The Role of Federal Courts in Changing State Law: The Employment at Will Doctrine in Pennsylvania," 133 *U. Pa. L. Rev.* 227, 234 (1984) (federal courts should participate in reforming state law by noting new developments and trends in analogous cases).

125. See 28 U.S.C. § 1367; Mine Workers v. Gibbs, 383 U.S. 715, 732–35 (1966) (discussion of state law of contractual interference in connection with plaintiff's federal claim under the Labor Management Relations Act); Moore v. New York Cotton Exch., 270 U.S. 593, 605–07 (1926) (discussion of contract law in connection with ancillary jurisdiction over defendants' counterclaim).

126. John Frank has observed:

> The success of the federal rules [of civil procedure] has led to their widespread emulation in the states, and the federally sponsored process of continued revision is keeping state procedure moving as well. This process is of tremendous importance because the necessary spade work on procedural studies may require national attention and national subsidization. . . . And interaction is by no means a one-way street. The present practice encourages the federal system to borrow state improvements and experiments. Many of the recent changes in federal procedure came from the states.

John Frank, "For Maintaining Diversity Jurisdiction," 73 *Yale L.J.* 7, 11 (1963).

127. See chapter 1, supra pp. 7–10.

128. U.S. Const. art. I, § 8, cl. 3

129. U.S. Const. art. I, § 8, cl. 18.

130. 426 U.S. 833 (1976) (Rehnquist, J.).

131. Pub. L. No. 93-259, 88 Stat. 55 (1974).

132. Fair Labor Standards Act of 1938, 52 Stat. 1060 (codified as amended at 29 U.S.C. §§ 201–19 (1982)).

133. *National League of Cities,* 426 U.S. at 840–41.

134. Id. at 845.

135. Id.

136. Id. at 852, n.17 (citing U.S. Const. art. I, § 8, cl. 1). It is difficult to understand why Congress would be interfering with state sovereignty any less if it passed the very same legislation under a different grant of national authority. Courts have asserted, however, that when Congress initiates legislation under the spending power, states' choices are respected because states can opt out of such programs. See, e.g., Montgomery County v. Califano, 449 F. Supp. 1230 (D. Md. 1978); North Carolina v. Califano, 445 F. Supp. 532 (E.D.N.C. 1977), aff'd mem., 435 U.S. 962 (1978); Goodin v. Oklahoma, 436 F. Supp. 583 (W.D. Okla. 1977). But see Lewis B. Kaden, "Politics, Money, and State Sovereignty: The Judicial Role," 79 *Colum. L. Rev.* 847, 896 (1979) (states no longer have a realistic choice to opt out of federal

programs). See generally La Pierre, supra note 7, at 838–60 (describing federal grants to states).

137. 426 U.S. at 856 (Blackmun, J., concurring). The Court subsequently incorporated the balancing approach into a four-prong test to determine whether federal legislation was invalid under *National League of Cities.* Hodel v. Virginia Surface Mining & Reclamation Ass'n, 452 U.S. 264, 287–88 & 288 n.29 (1981) (challenged statute must regulate "the States as States," federal regulation must address "matters that are indisputably 'attributes of state sovereignty,'" states' compliance would "directly impair their ability 'to structure integral operations in areas of traditional government functions,'" and relation of state and federal interests must not be such that "the nature of the federal interest . . . justifies state submission").

138. 469 U.S. 528 (1985).

139. Id. at 531, 539, 546–47.

140. Id. at 531.

141. Id. at 552.

142. Id.

143. Id. at 554.

144. See id. at 554–55.

145. Id. at 550–51.

146. Id. at 554 (citation omitted).

147. Id. at 556.

148. See Jesse Choper, *Judicial Review and the National Political Process* 175–84 (1980), cited in *Garcia,* 469 U.S. at 551 n.11. Professor Choper's theory is discussed in chapter 1, supra pp. 16–20.

149. At the outset of section II of its opinion, the Court stated: "Were SAMTA a privately owned and operated enterprise, it could not credibly argue that Congress exceeded the bounds of its Commerce Clause powers in prescribing minimum wages and overtime rates for SAMTA's employees." *Garcia,* 469 U.S. at 537. While the Court correctly noted that "it long has been settled that Congress' authority under the Commerce Clause extends to intrastate economic activities that affect interstate commerce," id., it engaged in absolutely no specific inquiry to determine whether interstate commerce actually was affected, or even whether Congress had made inquiry into this question prior to passage.

150. See, e.g., Presault v. Interstate Commerce Comm'n, 494 U.S. 1 (1990).

151. 112 S. Ct. 2408 (1992). See also Gregory v. Ashcroft, 111 S. Ct. 2395 (1991), where the Court found that Missouri's age seventy mandatory retirement requirement for judges does not violate the federal Age Discrimination in Employment Act of 1967, 29 U.S.C. §§ 623(a), 631(a). In dictum, Justice O'Connor, speaking for the Court, stated that "[a]s against Congress' power '[t]o regulate Commerce . . . among the several States', . . . the authority of the people of the States to determine the qualifications of their government officials may be inviolate." 111 S. Ct. at 2403. She acknowledged that the Court was "constrained" in its ability to consider such constitutional limits by *Garcia,* but noted that "there is no need to do so if we hold that the [act] does not apply to state judges." Id.

152. Pub. L. 99–240, 99 Stat. 1842, 42 U.S.C. § 2021b et seq.

153. 42 U.S.C. § 2021e(d)(2)(C).

154. 112 S. Ct. at 2420, quoting Hodel v. Virginia Surface Mining & Reclamation Assn., Inc., 452 U.S. 264, 288 (1981).

155. 112 S. Ct. at 2420.

156. Id.

157. Id. at 2441 (White, J., concurring in part and dissenting in part).

158. Id.

159. Id.

160. Id.

161. In another portion of its decision, the Court upheld provisions of the act in which Congress sought to induce state compliance by using noncoercive incentives. Justice O'Connor found that these incentives constituted legitimate "conditional exercise[s]" of Congress's spending and commerce powers. 112 S. Ct. at 2426–27.

162. See e.g., Schechter Poultry Corp. v. United States, 295 U.S. 495 (1935).

163. 426 U.S. 623 (1976).

164. See id. at 840.

165. See U.S. Const. art. I, § 8, cl. 3.

166. U.S. Const. amend. X.

167. John Hart Ely, "The Irrepressible Myth of *Erie*," 87 *Harv. L. Rev.* 693, 701–02 (1974).

168. See U.S. Const. art. I, § 8, cl. 3.

169. See Ely, supra note 167, at 701.

170. U.S. Const. amend. I, cl. 2.

171. Ely, supra note 167, at 701; see, e.g., United States v. Constantine, 296 U.S. 287, 295–96 (1935); Hammer v. Dagenhart, 247 U.S. 251, 276 (1918).

172. See, e.g., United States v. Darby, 312 U.S. 100, 124 (1941).

173. 426 U.S. at 833, 836.

174. 421 U.S. 542 (1975).

175. Id. at 547, n.7, quoted in *National League of Cities*, 426 U.S. at 842–43.

176. But see Robert Nagel, "Federalism as a Fundamental Value: *National League of Cities* in Perspective," 1981 *Sup. Ct. Rev.* 81, 97–98 (footnotes omitted) (defending *National League of Cities*).

177. See Ely, supra note 167, at 701–02.

178. See Garcia v. San Antonio Metro. Transit Auth., 469 U.S. 528, 568–69 (1985) (Powell, J., dissenting):

> Much of the initial opposition to the Constitution was rooted in the fear that the National Government would be too powerful and eventually would eliminate the States as viable political entities. This concern was voiced repeatedly until proponents of the Constitution made assurances that a Bill of Rights, including a provision explicitly reserving powers in the States, would be among the first business of the new Congress. . . .
>
> Antifederalists raised these concerns in almost every state ratifying convention. . . .
>
> As a result, eight states voted for the Constitution only after proposing amendments to be adopted after ratification. All eight of these included among their recommendations some version of what later became the Tenth Amendment.

Id. (footnote omitted).

In an accompanying footnote, Justice Powell noted that "'[o]pponents of the Constitution were particularly dubious of the Federalists' claim that the States retained powers not delegated to the United States in the absence of an express provision so providing." Id. at 569 n.14.

179. See generally William Rehnquist, "The Notion of a Living Constitution," 54 *Tex. L. Rev.* 693 (1976):

> Beyond the Constitution and the laws in our society, there simply is no basis other than the individual conscience of the citizen that may serve as a platform for the launching of moral judgments. There is no conceivable way in which I can logically demonstrate to you that the judgments of my conscience are superior to the judgments of your conscience, and vice versa.

Id. at 704.

180. 112 S. Ct. 2408 (1992). See discussion supra p. 23.

181. Pub. L. 99-240, 99 Stat. 1842, 42 U.S.C. § 2021b et seq.

182. 112 S. Ct. at 2420.

183. 112 S. Ct. at 2421.

184. 112 S. Ct. at 2419.

185. Id. at 2417.

186. See, e.g., United States v. Darby, 312 U.S. 100 (1941).

187. That Justice O'Connor was employing a pure enclave analysis is illustrated by her analogy between the Tenth Amendment and the First Amendment's limit on federal power. 112 S. Ct. at 2418. Clearly, the First Amendment imposes limits on federal power above and beyond those inherent in the concept of enumerated federal powers.

188. See Akhil Reed Amar, "Of Sovereignty and Federalism," 96 *Yale L.J.* 1425, 1447 (1987).

189. See Saikrishna Bangalore Prakash, "Field Office Federalism," 79 *Va. L. Rev.* 1957 (1993).

190. It has been argued that the Framers' intent should not control modern textual interpretation because it is impossible to know how that intent might have changed in light of subsequent developments. See Robert W. Bennett, "Objectivity in Constitutional Law," 132 *U. Pa. L. Rev.* 445 (1984).

191. U.S. Const. art. IV, § 4.

192. Justice O'Connor failed in her attempts to distinguish Testa v. Katt, 330 U.S. 386 (1947) and FERC v. Mississippi, 456 U.S. 742 (1982), which upheld the federal "commandeering" of the state courts and state administrative systems, respectively, to enforce federal law. See 112 S. Ct. at 2430. However, under a Guarantee Clause analysis one could conceivably distinguish these situations, because arguably neither state courts nor state administrative agencies must be representative in the sense in which a state legislature must in order to ensure the essence of republican government.

193. Justice O'Connor acknowledged the possibility that resolution of the Guarantee Clause issue was precluded by the "political question" doctrine. She correctly noted that "[i]n most of the cases in which the Court has been asked to apply the clause, the Court has found the claims presented to be nonjusticiable under the 'political question' doctrine." Id. at 2432. See, e.g., Luther v. Borden, 48 U.S. (7 How.) 1 (1849). She declined to reach the question of the doctrine's application in *New York*. Id. For criticism of this use of the political question doctrine, see Martin H. Redish, *The Federal Courts in the Political Order: Judicial Jurisdiction and American Political Theory* 115–16 (1991).

194. One final problem that might be raised under the "enumerated powers" analysis is that a congressional requirement that states legislate is not itself a regulation of "commerce." But when one adds the Necessary-and-Proper Clause to the analysis, it becomes clear that Congress's actions need not themselves regulate interstate commerce, as long as those actions are reasonably designed to have an impact on

interstate commerce. See, e.g., Wickard v. Filburn, 317 U.S. 111 (1942). Under this standard, there can be little doubt that Congress's "take title" provision meets this test.

195. See U.S. Const. art. I, § 8.

196. Cf. U.S. Const. art. I, § 8, cl. 18 ("Necessary-and-Proper" Clause by its terms extends to Congress only authority to do anything "necessary and proper" to exercise one of the specifically enumerated powers).

197. 22 U.S. (9 Wheat.) 1, 195 (1824).

198. See Laurence Tribe, *American Constitutional Law* § 5–8 (2d ed. 1988). ("[C]ontemporary commerce clause doctrine grants Congress such broad power that judicial review of the affirmative authorization for congressional action is largely a formality.").

199. See discussion supra p. 23.

200. U.S. Const. art. I, § 8, cl. 18.

201. 17 U.S. (4 Wheat.) 316 (1819).

202. Id. at 421.

203. Id.

204. The "dormant" Commerce Clause concerns the states' power to regulate interstate commerce in the absence of preemptive congressional action. See, e.g., Cooley v. Board of Wardens, 53 U.S. (12 How.) 299 (1851); Mark Tushnet, "Rethinking the Dormant Commerce Clause," 1979 *Wis. L. Rev.* 125. See generally chapter 3.

205. Ch. 104, 24 Stat. 379 (1887) (codified as amended at 49 U.S.C. §§ 10101–11917).

206. Ch. 647, § 1, 26 Stat. 209 (1890) (codified as amended at 15 U.S.C. §§ 1–7).

207. See, e.g., Hammer v. Dagenhart, 247 U.S. 251 (1918) (finding that attempt by Congress to regulate child labor unconstitutionally infringed upon state sovereignty).

208. See discussion infra pp. 51–59.

209. See, e.g., Swift v. United States, 196 U.S. 375 (1905).

210. See Hammer v. Dagenhart, 247 U.S. 251 (1918).

211. 317 U.S. 111, 127–28 (1942).

212. See Tribe, supra note 198, at 310.

213. 312 U.S. 100 (1941).

214. Id. at 114.

215. U.S. Const. art I, § 8, cl. 18.

216. See, e.g., Edward S. Corwin, *The Constitution and What It Means Today* 74–75 (11th ed. 1963).

217. Hodel v. Virginia Surface Mining & Reclamation Ass'n, 452 U.S. 264, 276 (1981) (citation omitted).

218. See, e.g., New York Times Co. v. United States, 403 U.S. 713 (1971) (holding prior restraint on publication of "Pentagon Papers" unconstitutional, despite executive's assertion that publication would adversely affect national security).

219. See, e.g., Korematsu v. United States, 323 U.S. 214 (1944) (allowing internment of Japanese-Americans during World War II); see also discussion infra pp. 54–57.

220. Such a theory finds its origin in Justice Stone's famed footnote 4 in United States v. Carolene Prods., 304 U.S. 144, 152–53 (1938):

> There may be narrower scope for operation of the presumption of constitutionality when legislation appears on its face to be within a specific prohibition of the Constitution, such as those of the first ten amendments, which

are deemed equally specific when held to be embraced within the Fourteenth.

It is unnecessary to consider now whether legislation which restricts those political processes which can ordinarily be expected to bring about repeal of undesirable legislation, is to be subjected to more exacting judicial scrutiny under the general prohibitions of the Fourteenth Amendment than are most other types of legislation.

Nor need we enquire whether similar considerations enter into the review of statutes directed at particular religious, or national, or racial minorities: whether prejudice against discrete and insular minorities may be a special condition, which tends seriously to curtail the operation of those political processes ordinarily to be relied upon to protect minorities, and which may call for a correspondingly more searching judicial inquiry.

Id. at 152 n.4 (citations omitted). For a criticism of the preference for constitutional protections of individual liberty at the expense of the Constitution's structural provisions, see Nagel, supra note 176, at 83–97.

221. See chapter 1, supra p. 16.

222. See discussion supra pp. 16–20.

223. See discussion supra pp. 16–20.

224. 323 U.S. 214 (1944).

225. Justice Black, writing for the Court, cited the earlier decision in Hirabayashi v. United States, 320 U.S. 81, 99 (1943), for the proposition that "'we cannot reject as unfounded the judgment of the military authorities and of Congress that there were disloyal members of that population, whose number and strength could not be precisely and quickly ascertained.'" 323 U.S. at 218. As Chief Justice Warren later concluded, cases like *Korematsu* "demonstrate dramatically that there are some circumstances in which the Court will, in effect, conclude that it is simply not in a position to reject descriptions by the Executive of the degree of military necessity." Earl Warren, "The Bill of Rights and the Military," in *The Great Rights* 89, 101 (Edmond Cahn ed., 1963).

226. *Korematsu*, 323 U.S. at 244–48 (Jackson, J., dissenting).

227. See Eugene Rostow, *The Sovereign Prerogative* 197 (1962) ("[The Court in *Korematsu*] upheld an act of military power, without a factual record in which the justification for the act may be analyzed.").

228. See *Korematsu*, 323 U.S. at 239 (Murphy, J., dissenting) ("[T]he main reasons relied upon by those for the forced evacuation . . . appear, instead, to be largely an accumulation of much of the information, half-truths and insinuations that for years have been directed against Japanese Americans by people with racial and economic prejudices.").

229. See, e.g., Williamson v. Lee Optical, Inc., 348 U.S. 483 (1955) (upholding prohibition on optician's filing or duplicating lenses without optometrist's or ophthalmologist's prescription). See generally Gerald Gunther, "The Supreme Court, 1971 Term—Foreword: In Search of Evolving Doctrine on a Changing Court: A Model for a Newer Equal Protection," 86 *Harv. L. Rev.* 1, 19–24 (1972) (noting Burger Court's apparent willingness to recognize equal protection claims on minimum rationality review, in contrast with Warren Court's greater deference to enactments not subject to strict scrutiny).

230. See, e.g., Zobel v. Williams, 457 U.S. 55, 61–63 (1982) (employing rational basis standard and holding that Alaska's scheme for distributing dividends from state's mineral resources violated equal protection clause because state's objectives were not

"rationally related to the distinctions Alaska seeks to make between newer residents and those who have been in the State since 1959" (footnote omitted)); see also Hooper v. Bernalillo County Assessor, 472 U.S. 612 (1985) (finding limitation of New Mexico tax exemptions for Vietnam veterans to persons who could establish residency for 1976 not rationally related to asserted state purpose of encouraging Vietnam veterans to move into state); City of Cleburne v. Cleburne Living Center, 473 U.S. 432 (1985) (concluding that zoning decision refusing special use permit for group home for mentally retarded was based on "irrational prejudice" and violated equal protection); Attorney Gen. v. Soto-Lopez, 476 U.S. 898, 912–16 (1986) (Burger, C.J., concurring) (holding New York's grant of preferential treatment only to veterans who lived in New York when they joined service not rationally related to asserted state interest).

231. More recently, however, the Court appears to have returned to an all but total deference in the use of its rationality review of at least federal economic legislations. See FCC v. Beach Communications, Inc., 113 S. Ct. 2096 (1993).

232. For an explanation of the Court's approach, see San Antonio School Dist. v. Rodriguez, 411 U.S. 1 (1973) (because wealth is not suspect classification and education is not "fundamental" interest, rational basis scrutiny, which Texas's educational finance system survives, is in order).

233. 452 U.S. 264 (1981).

234. 30 U.S.C. §§ 1201–1328.

235. *Hodel,* 452 U.S. at 268 (quoting 30 U.S.C. § 1202(a)).

236. Id. at 269.

237. Id. at 277.

238. Id.

239. Id. (quoting 30 U.S.C. § 1201(c)).

240. See Korematsu v. United States, 323 U.S. 214 (1944).

241. Hodel, 452 U.S. at 277.

242. Id. at 277–78 (footnote omitted).

243. Id. at 279.

244. Id.

245. See id. at 280 n.20. Significantly, even those Justices who traditionally decry the demise of the commerce clause limitation concurred, because while "we often seem to forget the doctrine that laws enacted by Congress under the Commerce Clause must be based on a substantial effect on interstate commerce . . . in these cases . . . the Court acknowledges and reaffirms that doctrine." Id. at 305 (Burger, C.J., concurring); See also at 307–13 (Rehnquist, J., concurring).

246. 29 U.S.C. § 201 et seq.

247. 312 U.S. at 117.

248. Id. at 117–18.

249. Houston & Texas Ry. v. United States, 234 U.S. 342 (1914).

250. 312 U.S. at 121.

251. 402 U.S. 146 (1971).

252. 18 U.S.C. § 891 et seq.

253. 402 U.S. at 153 (emphasis in original; footnote omitted).

254. Id. at 154 (emphasis in original; footnote omitted).

255. 234 U.S. at 351.

256. 402 U.S. at 157 (Stewart, J., dissenting).

257. 402 U.S. at 154–55.

258. See discussion supra pp. 53–57.

259. See id.

260. 402 U.S. at 157–58 (Stewart, J., dissenting).

261. Id. at 157 (Stewart, J., dissenting).

262. See, e.g., Richard Stewart,"Federalism and Rights," 19 *Ga. L.Rev.* 917 (1985)("Federalism seeks to maintain political decentralization and social diversity while simultaneously promoting national measures to meet national needs and prevent localized oppression.").

263. See discussion supra pp. 3–4.

264. Such a deprecation of the constitutional protection of free speech was in fact suggested by no less an authority than Dean Wigmore in his criticism of Justice Holmes's application of the "clear and present danger" test to leftists' expression during World War I. John Henry Wigmore, *"Abrams v. U.S.:* Freedom of Speech and Freedom of Thuggery in War-Time and Peace-Time," 14 *Ill. L. Rev.* 539, 546–61 (1920).

Chapter 3

1. See chapter 2, supra pp. 48–59.

2. See, e.g., CTS Corp. v. Dynamics Corp. of America, 481 U.S. 69 (1987) (regulation of purchase of corporate securities).

3. See, e.g., Pike v. Bruce Church, Inc., 397 U.S. 137 (1970); Bibb v. Navajo Freight Lines, 359 U.S. 520 (1959).

4. See generally John E. Nowak and Ronald D. Rotunda, *Constitutional Law* 274–303 (4th ed. 1991).

5. The label "dormant" has been criticized as misleading. See Julian Eule, "Laying the Dormant Commerce Clause to Rest," 91 *Yale L.J.* 425 n.1 (1982):

> The term connotes something with the potential for action, yet currently in repose. It is clear that what remains dormant is Congress, and not the commerce clause. The clause's limitation on state regulation can certainly be termed implicit, silent, or negative, but dormancy does not accurately describe the situation.

6. In Southern Pacific Co. v. Arizona ex rel. Sullivan, 325 U.S. 761 (1945), Chief Justice Stone, speaking for the Court, stated that Congress has "undoubted" power "to permit the states to regulate the commerce in a manner which would otherwise not be permissible." Id. at 769. See generally Prudential Insurance Co. v. Benjamin, 328 U.S. 408 (1946).

7. See, e.g., Eule, supra note 5; Daniel Farber, "State Regulation and the Dormant Commerce Clause," 3 *Const. Comm.* 395 (1986); Donald Regan, "The Supreme Court and State Protectionism: Making Sense of the Dormant Commerce Clause," 84 *Mich. L. Rev.* 1082 (1986); Earl Maltz, "How Much Regulation Is Too Much—An Examination of Commerce Clause Jurisprudence," 50 *Geo. Wash. L. Rev.* 47 (1981); Robert Sedler, "The Negative Commerce Clause as a Restriction on State Regulations and Taxation: An Analysis in Terms of Constitutional Structure," 31 *Wayne L. Rev.* 885 (1985); Bernard Schwartz, "Commerce, the States, and the Burger Court," 74 *Nw. U. L. Rev.* 409 (1979); Mark Tushnet, "Rethinking the Dormant Commerce Clause," 1979 *Wis. L. Rev.* 125.

8. In recent years, the Supreme Court's interest in the area appears to have been on the dramatic increase. See, e.g., Brown-Forman Distillers Corp. v. New York St. Liquor Authority, 476 U.S. 573 (1986); Maine v. Taylor, 477 U.S. 131 (1986); South-

Central Timber Dev., Inc. v. Wunnicke, 467 U.S. 82 (1984). See Farber, supra note 7, at 400.

9. Professor Eule, for example, emphasizes "the process-oriented protection of representational government" as the concept's ultimate rationale (Eule, supra note 5, at 443), as does Professor Tushnet (Tushnet, supra note 7). Professor Regan, on the other hand, has argued that in interpreting the dormant Commerce Clause "the Court is concerned and should be concerned only with preventing purposeful [state] protectionism." Regan, supra note 7, at 1093.

10. Professor Regan has expended the greatest effort in this attempt. See discussion infra pp. 85–86. See also Sedler, supra note 7 at 968–99.

11. See generally Thomas G. Grey, "Do We Have an Unwritten Constitution?," 27 *Stan. L. Rev.* 703 (1975). See also Michael J. Perry, *The Constitution, the Courts and Human Rights* (1982).

12. See Regan, supra note 7, at 1110–25; Sedler, supra note 7, at 977–82.

13. See discussion supra pp. 7–9. See also discussion infra p. 86.

14. See chapter 1, supra pp. 7–9.

15. See discussion infra pp. 79–81.

16. See, e.g., U.S. Const., art. I, § 10, cls. 1–8; art. IV, § 2. See discussion infra p. 80.

17. See U.S. Const., art. I, § 10, cl. 9. See discussion infra p. 79.

18. See U.S. Const., art. I, § 8, cl. 3 (the commerce power). See discussion infra p. 80.

19. It should be noted that certain exercises by a state of the commerce power may conceivably run afoul of a specific constitutional prohibition, such as the Privileges-and-Immunities Clause of Article IV, Section 2. See discussion infra pp. 89–93.

20. U.S. Const., art. V.

21. See discussion infra pp. 81–83.

22. See discussion infra pp. 82–83.

23. See discussion infra p. 82.

24. See generally Eule, supra note 5; Tushnet, supra note 7.

25. See discussion infra pp. 84–85.

26. The analysis may well be different, however, if the grounds for judicial invalidation is the discriminatory effect of state regulation on out-of-state residents. Such a situation might well implicate the Privileges-and-Immunities Clause. See discussion infra at pp. 89–93.

27. U.S. Const., art. IV, § 2.

28. See Eule, supra note 5; Tushnet, supra note 7.

29. Eule, supra note 5 at 446–47.

30. See infra pp. 96–97.

31. Buck v. Kuykendall, 267 U.S. 307 (1925); DiSanto v. Pennsylvania, 273 U.S. 34 (1927) (steamship ticket sales requirement).

32. Southern Pacific Co. v. Arizona, 325 U.S. 761 (1945).

33. Bibb v. Navajo Freight Lines, Inc. 359 U.S. 520 (1959).

34. Kassel v. Consolidated Freightways Corp., 450 U.S. 662 (1981).

35. Hunt v. Washington State Apple Advertising Commission, 432 U.S. 333 (1977) (apple packaging requirement); Dean Milk v. City of Madison, 340 U.S. 349 (1951) (milk pasteurization and sale requirements); Baldwin v. G.A.F. Seelig, Inc., 294 U.S. 511 (1935) (milk price regulation).

36. See, e.g., Pike v. Bruce Church, Inc., 397 U.S. 137 (1970). For a thorough

discussion of the Court's dormant Commerce Clause tests, see Sedler, supra note 7 at 895–968.

37. 22 U.S. (9 Wheat.) 1 (1824).

38. Id. at 186.

39. Id. at 199–200.

40. Id. at 200.

41. Id. at 200–22. Justice Johnson, concurring in the judgment, would have invalidated the New York monopoly on the grounds that the constitutional grant of power to regulate commerce among the states precluded a state from exercising a concurrent power to regulate such commerce. Id. at 222–39.

42. Id. at 199–210.

43. Felix Frankfurter, *The Commerce Clause Under Marshall, Taney and Waite* 16 (1937).

44. 22 U.S. (9 Wheat.) at 197–209.

45. Id. at 199–200.

46. Id.

47. Id. at 209. This argument has given rise to the view that Congress's power to regulate interstate commerce in exclusive. See Frankfurter, supra note 43, at 17.

48. 22 U.S. (9 Wheat.) at 203.

49. Id. at 204.

50. Id.

51. 27 U.S. (2 Pet.) 245 (1829). The Marshall Court had one other opportunity to consider the commerce power before deciding *Black Bird Creek*. In Brown v. Maryland, 25 U.S. (12 Wheat.) 419 (1827), Marshall maintained that the sole question before the Court was whether a state could constitutionally require an importer to take out a license before selling imported goods in that state. Id. at 436. The Court held that a Maryland license fee for the sale of imports was a tax on imports that violated the Constitution's Article I, Section 10, Clause 2 limitation on the states, which proscribed the states from levying imposts or duties on imports without the consent of Congress. Id. at 445. The Court also held that the license fee was invalid because it "must be in opposition to to the act of Congress which authorizes importation" passed pursuant to Congress's article I, section 8, clause 3 power to regulate commerce. Id. at 447–48.

52. 27 U.S. (2 Pet.) at 250–51.

53. Id. at 251–52. Noting that Congress had not passed any act which would preempt the Delaware statute, the Court maintained that "[t]he repugnancy of the law of Delaware to the constitution is placed entirely on its repugnancy to the power to regulate commerce with foreign nations and among the several states; a power which has not been so exercised as to affect the question." Id. at 252.

54. Id. at 252.

55. See id.

56. Marshall did hear the first oral argument in New York v. Miln, 36 U.S. (11 Pet.) 102 (1837), but died before a decision had been reached.

57. See, for example, the opinion of Chief Justice Taney in *The License Cases*, 46 U.S. (5 How.) 504, 578–79 (1847).

58. 53 U.S. (12 How.) 299 (1851).

59. See id. at 311–12.

60. Id. at 312–15. First, the statute was attacked as an impermissable impost or duty on imports, exports, or tonnage under Article I, Section 10, Clauses 2 and 3. Curtis wrote that the portion of the Pennsylvania statute which required the payment

of a pilotage fee was "an appropriate part" of pilotage regulations generally. Id. at 312. He reasoned that the statute was based upon a desire to save lives and property by providing skilled and experienced pilots to safely navigate ships entering the port of Philadelphia. Id. The pilotage requirement and fee were designed to

> discourag[e] the commanders of vessels from refusing to receive such persons . . . and upon the expediency, and even the injustice, of not suffering those who have incurred labor, and expense, and danger, to place themselves in a position to render important service generally necessary, to go unrewarded, because the master of a particular vessel either rashly refuses their proffered assistance, or, contrary to the general experience, does not need it.

Id.

61. Id. at 321.

62. See Nowak and Rotunda, supra note 4, at 279–80.

63. See *Cooley*, 53 U.S. (12 How.) at 311–13.

64. Id. at 315–16.

65. 1 Stat. 54 (1789).

66. *Cooley*, 53 U.S. (12 How.) at 317–18.

67. Id. at 318.

68. Id. at 319 (citing Sturges v. Crowninshield, 17 U.S. (4 Wheat.) 193 (1819); Houston v. Moore, 18 U.S. (5 Wheat.) 1 (1820); Willson v. Black-Bird Marsh Creek Co. 27 U.S. (2 Pet.) 251 (1829)). Justice Curtis noted that a state power to regulate the District of Columbia, for example, would be incompatible with the grant of such a power to Congress. Id. at 318.

69. Id. at 319.

70. Id. Justice Curtis maintained that the Pennsylvania statute did not regulate the type of commerce falling into the "exclusive" category. He further noted that the federal act of 1789 "manifest[ed] the understanding of Congress, at the outset of the government, that the nature of th[e] subject [before the Court] is not such as to require its exclusive legislation." Id. at 319–20.

71. Id. at 320. Justice Curtis failed to consider Chief Justice Marshall's view of the Commerce Clause, which permitted the states to enact legislation pursuant to their "police power" that could have a substantial effect on commerce. See id.

72. Id.

73. Id. The Court in *Cooley* noted that the state statute had a nondiscriminatory effect since the statute applied to residents and nonresidents alike, despite an exemption for any vessels engaged in the Pennsylvania coal trade. Id. at 313. The "nondiscriminatory" effect of the Pennsylvania statute has been considered an important element in the *Cooley* decision. See Nowak & Rotunda, supra note 4, at 279–80.

74. See discussion infra p. 75.

75. 91 U.S. 275 (1875).

76. Id. at 280.

77. Id. at 282 (emphasis added).

78. Id. at 282. Justice Field cited three cases in support of the "views here expressed": The State Freight Tax Cases, 82 U.S. (15 Wall.) 232 (1872); Woodruff v. Parham, 75 U.S. (8 Wall.) 123 (1868); Brown v. Maryland, 25 U.S. (12 Wheat.) 419 (1827). Id. Yet not one of the cases that Field cited in support actually alluded to such a proposition.

79. 325 U.S. 761 (1945).

80. Id. at 767 (citations omitted).

81. Id. at 769 (citations omitted). "[I]n general Congress has left it to the Courts to formulate the rules thus interpreting the commerce clause in its application, doubtless because it has appreciated the destructive consequences to the commerce of the nation if their protection were withdrawn . . . ." Id. at 770 (citing Gwin, White & Prince v. Henneford, 305 U.S. 434, 441 (1837)). "Congress is more leary of impeachment, removing appellate jurisdiction, or is too occupied to bother." Id. at 769. "Congress has undoubted power to redefine the distribution of power over interstate commerce. It may either permit the states to regulate the commerce in a manner which would not otherwise be permissable, or exclude state regulation even of matters peculiarly of local concern which nevertheless affect interstate commerce." Id. at 769 (citations omitted). "There has thus been left to the states wide scope for the regulation of matters of local state concern, even though it in some measure affects the commerce, provided that it does not materially restrict the free flow of commerce across state lines, or interfere with it in matters with respect to which uniformity of regulation is of predominant national concern." Id. at 770.

82. See, e.g., Kassel v. Consolidated Freightways Corp., 450 U.S. 662 (1981); City of Philadelphia v. New Jersey, 437 U.S. 617 (1978); Pike v. Bruce Church, Inc., 397 U.S. 137 (1970); Bibb v. Navajo Freight Lines, 359 U.S. 520 (1959).

83. U.S. Const. art. VI, cl. 2. See, e.g., Perez v. Campbell, 402 U.S. 637 (1971).

84. U.S. Const. Art. I, § 10.

85. U.S. Const. Art. IV, § 2.

86. See Hicklin v. Orbeck, 437 U.S. 518 (1978); discussion infra pp. 89–94.

87. Interestingly, the dormant Commerce Clause operates in much the same manner as the conditional prohibitions in Article I, Section 10, clauses 2–3. In those situations, states are prohibited from taking certain actions, unless Congress affirmatively authorizes such behavior. However, neither of these clauses concerns the general power to regulate interstate commerce.

88. See discussion supra pp. 69–72.

89. The Court's subsequent supposition that congressional silence manifests Congress's intention that these objects of commerce remain unregulated does not rise to the level of constitutional interpretation. That issue is addressed separately. See discussion infra pp. 77–79.

90. See In re Rahrer, 140 U.S. 545 (1891).

91. Cooley v. Board of Wardens, 53 U.S. (12 How.) 518–21 (1851).

92. U.S. Const. art. I, § 8, cl. 3.

93. See discussion infra pp. 79–80.

94. Alpheus Mason, "Federalism: The Role of the Court," in *Federalism: Infinite Variety in Theory and Practice* 24–25 (Valerie A. Earle ed., 1968). See the discussion in chapter 2, supra pp. 26–30.

95. U.S. Const. art. VI, cl. 2.

96. It should be noted that the absence of a direct constitutional prohibition on state power does not automatically vest a state with power it never possessed prior to the adoption of the Constitution. The state of Illinois, for example, could not purport to regulate commerce between Maryland and Virginia, having no impact on Illinois, solely because the Constitution does not expressly deny such power. The state of Illinois never had this power in the first place. An argument that the absence of a direct constitutional prohibition automatically empowers the states to act in ways they never could previously is reminiscent of Groucho Marx's famous exchange with a

doctor. After being treated for an accident, Groucho asked the doctor whether, after the accident, he would be able to play the piano. "Certainly," the doctor replied. "That's good," Groucho responded, "because I never could before."

97. See generally Daniel Elazar, *The American Partnership* (1962). See the discussion in chapter 2, supra p. 26.

98. Elazar, supra note 97, at 22.

99. Edward S. Corwin, "The Passing of Dual Federalism," 36 *Va. L. Rev.* 1, 4 (1950).

100. As indicated in the previous chapter, I do not believe that dual federalism does accurately reflect American constitutional or political theory. See discussion supra pp. 27–28.

101. See discussion supra pp. 69–72.

102. See the discussion in chapter 2, supra pp. 27–38.

103. See Daniel Elazar, *American Federalism: A View from the States* 51 (3d ed. 1984); Elazar, supra note 97, at 304.

104. It should once again be emphasized that state regulation of interstate commerce could conceivably come into conflict with a specific constitutional prohibition, and therefore be void.

105. Regan, supra note 7, at 1125.

106. Id.

107. Id.

108. Defenders of the dormant Commerce Clause point to Madison's statement forty years after the ratification of the Constitution that the commerce power "was intended as a negative and preventive provision against injustice among the States themselves," letter from James Madison to Joseph C. Cabell (Feb. 13, 1829), in 4 *Letters and Other Writings of James Madison* 14–15 (Gaillard Hunt ed., 1910) [hereinafter *Writings*], as historical support for the dormant Commerce Clause. See, e.g., Eule, supra note 5, at 431. While a fair reading of Madison's letter might be thought to indicate that the Commerce Clause was intended to be a negative on the states, such an interpretation goes too far. On its face, Madison's language can be construed to mean that Congress *alone* was given the power to negate state regulations of commerce. Madison's letter must be considered in its entirety and in the context in which it was written in order to understand the type of negative on the states imposed by the Commerce Clause.

In his letters to Joseph Cabell, Madison discussed Congress's power to regulate commerce. In his first letter, Madison attempted to explain the constitutionality of "the power in Congs. to impose a tariff for the encouragement of Manufacturers." 9 *Writings* at 316–40. Madison noted that "[t]he Constitution vests in *Congress expressly* 'the power to lay & collect taxes[,] duties[,] imposts & excises;' and 'the power to regulate trade[.]'" Id. The important point is that Madison referred to the "granting to Congress" of power over commerce as a power that Congress would "exercise" and "use." Id. He declined to comment on the wisdom of the tariff and closed, "In the exercise of the power, . . . [the members of Congress] are responsible to their Constituents whose right & duty it is, in that as in all cases, to bring their measures to the test of justice & the general good." Id. Conspicuously absent was any discussion of the clause itself as a limit on the states. Nor was the clause discussed in terms that would indicate that it was a self-executing provision.

In another letter, Madison addressed Congress's power over interstate commerce. He wrote:

Being in the same terms with the power over foreign commerce, the same extent if taken literally, would belong to it. Yet it is very certain that it grew out of the abuse of the power by the importing States in taxing the non-importing, and was intended as a negative and preventive provision against injustice among the States themselves, rather than as *a power to be used* for the positive purposes of the General Government, in which alone, however, the remedial power could be lodged.

Id. (emphasis added).

Taken together, Madison's letters reveal an understanding of the Commerce Clause providing little support to the dormant Commerce Clause's proponents. While the power over interstate commerce may have been intended to have been a negative on state legislation, Madison apparently believed—as the text itself indicates—that the power was to be exercised by Congress, not the Court.

109. Regan, supra note 7, at 1125.

110. See generally H. Jefferson Powell, "The Original Understanding of Original Intent," 98 *Harv. L. Rev.* 885 (1985).

111. See discussion infra pp. 79–85.

112. This fact distinguishes the dormant Commerce Clause cases from the analysis employed by the Court in Flood v. Kuhn, 407 U.S. 258 (1972), where the Court refused to overturn its earlier decisions finding that baseball was not a business for purposes of the antitrust laws, in light of Congress's failure to overrule those decisions, despite numerous legislative attempts to do so. In any event, with the exception of this one difference *Flood* is itself subject to much of the same criticisms made here of the dormant Commerce Clause as an inference of congressional intent.

113. See discussion infra pp. 159–60.

114. U.S. Const. art. VI, cl. 4.

115. Martin H. Redish, "Abstention, Separation of Powers, and the Limits of the Judicial Function," 94 *Yale L.J.* 71, 82 (1984).

116. Id.

117. Thomas Merrill, "The Common Law Powers of Federal Courts," 52 *U. Chi. L. Rev.* 1, 22–23 (1985) (footnotes omitted).

118. For example, during the 98th Congress 11,156 measures were introduced into both Houses of Congress. U.S. Dep't Commerce, Bureau of the Census, *Statistical Abstract of the United States 1986* 247 (1987). Of these *only* 677 measures were enacted—roughly 6 percent.

119. U.S. Const. art. I, § 10, cl. 1.

120. U.S. Const. art. V, § 2.

121. U.S. Const. art. I, § 10, cls. 2–3.

122. See discussion infra p. 81.

123. U.S. Const. art. VI, cl. 2.

124. See supra note 118.

125. See generally Roger H. Davidson & Walter J. Oleszek, *Congress and Its Members* 263–85 (2d ed. 1985).

Congress has a highly decentralized power structure. Walter J. Oleszek, *Congressional Procedures and the Policy Process* (1978). When a bill is introduced, it is referred to the appropriate committee, which in turn frequently will refer the bill to the appropriate subcommittee. Id. at 14. Sometimes, a bill is referred to more than one committee in either the House or Senate because of overlapping committee resonsibilities. Id. at 13. Once the bill has been referred to the appropriate committee or subcommittee, the committee members will often solicit the opinions of the government agencies that would be affected by the passage of the bill. Jack R. Van Der Slik, *American Legislative Process* 208 (1977). The committee will probably hold its own hearings on the bill as well. Id. At some point, the committee will "mark-up" or rework the bill before voting on it and, if the mark-up has been extensive, the committee may reintroduce the bill in its "clean" form. Id. After the committee has taken action on the bill, a report is issued and the bill is placed on the House's calendar for consideration by all of the members of the House in which the bill was introduced. Once one House has passed a bill, it is introduced in the second House, provided that the bill was not simultaneously introduced into both Houses of Congress. Id. at 14. After the bill has been introduced in the second House, the bill undergoes the same basic process and at any point in the legislative process, can be delayed, defeated, or substantially modified. Id. Coalitions must be built and maintained in order to garner the votes necessary to ensure passage of a bill: Various committees, interest groups, or influential individuals may be able effectively to kill a bill by forming and sustaining an opposition coalition on the committee or subcommittee level. Id at 14–17.

126. Lewis Froman, *The Congressional Process* 17 (1967).

127. Oleszek, supra note 125, at 17.

128. Id. at 17–18.

129. Merrill, supra note 117, at 22–23 (citing Grant Gilmore, *The Ages of American Law* 95–96 (1977)).

130. By "evenhanded,"I mean that the enactment would survive Article IV Privileges-and-Immunities Clause scrutiny.

131. Thomas Anson & P. M. Schenkkan, "Observation: Federalism, the Dormant Commerce Clause, and State-Owned Resources," 59 *Tex. L. Rev.* 71, 84 (1980).

132. McCarroll v. Dixie Greyhound Lines, Inc., 309 U.S. 176, 189 (1940) (Black, Frankfurter, and Douglas, J.J., dissenting).

133. Herbert Wechsler, "The Political Safeguards of Federalism: The Role of the States in the Composition and Selection of the National Government," 54 *Colum. L. Rev.* 543, 546 (1954). See the discussion in chapter 1.

134. Wechsler, supra note 133, at 546.

135. Id.

136. Id. at 558.

137. Jesse Choper, *Judicial Review and the National Political Process* 176–77 (1980). See also Joseph Grano, "Prophylactic Rules in Criminal Procedure: A Question of Article III Legitimacy," 80 *Nw. U. L. Rev.* 100, 126 (1985).

138. Garcia v. San Antonio Metropolitan Transit Authority, 469 U.S. 528 (1985).

139. Letter from James Madison to Edward Everett, (1830), in 9 *Writings* 338, 395–96 (as quoted in Wechsler, supra note 133, at 558).

140. See Lawrence Sager, "The Supreme Court, 1980 Term—Foreword: Constitutional Limitations on Congress' Authority to Regulate the Jurisdiction of the Federal Courts," 95 *Harv. L. Rev.* 17, 51–52 (1981).

141. See the discussion in chapter 1.

142. Paul M. Bator et al., *Hart & Wechsler's The Federal Courts and the Federal System* 10 (3d ed. 1988).

143. 1 *Records of the Federal Convention* 124 (James Madison, 5 June).

144. 2 *Records of the Federal Convention* 41

145. James Monroe, "Some Observations on the Constitution," in 5 *The Complete Antifederalist* 278, 304 (Herbert Storing ed., 1981).

146. "Essays by the Impartial Examiner," *Virginia Independent Chronicle*, 27

February 1788, in 5 *The Complete Antifederalist* 172, 180.

147. "Essay by a Georgian," *Gazette of the State of Georgia,* 15 November 1787, in 5 *The Complete Antifederalist* 129, 134.

148. See John E. Nowak, "The Scope of Congressional Power to Create Causes of Action Against State Governments and the History of the Eleventh and Fourteenth Amendments," 75 *Colum. L. Rev.* 1413 (1975). Professor Nowak contends that

> a convincing argument can be made that the drafters of the eleventh amendment were only responding to the judicial assumption of jurisdiction in suits brought by Tories against states. It is also probable that the states' interest in the amendment was similarly limited. The states were concerned that the federal courts, with whom they had no lobbying power, would, if *Chisholm* were not overruled, impose other retroactive liabilities on them. They feared that they would have no political recourse if life-tenured judges could assume jurisdiction in controversial actions, such as Tory suits. No evidence exists that the states had the same fear of congressional authorization of suits against states. Indeed, given the assumption of state debts by the Congress in the period following the Revolutionary War it is most likely that these representatives had implicit faith in the congressional ability to balance the interests of the state and federal governments.

Id. at 1440–41. See *also* Laurence Tribe, "Intergovernmental Immunities in Litigation, Taxation, and Regulation: Separation of Powers Issues in Controversies About Federalism," 89 *Harv. L. Rev.* 682 (1976).

149. U.S. Const. amend XI: "The judicial power of the United States shall not be construed to extend to any suit in law or equity, commenced or prosecuted against one of the United States by citizens of another State, or by citizens or subjects of any foreign State."

150. See U.S. Const. art. I, § 10; art. IV, § 2; discussion supra pp. 73–74.

151. U.S. Const. art. VI, cl. 2 (the Supremacy Clause).

152. See discussion supra pp. 73–74.

153. See discussion infra pp. 89–93.

154. See, for example, Bibb v. Navajo Freight Lines, 359 U.S. 520 (1959). Illinois had enacted a statute requiring the use of a contour rear fender mudguard on trucks and trailers operated on the highways of the state. The Supreme Court held the statute invalid under the dormant Commerce Clause, noting that the state "did not attempt to rebut the . . . showing that the statute in question severely burden[s] interstate commerce," despite the fact that the statute was clearly non-discriminatory.

155. See generally Richard Stewart, "Federalism and Rights," 19 *Ga. L. Rev.* 917 (1985).

156. Regan, supra note 7, at 1124.

157. *Id.* at 1124.

158. *Id.* at 1122–25.

159. *Id.* at 1094.

160. *Id.* at 1113.

161. *Id.* at 1114.

162. *Id.*

163. *Id.* at 1119.

164. See the discussion in chapter 1, supra pp. 7–9. I have articulated this position in earlier writing. See Martin H. Redish, "Due Process, Federalism, and Personal Jurisdiction: A Theoretical Evaluation," 75 *Nw. U. L. Rev.* 1112, 1130 (1981):

[W]hile the Court may necessarily exercise considerable freedom in defining and applying constitutional language, it does not follow that it can supplement the specific provisions of the Constitution by writing new ones, rather than interpreting existing ones. For, if recognized, such a power knows no logical bounds: if the Court's constitutional pronouncements are not required to have at least an arguable basis in the document's language, the Court's decisions inescapably become mere fiat, insulated from reasoned debate other than in the purely legislative sense of debating the normative wisdom of whatever "constitutional" rule the Court is considering devising.

See also Martin H. Redish, "The Federal Courts, Judicial Restraint, and the Importance of Analyzing Legal Doctrine," 85 *Colum. L. Rev.* 1378, 1400 (1985):

Neither theoretically nor practically does the judiciary have a freedom to function equivalent to that possessed by the executive and legislative branches. While those branches are authorized and able to act on an ad hoc basis and usually to decide solely on the basis of their views of normative policy, the judiciary is confined institutionally by the flow of past legal developments, by the concern about futures applications of its decisions, and by the constraints of the governing documents that it interprets. . . . The unrepresentative nature of the federal judiciary largely confines the legitimacy of the judiciary's operation. Once the judiciary departs from this practice and instead attempts to operate without concern for any factor other than its own personal and isolated preferences, it has abandoned its role and therefore its legitimacy in a democratic system.

165. See generally Powell, supra note 110.

166. See generally Regan, supra note 7.

167. See, e.g., Pike v. Bruce Church, Inc., 397 U.S. 137 (1970).

168. Professor Regan argues that he is "not vehemently opposed" to founding his antiprotectionism principle in the Privileges-and-Immunities Clause, because he is "not overly concerned with what textual hook we hang the principle on." Indeed, he believes "it can be a mistake to insist too strongly on identifying a particular textual hook." Regan, supra note 7, at 1202. However, for reasons already discussed (see, e.g., note 164), this is an unacceptable approach to the performance of the judicial review function.

169. See discussion infra pp. 89–93.

170. Henry P. Monaghan, "The Supreme Court 1974 Term—Foreword: Constitutional Common Law," 89 *Harv. L. Rev.* 1, 2–3 (1975).

171. Id. at 3–10.

172. Id. at 10.

173. Id. Monaghan believed that it "was too late in the day to conclude" that the Court was mistaken. Id.

174. Id. at 15.

175. Id.

176. Id. at 15–16.

177. Id. at 16–17.

178. Id. Monaghan explained that the reason the dormant Commerce Clause cases were not deemed to be the result of common law jurisprudence was that traditional *Marbury* nullification was the accepted norm and that the dormant Commerce Clause invalidation did not "look like the affirmative creation of federal rules." Id.

179. Henry J. Friendly, "In Praise of *Erie*—and of the New Federal Common Law," 39 *N.Y.U. L. Rev.* 383, 405 (1964). See Monaghan, supra note 170, at 10.

180. Id. at 12.

181. Id. at 12–13.

182. Under the Rules of Decision Act, 28 U.S.C. § 1652, federal courts are required to employ state law as the "rule of decision" "except where the Constitution or treaties of the United States or Acts of Congress otherwise require or provide . . . ."

183. Monaghan, supra note 170, at 12.

184. See D'Oench, Duhme & Co. v. FDIC, 315 U.S. 447, 472 (1942) (Jackson, J., concurring) (footnote omitted): "Federal common law implements the federal Constitution and statutes, and is conditioned by them."

185. See discussion supra pp. 79–83.

186. U.S. Const. art. IV, § 2.

187. Hicklin v. Orbeck, 437 U.S. 518, 531–32 (1978).

188. United Building & Construction Council v. Mayor of Camden, 465 U.S. 208, 220 (1983).

189. Gary Simpson, "Discrimination Against Nonresidents and the Privileges and Immunities Clause of Article IV," 128 *U. Pa. L. Rev.* 379, 383 (1979).

190. Id.

191. 3 *Records of the Federal Convention* 112. This excerpt is taken from a pamphlet written in 1787 by Pinckney and originally printed in New York and reprinted in South Carolina for public consumption. Id. at 106 n.1. The pamphlet was probably the basis for a speech that Pinckney was unable to deliver in the Convention because of a lack of time. Id.

192. Simpson, supra note 189, at 384 (citing 3 *Records of the Federal Convention* 437, 443, 456).

193. Id. at 384.

194. See discussion supra pp. 67–72.

195. See Regan, supra note 17; Eule, supra note 5.

196. See discussion supra pp. 69–72.

197. See supra note 6.

198. See, e.g., Baldwin v. Fish & Game Commission, 436 U.S. 371 (1978).

199. See, e.g., Ward v. Maryland, 79 U.S. (12 Wall.) 418 (1870); Paul v. Virginia, 75 U.S. (8 Wall.) 168 (1869).

200. Toomer v. Witsell, 334 U.S. 385 (1948). See Simpson, supra note 189 at 379.

201. 6 F. Cas. 546 (C.C.E.D. Pa. 1823).

202. Simpson, supra note 189, at 379–80.

203. 6 F. Cas. at 552.

204. Id.

205. See, e.g., Hicklin v. Orbeck, 437 U.S. 518 (1978).

206. See Regan, supra note 7, at 1202.

207. Hicklin v. Orbeck, 437 U.S. 518, 531 (1978).

208. United Building & Construction Council v. Mayor of Camden, 465 U.S. 208, 220 (1983).

209. Id. at 220.

210. Id. (emphasis added).

211. Id. Similarly, Professor Varat argues that "[a]t the most elementary level, the primary concern of the commerce clause is business that involves more than one state, whereas the core concern of the interstate privileges and immunities is the

treatment received within a state by citizens of other states." Jonathan Varat, "State 'Citizenship' and Interstate Equality," 48 *U. Chi. L. Rev.* 487, 499 (1981).

212. Baldwin v. Fish & Game Commission, 436 U.S. 371, 383 (1978).

213. Baldwin v. G.A.F. Seelig, Inc., 294 U.S. 511, 523 (1935) (quoting 2 *Records of the Federal Convention* 308).

214. Bacchus Imports, Ltd. v. Dias, 468 U.S. 263, 276 (1984).

215. Baldwin v. G. A. F. Seelig, 294 U.S. at 511, 523.

216. In Hope Insurance Co. v. Boardman, 9 U.S. (5 Cranch) 57 (1809), and in Bank of United States v. Deveaux, 9 U.S. (5 Cranch) 61 (1809), the Supreme Court held that a corporation was not a citizen because a corporation was an artificial legal entity, and as such, could not sue or be sued in federal court. Id. at 86. The Court, however, concluded that the corporation's stockholders could sue and be sued in federal court under the corporation's name. Id. at 91–93. The Court noted that the incorporating statute empowered the corporation's officers to sue and be sued. Id. at 85–86.

Thirty years later in Bank of Augusta v. Earle, 38 U.S. (13 Pet.) 519, 586–87 (1839), the Court refused to extend *Deveaux* in order to recognize that corporations enjoy the protection of the Privileges-and-Immunities Clause. Chief Justice Taney, writing for the Court, maintained that if a corporation were permitted to enjoy the privileges and immunities of citizens, it must also bear the accompanying liabilities of citizens. Id. at 587. This result, he concluded, would have reduced the corporation to "a mere partnership in business" and the corporation's stockholders would be liable for the full extent of the corporation's obligations. Id. Consequently, the Chief Justice refused to extend to corporations the protection of Article IV's Privileges-and-Immunities Clause. See id. at 586–91.

Similarly, in Paul v. Virginia, 75 U.S. (8 Wall.) 168 (1868), the Court responded to the assertion that the Privileges-and-Immunities Clause applied to corporations by declaring that "[t]he term citizens . . . [in the Privileges-and-Immunities Clause] only applies to natural persons, members of the body politic, owing allegiance to the State, not to artificial persons created by the legislature, and possessing only the attributes that the legislature has prescribed." Id. at 177. The Court continued that corporations only possess those rights contained in their charters and its shareholders' rights as citizens of a state. See id. at 180. The Court has maintained this position to date. Nowak and Rotunda, supra note 4, at 322.

217. U.S. Const. amend. XIV, § 1, cl. 4 ("No State shall . . . deny to any person within its jurisdiction the equal protection of the laws.")

218. See, e.g., Railway Express Agency v. New York, 336 U.S. 106 (1949).

219. 28 U.S.C. § 1332.

220. U.S. Const. Art. III, § 2, cl. 7.

221. Roe v. Wade, 410 U.S. 113 (1973).

222. Eule, supra note 5.

223. Id. at 435.

224. Id. at 443.

225. 303 U.S. 177, 185 n.2 (1938).

226. Eule, supra note 5 at 445. Professor Tushnet has argued for a similar rationale. See generally Tushnet, supra note 7. However, unlike Professor Eule, Professor Tushnet apparently intends not to shift the analysis to the umbrella of the Privileges-and-Immunities Clause but rather to infuse traditional dormant Commerce Clause jurisprudence with his "representational" analysis.

227. Tushnet, supra note 7, at 129 n.14.

228. A possible illustration would be anti-union legislation, enacted in a weak union state, that affects various workers in neighboring states where unions are politically powerful.

229. Regan, supra note 7, at 115 n.56.

230. This, at least, is the view taken by the so-called public choice literature. See generally Daniel Farber & Phillip Frickey, "The Jurisprudence of Public Choice," 65 *Tex. L. Rev.* 873 (1987).

231. See, e.g., Jack L. Walker, "A Critique of the Elitist Theory of Democracy," 60 *Am. Pol. Sci. Rev.* 285, 288 (1966) (emphasis in original):

> The most distinctive feature, and the principal orienting value, of classical democratic theory was its emphasis on individual participation in the development of public policy. . . . Although the classical theorists accepted the basic framework of Lockean democracy with its emphasis on limited government, they were *not* primarily concerned with the *policies* which might be produced in a democracy; above all else they were concerned with *human development,* the opportunities which existed in political activity to realize the untapped potentials of men . . . .

See also Peter Bachrach, "Interest, Participation, and Democratic Theory in Participation in Politics," Nomos 16 at 39 (1975) ("Democratic participation . . . is a process in which persons formulate, discuss, and decide public issues that are important to them and directly affect their lives.").

232. See, e.g., John Stuart Mill, *Considerations on Representative Government* 62–63, 69–80 (1882). See also Peter Bachrach, *The Theory of Democratic Elitism: A Critique* 98 (1967).

233. This is clearly true of Professor Tushnet. See generally Tushnet, supra note 7. Professor Eule acknowledges the possible textual difficulties with the dormant Commerce Clause, Eule, supra note 5, at 430, but does not seem to find them dispositive, largely because of what he understands to be Madison's intent. Id. at 431. Moreover, he suggests that "[l]ogic points inexorably to the courts" as the federal governmental body that "was to bring the states back in line when they transcend their authority." Id. It appears clear that if the absence of textual support were the only problem with the dormant Commerce Clause, Professor Eule would not favor its rejection.

234. Professor Eule assumes the justification for the dormant Commerce Clause to be the value of free trade, and then proceeds to reject it. Id. at 432–37. He concludes that "[i]n the end . . . we are left with only a single justification for judicial displacement of state legislative judgments in the commercial area—the process-oriented protection of representational government." Id. at 443.

235. See Edward S. Corwin, *The Constitution and What It Means Today* 46 (1963).

236. Pike v. Bruce Church, Inc., 397 U.S. 137 (1970).

237. See supra note 233.

238. See chapter 1, supra pp. 9–10.

239. See supra note 233.

240. In his opinion concurring in part in CTS Corp. v. Dynamics Corp. of America, 481 U.S. 69, 94–97 (1987), Justice Scalia advocated a position similar, though not identical, to the one advocated here. Also unlike the analysis adopted here, Justice Scalia did not ground his conclusion in a construction of the Privileges-and-Immunities Clause.

Chapter 4

1. See, e.g., Henry P. Monaghan, "Our Perfect Constitution," 56 *N.Y.U. L. Rev.* 353 (1981).

2. See discussion infra pp. 108–13.

3. See Mistretta v. United States, 488 U.S. 361 (1989).

4. "Formalism" in the separation-of-powers context has been described in the following manner:

> Any exercise of governmental power, and any governmental institution exercising that power, must either fit within one of the three formal categories [i.e., legislative, executive, or judicial] or find explicit constitutional authorization for such deviation. The separation of powers principle is violated whenever the categorizations of the exercised power and the exercising institution do not match and the Constitution does not specifically permit such blending.

Gary Lawson, "Territorial Governments and the Limits of Formalism," 78 *Cal. L. Rev.* 853, 858, (1990) (footnotes omitted). See also Lee S. Liberman, "*Morrison v. Olson:* A Formalist Perspective on Why the Court Was Wrong," 38 *Am. U. L. Rev.* 313 343 (1989) ("A decision uses a syllogistic, definitional approach to determining whether a particular exercise of power is legislative, executive or judicial. It assumes that all exercises of power must fall into one of these categories. . . .")

5. See, e.g., Rebecca L. Brown, "Separated Powers and Ordered Liberty," 139 *U. Pa. L. Rev.* 1513, 1524–27 (1991); Thomas O. Sargentich, "The Contemporary Debate About Legislative-Executive Separation of Powers," 72 *Cornell L. Rev.* 430 (1987); Paul Gewirtz, "Realism in Separation of Powers Thinking," 30 *William & Mary L. Rev.* 343 (1989); discussion infra pp. 115–16.

6. In this sense, this approach may be distinguished from those who urge a more "syllogistic" brand of formalism. See, e.g., Liberman, supra note 4, at 343. As subsequent discussion will show, the version of formalism advocated here also rejects use of an originalist perspective, sometimes thought to be an inherent element of formalism in general (see Paul Brest, "The Misconceived Quest for the Original Understanding," 60 *B.U. L. Rev.* 204 (1980)) or in the separation-of-powers context in particular (see generally Arthur C. Leahy, "Note, *Mistretta v. United States:* Mistreating the Separation of Powers Doctrine?," 27 *San Diego L. Rev.* 209 (1990)).

7. See, e.g., E. Donald Elliott, "Why Our Separation of Powers Jurisprudence Is So Abysmal," 57 *Geo. Wash. L. Rev.* 506, 508, 530–32 (1989).

8. See, e.g., Mathews v. Eldridge, 424 U.S. 319 (1976) (establishing utilitarian calculus by which to measure procedural due process).

9. See, e.g., Texas v. Johnson, 491 U.S. 397, 417–18 (1989) (extending free speech protection to flag desecration).

10. See, e.g., Trop v. Dulles, 356 U.S. 86, 101 (1958) (Eighth Amendment prohibition against cruel and unusual punishment "must draw its meaning from the evolving standards of decency that mark the progress of a maturing society").

11. See Frederick Schauer, "An Essay on Constitutional Language," 29 *U.C.L.A. L. Rev.* 797, 828 (1982). See also the discussion in chapter 1, supra pp. 9–10.

12. An additional analytical model, the "judicial abdication" approach advocated by Professor Choper, is criticized in chapter 1, supra pp. 16–20.

13. See Brown, supra note 5 at 1515–16; see text accompanying note 5. As Thomas Jefferson warned the Virginia legislature,

[Do not] be deluded by the integrity of their own purposes, and conclude that these unlimited powers will never be abused, because [they] themselves are not disposed to abuse them. They should look forward to a time, and that not a distant one, when corruption in this, as in the country from which we derive our origin, will have seized the heads of government. . . . Human nature is the same on every side of the Atlantic. . . .

Thomas Jefferson, *Notes on the State of Virginia* 121 (William Peden ed., 1955).

14. See *The Federalist* Nos. 37, 47 (Roy P. Fairfield ed., 2d ed. 1966) (citing Montesquieu); "The Address and Reasons of Dissent of the Minority of the Convention of Pennsylvania to their Constituents," *Pennsylvania Packet and Daily Advertiser* (18 Dec. 1787) reprinted in 3 Herbert J. Storing, *The Complete Anti-Federalist* 17 145, 160–61 (1981) (citing Montesquieu). Locke's influence is most evident in the Declaration of Independence. In Massachusetts in 1762 in a conflict over the appointment of the lieutenant governor to the chief justiceship, opponents emphasized the need for proper separation of powers and drew on Locke and Montesquieu as authority: "Mr. Locke is an oracle as to the principles, Harrington and Montesquieu are oracles as to the forms of government." M.J.C. Vile, *Constitutionalism and the Separation of Powers* 147 (1967) (quoting Benjamin Rush, "Observations on the Present Government of Pennsylvania" (1777) quoted in R. L. Brunhouse, *The Counter-Revolution in Pennsylvania, 1776–1790*, at 20 (1942)).

15. In *The Federalist,* Madison examined the various state constitutions, where, despite constitutional requirements, the legislatures had been widely overstepping the bounds of their power. "Experience assures us," he wrote "that the efficacy of the provision [of merely marking the boundaries of power] has been greatly overrated." *The Federalist* No. 48, at 146 (James Madison), supra note 14. In *The Federalist* 51, Madison harked back to simple human nature to explain the proposed structure:

But the great security against a gradual concentration of the several powers in the same department, consists in giving those who administer each department the necessary constitutional means, and personal motives, to resist encroachments of the others . . . . The policy of supplying by opposite and rival interests, the defect of better motives, might be traced through the whole system of human affairs.

The Federalist No. 51, at 160.

16. William B. Gwyn, "The Indeterminacy of the Separation of Powers in the Age of the Framers," 30 *Wm. & Mary L. Rev.* 263, 263 (1989) (quoting Louis Fisher, *President and Congress: Power and Policy* 4–5 (1972)).

17. *The Records of the Federal Convention of 1787*, at 278 (Max Farrand ed. 1911) (quoting John Dickinson of Delaware).

18. Vile, supra note 14 at 23.

19. Id. at 35. Vile asserts that Plato was one of the first to emphasize the class system as the basic element of mixed government.

20. Id. at 36.

21. Id.

22. Marchamont Nedham, *The Excellence of a Free-State* (1656), reprinted in 1 *The Founders' Constitution: Major Themes* 314 (Philip B. Kurland & Ralph Lerner eds., 1987). Nedham defined legislative power as the "making, altering, or repealing of Laws." Executive power was "derived from the other [legislative power] . . . for the administration of Government." Id.

23. Id. at 315.

24. See George Lawson, *An Examination of the Political Part of Mr. Hobbs' Leviathan* (London 1657); George Lawson, *Politica Sacra et Civilis* (London 1660).

25. John Locke, *Two Treatises on Government* (Peter Laslett ed., student ed. 1988) (3d ed. 1698).

26. Lawson, *An Examination,* supra note 24, at 8.

27. Id. at 41. "Execution" includes inflicting penalties dispensations of judgment, suspension of execution, and pardons. Vile, supra note 14 at 55.

28. Vile, supra note 14 at 56.

29. Id. at 57–58.

30. Locke, supra note 25, at 350–51. The first was the legislative branch—responsible for making law—analogous to man in the state of nature doing whatever he thought fit for the preservation of himself and others. The second power was the power to punish those who had violated the law, which Locke called the executive. The function of Locke's executive was to support the sentences of those who violated the law. According to Locke, man formed "civilized" societies because he was unable to exercise these rights effectively on his own. There was no known settled law and no indifferent judge with authority to determine the differences according to law. Locke's formulation may have been derived largely from Lawson's work.

31. Vile, supra note 14 at 58.

32. Locke, supra note 25 at 364.

33. Id.

34. See generally *The Federalist* No. 47, supra note 14; *The Federalist* No. 48, supra note 14; *The Federalist* No. 51, supra note 15.

35. John Adams, *Thoughts on Government* (1776) reprinted in 1 *Founders' Constitution* supra note 22; Jefferson, supra note 13.

36. Locke, supra note 25, at 364.

37. Id. at 365.

38. Id. at 368.

39. "The legislative department is everywhere extending the sphere of its activity, and drawing all power into its impetuous vortex." *The Federalist* No. 48 (James Madison) supra note 15, at 147.

40. Locke, supra note 25, at 374–75.

41. The proper scope of executive power is discussed at length infra pp. 117–19.

42. 1 *Founders' Constitution,* supra note 22, at 312.

43. Id.

44. Charles-Louis de Montesquieu, *The Spirit of the Laws* 75 (David W. Carrithers ed., 1977).

45. Id.

46. See id. at 76.

47. Id. at 77.

48. Id. at 201.

49. Id.

50. Id. at 202.

51. Id. at 200.

52. Id.

53. *The Federalist* No. 51 (James Madison), supra note 15, at 160.

54. See discussion infra pp. 102–03.

55. Montesquieu, supra note 44, at 202.

56. Id.

57. *The Federalist* No. 51 (James Madison), supra note 15 at 160.

58. See, e.g., *The Federalist* No. 47 (James Madison), supra note 14 at 139 (discussing "the celebrated Montesquieu").

59. See discussion supra pp. 99–100.

60. See, e.g., *The Federalist* No. 5.

61. See discussion supra pp. 102–05.

62. See discussion infra pp. 107–08.

63. In Virginia, for example, where the state constitution had failed to provide barriers between the branches (the executive and judiciary were both dependent upon the legislature), the legislative branch had accumulated a dangerous level of power. This led Jefferson to warn that "[a]n *elective despotism* was not the government we fought for; but one which should not only be founded on free principles, but in which the powers of government would be so divided and balanced among several bodies . . . that no one could transcend their legal limits, without being effectually checked and restrained by the others." Thomas Jefferson, "Notes on the State of Virginia," Query 133 (1784), in 1 *Founders' Constitution,* supra note 22, at 319. See also *The Federalist* No. 48 (James Madison), supra note 15.

64. "The accumulation of all powers, legislative, executive, and judiciary, in the same hands, whether of one, a few, or many, and whether hereditary, self-appointed, or elective, may justly be pronounced the very definition of tyranny." *The Federalist* No. 47 (James Madison), supra note 14 at 139.

65. Jefferson, supra note 63 at 121.

66. *The Federalist* No. 48 (James Madison), supra note 15, at 146.

67. See discussion infra pp. 124–25.

68. See David F. Epstein, *The Political Theory of the Federalist* 135 (1984):

> [T]he "tyrannical concentration" of power . . . precedes the tyrannical exercise of that power, so that the danger of concentration may not be clear to the people at the time their trusted representatives are concentrating it. Madison also describes legislative encroachment stemming not from cleverly concealed ambition but from legislators "eagerly bent on some favorite object, and breaking through the restraints of the Constitution in pursuit of it." . . . The object may also be a favorite of the people themselves, and its attractiveness may obscure the danger of concentrating power in pursuit of it.

69. The exclusivity of branch power may seem problematic, because common sense tells us that there are certain activities that more than one branch may undertake. However, as subsequent discussion in this chapter will demonstrate, while there are numerous activities that, when described in the abstract, can be performed by more than one branch, each branch's performance of that activity is limited by the surrounding structural context, rendering the performance of the same activity either legislative, executive or judicial. But see discussion infra p. 119.

70. Examples include the President's power to veto congressional legislation (U.S. Cont. art. I, § 7, cl. 2) and Congress's power to impose limitations on federal court jurisdiction (U.S. Const. art. III, §§ 1,2).

71. Lawrence C. Dodd & Richard L. Schott, *Congress and the Administrative State* (1979); C. Douglas Dillon, "The Challenge of Modern Governance," in *Reforming American Government* 24 (Donald L. Robinson ed., 1985); Lloyd N. Cutler, "To Form a Government," in *Separation of Powers: Does It Still Work?* 1 (Robert A. Goldwin & Art Kaufman eds., 1986); Charles M. Hardin, "The Separation of Powers Needs Major Revision," in id. at 465; James Q. Wilson, "Political Parties and the Separation of Powers," in id. at 18; Sargentich, supra note 5, at 465 ("[I]t is difficult to

contest that separation is by design an inefficient basis of national government."). Lester Thurow, "The Moral Equivalent of Defeat," in *Reforming American Government,* 33 (1985), argues that separation of powers must be discarded in order to "regain our economic vigor." Id. at 38.

72. Cutler, supra note 71 at 1.

73. Id. at 2–3.

74. Wilson, supra note 71 at 18.

75. Donald L. Robinson, "The Renewal of American Constitutionalism," in *Separation of Powers,* supra note 71, at 38, 38–50.

76. Wilson, supra note 71, at 18.

77. Robinson, supra note 75, at 54.

78. Candace H. Beckett, "Separation of Powers and Federalism: Their Impact on Individual Liberty and the Functioning of Our Government," 29 *Wm. & M. L. Rev.* 635, 640 (1988).

79. Cutler, supra note 71, at 13.

80. Id. at 15.

81. Id.

82. Id.

83. Arthur M. Schlesinger, "Leave the Constitution Alone," in *Reforming American Government,* supra note 71, at 50, 51.

> Parliament's superiority over Congress in delivering whatever the executive requests is a function of weakness not of strength. . . . Thus the prime minister appoints people to office without worrying about parliamentary confirmation, concludes treaties without worrying about parliamentary ratification, declares war without worrying about parliamentary authorization, withholds information without worrying about parliamentary subpoenas, is relatively safe from parliamentary investigation and in many respects has unlimited authority that once belonged to the absolute monarch.

84. Id. at 51: "Parliament has really no control over the executive; it is a pure fiction." (quoting statement by Lloyd George to select committee in 1931).

85. Id.

86. Id.

87. See 11 Will Durant & Ariel Durant, *The Story of Civilization: The Age of Napoleon* 507–11 (1975) ("Rarely in history has a nation been so oppressed as the Irish."). See also 9 Will Durant & Ariel Durant, *The Story of Civilization: The Age of Voltaire* 103–07 (1965).

88. Cutler, supra note 71 at 5.

89. Jane J. Mansbridge, *Beyond Adversary Democracy* 15 (1983).

90. Id. at 16.

91. One scholar has contrasted the American with the British system in the following manner:

> Constitutional norms, and the practices influenced by these norms vary in the extent to which authority is partitioned among and within such major institutions as executive, legislative, bureaucracy, and judiciary as well as such territorial structures as . . . states . . . . At one extreme in countries like . . . the United States, constitutional norms provide for an extensive division of authority by means of both federalism and separation of powers. As a result the government . . . is . . . fragmented into a number of separate subsystems, each possessing a good deal of autonomy in

relation to the others. At the other extreme, in countries like . . . Britain, a unitary rather than a federal system combined with parliamentary government rather than strict separation of powers between executive and legislature, make for considerably greater concentration of constitutional authority.

Robert A. Dahl, *Dilemmas of Pluralist Democracy* 65–66 (1982).

92. The system of Lords, Commons and monarch is based upon a theory of mixed government founded on a class system. Granted the influences of class have lessened in England, but here, at least officially, they have been rejected from the founding.

93. Dan K. Price, "Words of Caution About Structural Change," in *Reforming American Government,* supra note 71 at 39, 43.

94. Id.

95. See Wilson, supra note 71.

96. James L. Sundquist, *Dynamics of the Party System: Alignment & Realignment of the Political Parties in the United States* 342–411 (1983).

97. Price, supra note 93.

98. Id. at 40.

99. Id.

100. Id. at 44–45.

101. "[I]n political practice Americans followed Burke in making their main adjustments in their unwritten constitution on the basis of Burke's 'computing principle'—the unquantifiable process of working out 'balances between differences in good; in compromise between good and evil, and sometimes between evil and evil.'" Id. at 47.

102. Id. at 44.

103. I do not necessarily mean personal self-interest here, but rather political self-interest, i.e., seeking to represent one's constituents to ensure re-election.

104. In a sense, this analysis is parallel to Learned Hand's formula for determining negligence. See United States v. Carroll Towing Co., 159 F.2d 169, 173 (2d Cir. 1947).

105. John Rawls, *A Theory of Justice* 136–42 (1971).

106. It might be argued that the examples of threats to liberty in the nation's political history that have occurred despite the existence of a separation-of-powers structure only demonstrate the ineffectiveness of separation of powers as a means of preserving liberty. However, the examples to which we point are, for the most part, for the most part, cases in which the judiciary failed to enforce the limits on branch power imposed in the Constitution. Obviously, no system can work if the body obligated to enforce it chooses not to do so. In certain instances, however, the judiciary may attempt to enforce separation of powers yet be rebuffed by the stronger political branches. All this proves, however, is that separation of powers, like every other constitutional protection, is not foolproof. That hardly constitutes a basis for concluding that it serves no valuable positive function. Separation of powers is little more than the equivalent of a "speed bump" to tyranny. But speed bumps perform valuable preventative functions, even though someone determined to ignore them will ultimately not be stopped.

107. President Lincoln suspended the writ of habeas corpus on April 27, 1861, leading to the military arrests of thousands, even though it had been widely thought that only Congress had the authority to suspend the writ. Joseph Story, *Commentaries on the Constitution of the United States* 482–89 (1845). Lincoln's suspension

was not public. He authorized the General in Chief of the Union forces, who in turn delegated the authority to other commanders, to arrest citizens without the protections of the writ. "No one informed the courts or other civil authorities." Mark E. Neely, Jr., *The Fate of Liberty: Abraham Lincoln and Civil Liberties* 9 (1991). "Once [Lincoln] suspended the writ of habeas corpus without suffering dire political consequences, similar actions grew easier and easier." Id. at 10. He made individual suspensions of the writ and quickly overcame any initial hesitation to use his power to suspend it. Although the suspension was originally limited to areas near the battle lines, it was soon extended nationwide. Id. at 15.

First in Missouri and then in other states, Lincoln permitted military commissions, "essentially courts-martial," to try civilians. Id. at 35. Suspension of the writ only permitted imprisonment without charge. The military trials determined the final disposition of the prisoner. Lincoln authorized a mass relocation of all the inhabitants of certain Missouri counties. These "mischievous" citizens were deemed to be consorting with the enemy. Id. at 48.

Moreover, "any person . . .who may engage by act, speech or writing, in discouraging voluntary enlistments" was to be arrested and imprisoned. Id. at 53. A series of orders "allow[ed] a horde of petty functionaries to decide without any legal guidelines one of the highest matters of state: precisely who in this Civil War was loyal or disloyal." Id. at 54.

108. See generally Peter E. Quint, "The Separation of Powers Under Nixon: Reflections on Constitutional Liberties and the Rule of Law," 1981 *Duke L.J.* 1.

109. U.S. Const. art. II, § 2, cl. 1.

110. U.S. Const. art. I, § 8, cl. 11.

111. See generally J. Gregory Sidak, "To Declare War," 41 *Duke L.J.* 27 (1991).

112. See discussion infra at pp. 125–33.

113. "No one pretends that democracy is perfect or all-wise. Indeed, it has been said that democracy is the worst form of government except all those other forms that have been tried from time to time." Winston Churchill, Speech to the House of Commons, Nov. 11, 1947 (as quoted in the *Oxford Dictionary of Quotations* 150 (3d. ed. 1979)).

114. Sargentich, supra note 5, at 458 n.31.

115. Id. at 439. See also Gewirtz, supra note 5, at 343, suggesting that a rigid categorization of branch power "simplistically disregard[s] the real complexities of government structure as we know it and as our country has known it for a very long time."

116. For a description of the negatives of formalism, See Frederick Schauer, "Formalism," 97 *Yale L.J.* 509, 510 (1988).

117. See discussion supra pp. 111–13.

118. See discussion supra pp. 111–13.

119. See discussion supra pp. 107–08.

120. 487 U.S. 654 (1988).

121. 28 U.S.C. §§ 591–99.

122. Id. at § 593(b)(1); 487 U.S. at 678.

123. Id. at 695.

124. Id. at 696.

125. Id.

126. Brown, supra note 5 at 1525.

127. Id. at 1526.

128. Dean Alfange, Jr., "The Supreme Court and the Separation of Powers: A Welcome Return to Normalcy?," 58 *Geo. Wash. L. Rev.* 668, 670 (1990).

129. In particular, this refers to the Constitution's protections of federalism. See the discussion in chapter 2.

130. See discussion supra pp. 111–13.

131. See Martin H. Redish, *The Federal Courts in the Political Order: Judicial Jurisdiction and American Political Theory* 7 (1991).

132. Professor Brown has suggested an additional criticism of the use of formalism in separation of powers, that it "supports majoritarianism." Brown, supra note 5, at 1526. She explains that "[i]t is no accident that many of those who advocate the formalist view of constitutional interpretation for separation-of-powers issues also strongly favor greater strength for the Executive Branch—a majoritarian institution—through a 'unitary' theory of executive power." Id.

However, it is difficult to understand a criticism of constitutional doctrine for no reason other than that it "supports majoritarianism"—as if that description were somehow thought to be inherently damning. While it is true that the use of formalism would generally provide support to the theory of the unitary executive (under which "the President has unfettered control over any officer who can be said to exercise executive power," Id. at 1526 n.53), see discussion infra pp. 128–31, it is unclear why that renders the formalist model inherently defective, as Professor Brown appears to assume. In any event, to the extent that Professor Brown fears that formalism would lead to the dangerous expansion of executive power, she should note that use of a formalist model would also logically reject a theory of inherent and unenumerated executive power in general and a theory of unlimited executive power in the foreign policy area in particular. Thus, it is by no means clear that use of a formalist model would lead to dramatic expansion of executive power.

133. See generally the discussion in chapter 1.

134. See, e.g., Brown, supra note 5, at 1524, suggesting that "a belief that legislative, executive and judicial powers are inherently distinguishable as well as separable from one another [is] itself a highly questionable premise." See also Gewirtz, supra note 5, at 343, 346.

135. See chapter 1, supra pp. 9–10.

136. See generally the discussion in chapter 1.

137. It is important to emphasize that the separation-of-powers protections are not, as certain commentators have suggested, merely implied in the structure of the Constitution, but rather derive from the Constitution's affirmative grants of political power to the respective branches, construed in light of the background understanding of delegated powers.

138. The main historical exception to this requirement is the use of so-called private bills, by which Congress voted to award funds to individuals harmed by governmental action. Such legislative awards, however, were necessary because sovereign immunity precluded private suits against the federal government. This problem was resolved by a limited congressional waiver of sovereign immunity and the creation of the Court of Claims. See Glidden Co. v. Zdanok, 370 U.S. 530 (1962).

139. As Justice Rehnquist wrote in Valley Forge Christian College v. Americans United for Separation of Church and State, Inc., 454 U.S. 464, 472 (1982), the federal courts are not "debating societies."

140. For example, in the Civil Rights Act of 1991, Pub. L. No. 102–166 (1991), one of Congress's express purposes was "to respond to recent Supreme Court deci-

sions by restoring the civil rights protections that were dramatically limited by those decisions." H.R. Rep. No. 40, 102d Cong., 1st Sess. 1 (1991).

141. In addition to the obligation to execute the laws, Article II expressly vests in the executive branch such authority as the power to serve as commander in chief, to make treaties (with the advice and consent of two-thirds of the Senate) to appoint ambassadors and other executive officers, and to issue pardons. U.S. Const. art. II.

142. While it has been suggested that the president also may exercise inherent executive authority not specifically enumerated in Article II, for reasons of textual analysis as well as political theory I reject this interpretation. See discussion infra pp. 120–21.

143. See the discussion in chapter 5.

144. See id.

145. 299 U.S. 304 (1936). *Curtiss-Wright* is most widely known for its holding that the executive branch possesses broad, unenumerated power to control foreign affairs. See discussion infra pp. 120–21.

146. Ch. 365, 48 Stat. 811, quoted in 299 U.S. at 312.

147. See discussion infra pp. 120–21.

148. 299 U.S. at 319–21.

149. The argument might be made that the goal of reestablishing peace is so vague and nebulous that it effectively provides no meaningful legislative limitation on executive power. However, if we were to transport the goal of the congressional resolution involved in *Curtiss-Wright* to a hypothetical resolution enacted during the period immediately prior to the Gulf War, we could see how dramatic a limitation it could have imposed on the president's options.

150. See discussion supra pp. 113–16.

151. See, e.g., Geoffrey R. Stone et al., *Constitutional Law* 3 (2d ed. 1991), referring to "the perceived need for executive authority to provide energy and resolution in domestic and foreign affairs" as one of the problems encountered under the Articles of Confederation.

152. 343 U.S. 579 (1952).

153. Id. at 667.

154. Id. at 587.

155. See, e.g., Charles M. Hardin, *Presidential Power and Accountability: Toward a New Constitution* (1974); Louis Fisher, *President and Congress* (1972); Eugene V. Rostow, "What the Constitution Means By Executive Power," 43 *U. Miami L. Rev.* 138, 190–91 (1988).

156. See, e.g., United States v. Curtiss-Wright Export Corp., 299 U.S. 304 (1936) (executive power over foreign affairs).

157. The argument premised on the language of the vestiture clause is described in Edward S. Corwin, *The President: Office and Powers 1787–1984*, at 440 (5th ed. 1984). See also Thomas E. Cronin, *Inventing the American Presidency* 180, 193 (1989).

158. U.S. Const. art. I, § 1: "All legislative powers herein granted shall be vested in a Congress of the United States . . . ."

159. See sources cited in note 157.

160. See, e.g., National Mutual Ins. Co. v. Tidewater Transfer Co., 337 U.S. 582, 615, 646–47 (1949) (Rutledge, J., concurring) (Frankfurter, J., dissenting). See generally Martin H. Redish, *Federal Jurisdiction: Tensions in the Allocation of Judicial Power* 23–25 (2d ed. 1990).

161. U.S. Const. art. II, § 3, cl. 4, directing the president to "take care that the laws be faithfully executed . . . ."

162. See discussion supra pp. 105–08.

163. In the words of one commentator, "[a] representative republic is constructed with an eye on the dangers of kings, and thus carefully limits the executive power." Epstein, supra note 68 at 132.

It is true that in the Federalist Papers, Madison expressed primary concern about the dangers posed by the legislative branch. See, e.g., *The Federalist* No. 48. However, this was only because the executive branch had already been sufficiently curbed in the body of the Constitution. See Epstein, supra 131–32.

164. See Laurence Tribe, *American Constitutional Law* 298 (2d ed. 1988).

165. U.S. Const. amend. X: "The powers not delegated to the United States by the Constitution, nor prohibited by it to the States, are reserved to the States respectively, or to the people."

166. See Tribe, supra note 164, at 379.

167. For a parallel argument against an unlimited construction of Congress power under Article I, see the discussion in chapter 2.

168. In using this terminology, we intend to distinguish its use here from its more common usage in Commerce Clause jurisprudence. See Wickard v. Filburn, 317 U.S. 111 (1942).

169. 343 U.S. 579 (1952).

170. The facts of the case are discussed in text at note 152, supra. See also Edward S. Corwin, *"The Steel Seizure Case:* A Judicial Brick Without Straw," 53 *Colum. L. Rev.* 53 (1953).

171. 343 U.S. at 635–37 (Jackson, J., concurring).

172. See discussion supra pp. 117–19.

173. 343 U.S. at 635 (Jackson, J., concurring).

174. See discussion supra p. 122.

175. In effect, this reasoning provides a key assumption behind Professor Choper's proposed "Separation Principle." See the discussion in chapter 1, supra pp. 16–20.

176. See Erwin Chemerinsky, *Federal Jurisdiction* § 5.1 at 219 (1989).

177. For a more detailed discussion of this issue, see chapter 5.

178. 478 U.S. 714 (1986).

179. Balanced Budget and Emergency Deficit Control Act of 1985, Pub. L. No. 99–177, § 251, 99 Stat. 1038, 1063.

180. Id. §§ 241(b); 251(Q)(2).

181. Id. at 252.

182. Id. § 254(b).

183. 478 U.S. at 726–27, 732.

184. Id. at 722.

185. Id. at 726.

186. The Court noted that although the comptroller general is nominated by the president and confirmed by the Senate, "he is removable only at the initiative of Congress," not only through impeachment but also by joint resolution for permanent disability, inefficiency, neglect of duty, malfeasance and felony or conduct involving moral turpitude. 478 U.S. at 728. These criteria, the Court reasoned, would allow removal for any number of real or perceived "transgressions of the legislative will." Id. at 729. The Court further noted that Congress had consistently viewed the comptroller general as an officer of the legislative branch. "Against this background,"

it concluded, "we see no escape from the conclusion that, because Congress has retained removal authority over the Comptroller, he may not be entrusted with executive power." Id. at 732.

187. Id. at 737 (Stevens, J., concurring).

188. Id. at 763 (White, J., dissenting).

189. 478 U.S. at 754–55 (Stevens, J., concurring).

190. This was the import of the Court's decision in INS v. Chadha, 462 U.S. 919 (1983), invalidating the one-house legislative veto. See also Metropolitan Washington Airports Authority v. Citizens for the Abatement of Aircraft Noise, Inc., 111 S. Ct. 2298, 2312 (1991) (use of nine-member congressional board with power to veto Metropolitan Washington Airports Authority decision unconstitutionally fails to adhere to bicameral and presentment procedures).

191. See discussion supra pp. 3–5.

192. 487 U.S. 654 (1988).

193. Id. at 670–77.

194. Id. at 671.

195. See sources cited in note 118, supra.

196. For a detailed discussion of these submodels of functionalism in the particular context of Article III, see Martin H. Redish, supra note 160 at 13–19.

197. See discussion supra pp. 106–08.

198. See Stephen L. Carter, "From *Sick Chicken* to *Synar:* The Evolution and Subsequent De-Evolution of the Separation of Powers," 1987 *B.Y.U. L. Rev.* 719.

199. See, e.g., Monaghan, supra note 1. According to one commentator, under the theory of originalism,

> the constitutional text is the verbal or linguistic embodiment of various beliefs about how the polity ought to live various aspects of its life. In proposing and ratifying particular constitutional provisions . . . the proposers and ratifiers . . . were, on this view, according authoritative status to particular beliefs about how the polity ought to live its life.

Michael J. Perry, "The Authority of Text, Tradition and Reason: A Theory of Constitutional 'Interpretation'," 58 *S. Cal. L. Rev.* 551, 597 (1985).

200. Carter, supra note 198, at 848.

201. Id. at 849–52.

202. Id. at 853.

203. Id. at 857.

204. Id. at 854.

205. Id. at 859.

206. See Robert W. Bennett, "Objectivity in Constitutional Law," 132 *U. Pa. L. Rev.* 445, 472 (1984):

> Even if we knew all the values the intenders consciously held *before* they encountered a constitutional case, that would not tell us how those intenders would have decided a case differently in non-trivial ways from ones they had actually considered; nor would it tell us the values they would have held *after* the decision. Only the process of decision can elicit and shape the relevant values, and only the interpreters—successive courts—go through that process. Over time, those courts could reach conclusions that seem dramatically opposed to the intenders' initial ones without being untrue to "original intentions" in the sense that those intentions would have informed the intenders' decisions had the decisions been theirs to make.

207. Stephen L. Carter, "The Independent Counsel Mess," 102 *Harv. L. Rev.* 105, 111 n.21 (1988).

208. Carter, supra note 198, at 801.

209. Id.

210. Id. at 719.

211. Id.

212. Bowsher v. Synar, 478 U.S. 714, 759 (1986) (White, J., dissenting). See Carter, supra note 198, at 731–32.

213. Id. at 720.

214. Id.

215. See id. at 744, suggesting that "the two traditions that have governed the separation of powers jurisprudence both raise analytical questions sufficiently grave as to cast doubt on whether either one, in its pure form, can supply the courts a relatively coherent analytical approach for cases involving this system of balanced and separated powers."

216. "[T]he aims of liberal democratic theory and of constitutionalism generally will best be served if interpretation of the structural provisions of the political Constitution begins, and frequently ends, with consideration of the text and its historical background." Id. at 765. See also id. at 761. Professor Carter contrasts this conclusion with the treatment required for interpretation of the individual rights provisions, where he believes that "judicial muddling . . . does not necessarily represent a threat to the legitimacy of constitutional democracy." Id. (footnote omitted).

217. Id. at 761, 764.

218. Id. at 722.

219. See generally H. Jefferson Powell, "The Original Understanding of Original Intent," 98 *Harv. L. Rev.* 885 (1985).

220. Paul R. Verkuil, "Separation of Powers, The Rule of Law and the Idea of Independence," 30 *Wm. & Mary L. Rev.* 301 (1989).

221. Id. at 304.

222. Id. at 303.

223. Id. at 304.

224. Id.

225. Id. at 307.

226. Id. at 305.

227. Id. at 307.

228. Id. at 304.

229. Id. at 315.

230. Verkuil, supra note 220, at 316–17.

231. Id. at 323–25.

232. Id. at 337.

233. Id. at 338.

234. Id. at 326.

235. Id. at 327.

236. See, e.g., Keyishian v. Board of Regents, 385 U.S. 589 (1967). See generally Jerold H. Israel, "*Elfbrandt v. Russell:* The Demise of the Oath?," 1966 *Sup. Ct. Rev.* 193, 217–19.

237. Verkuil, supra note 220, at 327.

238. See id. at 304–05.

239. See Gewirtz, supra note 5, at 344 (emphasis in original): "The problem with

Verkuil's approach is that it seeks to apply a *unitary* principle to an area of law where there really are *multiple* concerns."

240. See, e.g., Tumey v. Ohio, 273 U.S. 510 (1927). See generally Martin H. Redish & Lawrence Marshall, "Adjudicatory Independence and the Values of Procedural Due Process," 95 *Yale L.J.* 455 (1986).

241. See, e.g., Ng Fung Ho v. White, 259 U.S. 276 (1922).

242. See discussion supra pp. 3–5.

243. See Martin H. Redish, supra note 131, at 78–85.

244. An example would be the president's usurpation of Congress's power to declare war. See discussion supra p. 113.

245. For this reason, Humphrey's Executor v. United States, 295 U.S. 602 (1935), in which the Court rejected presidential removal of an FTC Commissioner contrary to statute, was incorrectly decided.

246. Brown, supra note 5.

247. Id. at 1513–14.

248. Id. at 1514.

249. Id. at 1515–16.

250. Id. at 1516.

251. Id. at 1520.

252. Id.

253. See discussion supra pp. 16–20.

254. Brown, supra note 5, at 1520.

255. Id.

256. Id. at 1522.

257. See note 137, supra. See also the discussion in chapter 2.

258. Even this conclusion might be subject to debate. As previously noted, separation of powers may be viewed as a means of protecting the majoritarian interest in avoiding tyrannical usurpations of power, as well as in avoiding infringements on individual liberty.

259. See Brown, supra note 5, at 1522–31; discussion supra p. 115.

260. See Randy E. Barnett, "Foreword: Unenumerated Constitutional Rights and the Rule of Law," 3 *Harv. J. of Law & Pub. Policy* 1401, 1402 (1991): "The legal realists charged that adhering to the rule of law resulted in a 'mechanical jurisprudence'—now widely called 'formalism.'"

Chapter 5

1. See West Coast Hotel Co. v. Parrish, 300 U.S. 379 (1973). See generally Robert McCloskey, "Economic Due Process and the Supreme Court: An Exhumation and Reburial," 1962 *Sup. Ct. Rev.* 34.

2. See, e.g., Wickard v. Filburn, 317 U.S. 111 (1942); United States v. Darby, 312 U.S. 100 (1941).

3. See, e.g., National Broadcasting Co. v. United States, 319 U.S. 190 (1943). See discussion infra, pp. 139–40.

4. See, e.g., Panama Refining Co. v. Ryan, 293 U.S. 388 (1934). See discussion infra pp. 138–39.

5. See generally James M. Landis, *The Administrative Process* (1938).

6. See the discussion in chapter 4.

7. See id.

8. See, e.g., Roe v. Wade, 410 U.S. 113 (1973). See the discussion of the role of textualism in judicial review in chapter 1.

9. See the discussion in chapter 1.

10. See chapter 4.

11. See the discussions in chapter 1 and chapter 4.

12. See the discussion in chapter 4.

13. U.S. Const. amend. XVII: "The Senate of the United States shall be composed of two Senators from each state, elected by the people thereof, for six years . . . ."

14. See the discussion in chapter 1.

15. U.S. Const. art. III, § 2. See Valley Forge Christian College v. Americans United for Separation of Church & State, 454 U.S. 464 (1982).

16. 28 U.S.C. § 1652.

17. See, e.g., A.L.A. Schechter Poultry Corp. v. United States, 295 U.S. 493 (1934).

18. National Broadcasting Co. v. United States, 319 U.S. 190 (1943).

19. See, e.g., Mistretta v. United States, 488 U.S.361, 371–72 (1989).

20. Jerry L. Mashaw, "Prodelegation: Why Administrators Should Make Political Decisions," 1 *J. L. Econ. & Org.* 81, 82 (1985).

21. United States v. Grimaud, 220 U.S. 506, 517 (1911).

22. 293 U.S. 388 (1934).

23. 48 Stat. 195.

24. 293 U.S. at 415.

25. Id. at 430.

26. 295 U.S. 495 (1934).

27. Id. at 521–22.

28. 298 U.S. 236 (1936).

29. 49 Stat. 991.

30. 298 U.S. at 311.

31. 307 U.S. 533 (1939).

32. 50 Stat. 704, 717.

33. Id.

34. Id.

35. 307 U.S. at 574.

36. 319 U.S. 190 (1943).

37. Federal Communications Act of 1934, 47 U.S.C. § 303.

38. 319 U.S. at 225.

39. See, e.g., American Power & Light Co. v. S.E.C., 329 U.S. 90 (1946), upholding the Public Utility Holding Company Act of 1935, 15 U.S.C. § 79(k)(b)(2), which directed the S.E.C. to require registered holding companies to take such steps as the commission finds do "not unduly or unnecessarily complicate the structure, or unfairly or inequitably distribute voting power among security holders. . . ."

40. See, e.g., Mistretta v. United States, 488 U.S. 361 (1989).

41. See, e.g., David Schoenbrod, "The Delegation Doctrine: Could the Court Give It Substance?," 83 *Mich. L. Rev.* 1223, 1224–26 (1985).

42. See generally chapter 4.

43. See chapter 1.

44. See discussion infra pp. 141–57.

45. See chapter 4.

46. See id.

47. This was largely the rationale employed by Chief Justice John Marshall to justify judicial review in Marbury v. Madison, 5 U.S. (1 Cranch) 137 (1803).

48. There currently exists a body of scholarship that argues that it is often difficult—if not impossible—to distinguish between the functions of statutory construction and common law development. See, e.g., Martha Field, "Sources of Law: The Scope of Federal Common Law," 99 *Harv. L. Rev.* 881 (1986); Peter Westen & Jeffrey Lehman, "Is There Life for *Erie* After the Death of Diversity?" 78 *Mich. L. Rev.* 311 (1980). However, this is a view that I have attempted to refute in previous writing. See Martin H. Redish, *The Federal Courts in the Political Order: Judicial Jurisdiction and American Political Theory* 36–42 (1991).

49. The case-or-controversy requirement is textually mandated by Article III, Section 2 of the Constitution.

50. See chapter 4 supra p. 117.

51. 28 U.S.C. § 1652.

52. See Redish, supra note 48, at 34–36.

53. There are, I should acknowledge, several debates over the scope of the Rules of Decision Act, which are beyond the scope of the present inquiry. For a discussion of these controversies, see Redish, supra note 48, at 29–46.

54. See generally U.S. Const. art. III.

55. See Martin H. Redish, *Federal Jurisdiction: Tensions in the Allocation of Judicial Power* 11–22 (2d ed. 1990).

56. See chapter 4 supra pp. 113–25.

57. Id.

58. U.S. Const. art. II, § 3, providing that the president "shall take care that the laws be faithfully executed. . . ."

59. See the discussion in chapter 4 supra p. 117.

60. See the discussion in chapter 1 supra p. 5.

61. See chapter 4.

62. See id.

63. See chapter 4.

64. See id.

65. See id.

66. U.S. Const. art. II, § 2, cl. 2.

67. Myers v. United States, 272 U.S. 52 (1926).

68. Such agencies were held constitutional in Humphrey's Executor v. United States, 295 U.S. 602 (1935).

69. Such an analysis might seem to apply as well to delegations to the federal judiciary, whose judges are insulated from direct political pressures. However, when delegations to the judiciary are viewed as nothing more than selective repeals of the Rules of Decision Act's bar to the creation of federal common law, they should be deemed permissible. Unlike agencies, courts can develop substantive law only as an incident to resolution of a live case or controversy. See discussion supra pp. 140–41.

70. See discussion infra pp. 150–54.

71. Mashaw, supra note 30.

72. Id. at 87.

73. Id.

74. See discussion supra pp. 142–43.

75. Mashaw, supra note 20, at 87.

76. U.S. Const. art. V.

77. See discussion infra pp. 157–58.

78. Mashaw, supra note 20, at 95.

79. See id.

80. Id.

81. Id. at 96.

82. See discussion supra p. 142.

83. See U.S. Const. art. I, § 7, cl. 2 (bicameralism and presentment require-ments). See discussion infra pp. 159–60.

84. See chapter 4.

85. Professor Pierce all but concedes as much. See Richard J. Pierce, Jr., "Politi-cal Accountability and Delegated Power: A Response to Professor Lowi," 36 *Am. U. L. Rev.* 391, 408 (1987).

86. See supra note 68.

87. Pierce, supra note 85, at 408 (footnote omitted).

88. Id.

89. Mashaw, supra note 20, at 98.

90. Id. at 98.

91. Id. at 99.

92. Id.

93. Id.

94. Id.

95. See generally John Stuart Mill, *Considerations on Representative Govern-ment* (1882).

96. Richard B. Stewart, "Beyond Delegation Doctrine," 36 *Am. U. L. Rev.* 323, 333 (1987) (footnote omitted).

97. Id.

98. Ethyl Corp. v. EPA, 541 F.2d 1, 68 (D.C. Cir. 1972) (en banc) (Leventhal, J., concurring) (footnote omitted).

99. 462 U.S. 919 (1983).

100. Id. at 953 n.16.

101. Schoenbrod, supra note 41, at 1240.

102. See discussion supra p. 142.

103. Pierce, supra note 85 at 404.

104. Amartya Sen, "Social Choice Theory: A Re-Examination," 45 *Econometrics* 53 (1977); Kenneth Arrow, *Social Choice and Individual Values* (2d ed. 1963).

105. Pierce, supra note 85 at 404 (footnote omitted).

106. William H. Riker, *Liberalism Against Populism: A Confrontation Between the Theory of Democracy and the Theory of Public Choice* (1982).

107. Cass R. Sunstein, "Beyond the Republican Revival," 97 *Yale L.J.* 1539, 1545–46 (1988).

108. Robert A. Dahl, *A Preface to Democratic Theory* 131–32 (1956).

109. Id. See also Alexander Bickel, *The Least Dangerous Branch: The Supreme Court at the Bar of Politics* 19 (1962).

110. Pierce, supra note 85, at 403.

111. Id.

112. Id. at 404.

113. Id. (footnote omitted).

114. Id. See also Stewart, supra note 96, at 341–42.

115. Pierce, supra note 85, at 404.

116. Id. at 405.

117. See discussion supra pp. 142–43.

118. See the discussion in chapter 4.

119. See the discussion in chapter 3.

120. Pierce, supra note 85, at 403.

121. See the discussion in chapter 1.

122. Robert A. Dahl, *Democracy and the Critics* 76 (1989).

123. Id. at 52.

124. Id. at 66.

125. Id. at 393, citing Industrial Union Dep't v. American Petroleum Inst., 448 U.S. 607, 686–87 (1980) (Rehnquist, J., concurring); American Textile Mfgrs. Inst. v. Donovan, 452 U.S. 490, 547 (1981) (Rehnquist, J., dissenting).

126. Pierce, supra note 85, at 394, citing, inter alia, Carl McGowan, "Congress, Court, and Control of Delegated Power," 72 *Colum. L. Rev.* 1119, 1128–30 (1977).

127. Pierce, supra note 85, at 394 (footnote omitted).

128. Id.

129. Id.

130. Ernest Gellhorn, "Returning to First Principles," 36 *Am. U. L. Rev.* 345 (1987).

131. Pierce, supra note 85, at 396.

132. Gellhorn, supra note 130, at 352–53.

133. George Stigler, *The Citizen and the State* 111 (1975).

134. U.S. Const. amend. XIV, § 1.

135. See U.S. Const. art. I, § 2, cl. 1 (providing for election of members of House of Representatives); art. II, § 3 (providing for appointment of electors to electoral college, which selects the president); amend. XVII (providing for direct election of senators).

136. Schoenbrod, supra note 41, at 1253.

137. Id.

138. Id.

139. Id. at 1255 (footnote omitted).

140. Id. (footnote omitted).

141. See Jerome A. Barron et al. *Constitutional Law: Principles and Policy* 2 (4th ed. 1992).

142. Of course, Professor Schoenbrod's categorical condemnation of "goals" statutes is valid, to the extent that it is applied to statutes in which Congress announces conflicting goals, without making clear the manner in which those goals are to be reconciled.

143. See the discussion in chapter 4.

144. American Textile Mfgrs. Inst. v. Donovan, 452 U.S. 490, 547 (Rehnquist, J., dissenting).

145. Id. See also Industrial Union Dept. v. American Petroleum Inst., 448 U.S. 607, 687 (1980) (Rehnquist, J., concurring in the judgment) (urging that the Court "reshoulder the burden of ensuring that Congress itself make the critical policy decisions. . . .").

146. See chapter 4.

147. 488 U.S. 361 (1989).

148. Id. at 368–69.

149. Id. at 372.

150. Id. at 374.

151. Id. at 417–19 (Scalia, J., dissenting).

152. Id. at 420.

153. 488 U.S. 420 (Scalia, J., dissenting).
154. See chapter 4.
155. 48 Stat. 881, 15 U.S.C. § 77b et seq.
156. See supra note 37.
157. 38 Stat. 717, 15 U.S.C. §§ 41–51.
158. 462 U.S. 919 (1983).
159. Id. at 956–58.
160. Id. at 958.
161. See chapter 4.
162. See discussion supra pp. 138–40.
163. 462 U.S. at 953 n.16.
164. See discussion supra pp. 149–50.

Chapter 6

1. See chapter 2. Compare this position with that taken in Robert Nagel, *Constitutional Cultures: The Mentality and Consequences of Judicial Review* 60–65 (1989). See, for example, the opinions of Justice Rehnquist in *National League of Cities,* discussed in chapter 2, supra pp. 38–39. The one glaring exception, I suppose, is my attack on the creation of a special enclave of constitutional protection for state governments from federal regulation in *National League of Cities v. Usery.*

2. Herbert Wechsler, "Toward Neutral Principles of Constitutional Law," 73 *Harv. L. Rev.* 1 (1959). For a more detailed examination of the concept, see Martin H. Redish, "Taking a Stroll Through Jurassic Park: Neutral Principles and the Minimalist-Originalist Fallacy in Constitutional Interpretation," 88 *Nw. U. L. Rev.* 165 (1993).

3. See the discussion in chapter 4, supra pp. 113–23.

4. See the discussion in chapter 4, supra pp. 111–13.

5. See Nagel, supra note 5, at 60–65. For a critical discussion of Professor Nagel's position, see Martin H. Redish, "Political Consensus, Constitutional Formulae, and the Rationale for Judicial Review," 88 *Mich. L. Rev.* 1340, 1360–63 (1990).

6. See the discussion in chapter 4, supra pp. 111–13.

7. See the discussion in chapter 4, supra pp. 111–12.

8. See chapters 1, 2, 4 and 5.

TABLE OF CASES

223

INDEX